U.S. STAMP YEARBOOK 1987

A comprehensive record of technical data, design development and stories behind all of the stamps, stamped envelopes, postal cards, souvenir cards and maximum cards issued by the United States Postal Service and the Bureau of Engraving and Printing in 1987.

By
Fred Boughner

Published by *Linn's Stamp News,* the world's largest and most informative weekly stamp newspaper, Post Office Box 29, Sidney, Ohio 45365. *Linn's* is a division of Amos Press, Inc., which also publishes the *Scott* catalogs and publications; *Coin World,* a weekly newspaper for the numismatic field; and *Cars & Parts,* a monthly magazine for auto enthusiasts.
Copyright 1988 by Amos Press Inc.

ISSN 0748-996X

ISBN 0-940403-07-2

With Grateful Thanks...

I am again beholden to many who helped with the facts, figures and fare contained between the covers of this book. My appreciation to all of those named here, and to others helping them whom I may not even know.

United States Postal Service, Washington, D.C.
  Joe Brockert, program manager, Philatelic Design
  Robert Brown, manager, Philatelic Sales Division
  Pete Davidson, director, Office of Stamps and Philatelic Marketing
  Linda Foster, Stamps Division
  Don McDowell, general manager, Stamps Division
  Hugh McGonigle, Stamp Information Branch
  Peter Papadopoulos, Stamp Information Branch
  Dickey Rustin, manager, Stamp Information Branch
  Frank Thomas, Stamp Information Branch
  Jack Williams, program manager, Philatelic Design

Bureau of Engraving and Printing
  Edward Felver, chief, Office of Engraving
  Tom Ferguson, chief, Stamp and Currency Printing
  Robert J. Leuver, director
  Ira Polikoff, Public Affairs

Special thanks to Elizabeth Lipscomb, Public Affairs, U.S. Fish & Wildlife Service; Jim Lamb, artist/illustrator; Robert Blanke, plant manager, Westvaco-USEnvelope Division; George Godin of the Bureau Issues Association; Stephen Esrati; and the indefatigable Charles Yeager, *Linn's* Washington Correspondent.

Fred Boughner

CONTENTS

Introduction — 5

Commemoratives — 7
22¢ Michigan Statehood, January 26 — 9
22¢ Pan American Games, January 29 — 15
22¢ Jean Baptiste Du Sable, February 20 — 21
22¢ Enrico Caruso, February 27 — 25
22¢ Girl Scouts, March 12 — 31
22¢ United Way, April 28 — 37
22¢ American Wildlife (50), June 13 — 42
22¢ Delaware Statehood, July 4 — 61
22¢ Morocco, July 17 — 65
22¢ William Faulkner, August 3 — 71
22¢ Lacemaking (4), August 14 — 75
22¢ Pennsylvania Statehood, August 26 — 81
22¢ Drafting Constitution booklet (5), August 28 — 85
22¢ New Jersey Statehood, September 11 — 93
22¢ Signing of Constitution, September 17 — 99
22¢ Certified Public Accountants, September 21 — 106
22¢ Locomotives booklet (5), October 1 — 110

Special Stamps — 117
22¢ Love, January 30 — 118
22¢ Special Occasions booklet (8), April 20 — 123
22¢ Christmas Madonna and Child, October 23 — 130
22¢ Christmas Greetings, October 23 — 134

Definitives — 138
Transportation coils plate numbers — 139
Great Americans plate numbers — 141
8.5¢ Tow Truck coil, January 24 — 142
7.1¢ Tractor coil (2 designs), February 6 — 147
14¢ Julia Ward Howe, February 12 — 152
2¢ Mary Lyon, February 28 — 157
10¢ Canal Boat coil, April 11 — 161
22¢ Flag with Fireworks, May 9 — 165
22¢ Flag Over Capitol (tagged paper test), May 23 — 168
10¢ Red Cloud, August 15 — 172
$5 Bret Harte, August 25 — 177

5¢ Milk Wagon coil, September 25 ——— 183
17.5¢ Racing Car, September 25 ——— 186
22¢ Flag with Fireworks Booklet (20), November 30 ——— 192

Revised Definitives ——— 195
2¢ Locomotive coil, March 6 ——— 197
22¢ John J. Audubon, June 1 ——— 200
12¢ Stanley Steamer coil, September 3 ——— 202

Migratory Bird Hunting
$10 Redhead Ducks stamp, July 1 ——— 205

Stamped Envelope
22¢ Official Savings Bond envelope, March 2 ——— 210

Postal Cards ——— 213
14¢ Self-scouring Steel Plow, May 22 ——— 215
14¢ Constitutional Convention, May 25 ——— 219
14¢ Flag, June 14 ——— 225
14¢ Take Pride in America, September 22 ——— 229
14¢ Timberline Lodge, September 28 ——— 232

Souvenir Cards ——— 235
125th Anniversary (BEP), January 7 ——— 236
CAPEX (USPS), June 13 ——— 238
SESCAL 87 (BEP), October 16 ——— 240
HAFNIA 87 (USPS), October 16 ——— 242
HSNA 87 (BEP), November 12 ——— 244
Monte Carlo (USPS), November 13 ——— 246

Maximum Cards ——— 248

Appendix
Items Withdrawn in 1987 ——— 251
USPS Exhibition Cards ——— 252

INTRODUCTION

When Assistant Postmaster General Gordon C. Morison announced the U.S. Postal Service's 1987 stamp program on May 26, 1986, at AMERIPEX, it embraced 86 different postal items spread over 24 separate issues. When 1987's last postal item — the 20-stamp Flag with Fireworks booklet of November 30 — came to market, the postal items had increased to 110 over 42 separate issues. The USPS issued more face-different stamps in 1987 than in any year since it was chartered under the Postal Reorganization Act of 1970. All of those new items, plus the workhorse Flag stamps and some older definitives, totaled some 38 billion stamps, the great majority of which were produced by the Bureau of Engraving and Printing.

The Postal Service estimates that, in 1988, booklets will account for 25 percent of all stamps (they were 19 percent in 1984); coils will be the format for 51 percent of all stamps (48 percent in 1984); and pane stamps (which were 33 percent of all stamp output in 1984) will drop to 24 percent in 1988.

The ubiquitous Flag stamps now account for almost half of all stamps sold. Christmas stamps add up to 5 percent, commemoratives are 7 percent, with other definitives accounting for the balance. (It is ironic to note that the 77 commemoratives of 1987 carried just 7 percent of the mail.)

Briefly, these 1987 happenings made news and may have effects on future stamps and designs:

The dedication of a new $2.6 million Design Center in the BEP on January 15, 1987, will speed and improve stamp-design editing. The prepress electronic system allows designers to manipulate artwork by computer — changing colors, image sizes, locations and shapes in seconds. Such redesigning formerly took days and weeks of repainting. Designers can now play "What if?" with artwork in seconds, and at lower costs.

The USPS and BEP successfully tested prephosphored paper through all Bureau, postal and private mailers' production and handling equipment in 1987. The test was made with the 22¢ Flag Over Capitol stamps, specially marked with a "T." When all tagged stamps are switched to this prephosphored paper, brighter, more eye-popping colors will result. The present on-press tagging of stamps is done in a varnish that dulls printing inks.

A BEP engraver revealed that he had carved a tiny Star of David to the right of the mouth in the bearded area of Bernard Revel on the $1 Revel definitive of 1986. Postal officials said it was the first time a symbol has been etched surreptitiously on a U.S. stamp. Collectors soon were searching through hundreds of other U.S. stamps and finding "secret marks" that existed mostly in their imaginations.

An upside-down Czeslaw Slania marking was found on a 1985 World War I Veterans stamp. Slania denied the marking, which was later proved to have existed in a pencil sketch given to Slania. The marking was not Slania's initials or signature. Close examination of the handstamp shown on stamp 4 from the 1986 Stamp Collecting booklet looked like "Hipschen" and "Masure" to some collectors. These engravers had, indeed, both worked on the stamp. The handstamp involved originally carried the name of a commercial maker, and the engravers were asked to substitute something else. They substituted their own names and showed the result to postal officials. The names were intentionally "trashed" so as to be unreadable. Or so the officials thought. They came out in print more legible than they were intended.

In the summer of 1987, it was discovered that employees of the Central Intelligence Agency (CIA) had purchased the famous partial pane of 95 inverted $1 Candleholder stamps from a post office in McLean, Virginia. One employee had been sent to buy the stamps for CIA postage needs. Employees replaced the inverts with regular $1 stamps, and sold the error stamps to Jacques C. Schiff, a New Jersey stamp dealer.

Nine CIA employees were involved, since Schiff was asked to make out nine separate checks for his purchase. The magic of the CIA name, along with the newsworthiness of the the inverted stamps, became front-page news. Television anchormen spread the story all over America. For a brief moment, stamps were making headlines. The CIA, which said it considered the whole affair an "internal matter," has still not commented on what — if anything — happened to those nine employees.

As you use the *Yearbook*, keep these facts in mind. The "Quantity Ordered" and "Quantity Distributed" figures for each postal item are for the 1987 postal fiscal year, which ran from September 27, 1986, through September 25, 1987. That's why stamps issued after September 25 show no distribution. Occasionally, more stamps will be distributed than had been ordered. The BEP always runs more stamps than are ordered to allow for spoilage. It will also rerun active definitives without a USPS purchase order whenever inventory runs low. That may be the reason that occasional design and perf changes were not reported in 1987 until the stamps were already on sale.

Shipments of 1987 postage stamps, by category, were:
Commemoratives: 3,886,000,000 (includes BEP and ABNC)
Special Stamps: 3,350,000,000
Definitives: 30,764,000,000

COMMEMORATIVES

U.S. commemorative stamps began with the 16-stamp Columbian issue of 1893. Collectors complained bitterly about the high face value of the set, $16.34, at a time when men's all-wool suits could be had for $12, sugar was 4¢ a pound, fine ladies' shoes sold for $1.75 a pair, and Dr. Sanford's Liver Invigorator was only 50¢ a bottle.

The 1893 Columbians were, of course, the only commemorative stamps of that year. Now, 94 years later, the 77 different commemoratives of 1987 cost collectors $16.94 to obtain. Collectors don't complain as much about the dollar amount (which hasn't changed that much) as they do about the number of stamps (which has steadily continued to escalate since the days of the Columbians).

U.S. commemoratives have had a checkered history. After the Columbians were introduced, no commemoratives at all appeared in 19 of the ensuing 30 years. In the next 30 years (1923-1952), only 288 commemoratives were released — fewer than 10 per year. From 1953 to 1972 (the next 20 years), the commemorative pace quickened a bit: 17 stamps per year.

The decade from 1973 to 1982 saw the first great proliferation of these stamps: 403 commemoratives over ten years, for an average annual output of more than 40 issues. It will perhaps come as no surprise that the last five years (1983-1987) have witnessed more than 240 commemoratives, taking the yearly average up again to almost 50 stamps per year.

With its 77 issues, the year 1987 ranks as the second most prolific year for U.S. commemorative stamps. The bicentennial year of 1976 counted 88 commemoratives, greatly aided by the 50-stamp State Flags pane and four souvenir sheets that each contained five perforated commemoratives. Three years have gone over the 70-commemoratives mark, and each has hosted a pane of 50 different stamps: the 1982 50 Birds and Flowers and the 50 Wildlife stamps of 1987.

Of 1987's 77 face-different stamps, 58 had nothing to do with any anniversary: the Pan American Games, Enrico Caruso, Lacemaking, Locomotives and Wildlife stamps. The rest of the year's commemoratives honored statehood anniversaries (Michigan's 150th and Delaware's, Pennsylvania's and New Jersey's 200th); the Constitution's 200th anniversary (six stamps); the 150th anniversary of the incorporation of Chicago; the 100th birthdays of the United Way and Certified Public Accountants national organizations; the 75th anniversary of the Girl Scouts and, unwittingly perhaps, the 90th year since author William Faulkner's birth.

The Delaware Statehood stamp of July 4 heralded an almost unnoticeable change in the size of printed areas for many ensuing commemoratives. While the perf-to-perf overall size of the stamps would remain the same, the longest dimension on both horizontal and vertical printed designs was reduced by 3/100 of an inch. Only commemoratives produced in panes of 50 would be affected. The Postal Service said the change was made to get more white space around the printed image, and thus to improve the centered appearance of the stamps.

Of the 77 commemoratives, 64 could have been purchased with another different stamp alongside, above or below. Se-tenant (from the French meaning "holding one another") is rapidly becoming an American word and a United States Postal Service policy.

Some commemorative stamps list no plate impressions. In those instances, Bureau records were incomplete at press time.

22¢ MICHIGAN STATEHOOD

Date of Issue: January 26, 1987

Catalog Numbers: Scott 2246   Minkus CM1210

Colors: magenta, cyan, yellow, black, special green

First-Day Cancel: Lansing, Michigan (Capitol Ballroom, Radisson Hotel)

FDCs Canceled: 379,117

Format: Panes of 50, vertical, 10 across, 5 down. Printing cylinders of 400.

Perf: 11.2 (Eureka off-press perforator)

Selvage Markings: U.S. Postal Service© 1986, Use Correct ZIP Code

Designer: Robert Wilbert

Art Director: Frank Thomas (USPS)

Modeler: Peter Cocci (BEP)

Printing: Andreotti 7-color gravure press

Quantity Ordered: 150,000,000
Quantity Distributed: 167,430,000

Plate Block Detail: 5-digit group over/under corner stamps

Tagging: block over vignette

Plate Impressions: Magenta: 1(991,600)
   Cyan: 1(991,600)
   Yellow: 1(991,600)
   Black: 1(991,600)
   Green: 1(991,600)

The Stamp

Michigan presents two faces to the world geographically, industrially and philatelically.

The mitten-like lower peninsula is of relatively low altitude and gently rolling. It possesses the state's largest lakes, rivers and sand dunes. The upper peninsula is rugged; along its north coast are the 2,000-foot cliffs of Lake Superior. It is veined with streams and waterfalls, often turbulent and raging.

The lower peninsula is both a farming and industrial beehive. The cars and tools of Detroit, the cereals and baby foods of Battle Creek and Fremont, and the furniture of Grand Rapids put something from the state of Michigan into every American home. The iron ranges of the upper peninsula make the state second only to Minnesota in iron ore shipments. Copper from the hills near western Lake Superior rank the state fifth in production of that mineral. But people are scarce in upper Michigan. Many are visitors, trying for the trout, sturgeon, muskellunge and coho salmon that make the region literally a fisherman's paradise.

A chronological history of Michigan on U.S. stamps. 1673: Marquette leaves Sault Ste. Marie to sail the Mississippi River with Joliet. 1701: Antoine de Cadillac lands at Detroit. 1958: The Mackinac Bridge, connecting Michigan's upper and lower peninsulas, is dedicated.

Philatelically, too, the state presents a dichotomy. The Post Office Department issued a stamp in 1935 for the 100th anniversary of Michigan statehood. Now, in 1987, the U.S. Postal Service begets one for Michigan's 150th statehood birthday. One or the other must be wrong; the mathematics don't add up. A quick overview of Michigan's history is necessary to clear up the two-year anomaly.

The Indians were there first. Indeed, the Chippewa gave the state its name, *michi gami*, meaning "Great Water" and applying to Lake Michigan. The Menominee, Ottawa, Miami and Potawatomi tribes — about 15,000 of them — also roamed the upper and lower peninsulas. A Frenchman, Etienne Brule, is thought to have been the first white man to venture the Michigan region. Dates of his entry are uncertain, ranging from 1615 to 1620.

Brule explored the upper peninsula, having been sent there from Quebec by French Governor Samuel de Champlain to seek a route to the Pacific. Other explorers followed, most seeking a route westward, but not until 1668 did Father Jacques Marquette and a company of

Jesuits found a first settlement on the site of Sault Ste. Marie. Marquette, Louis Joliet, Robert Sieur de la Salle and others explored and mapped many of the lakes and rivers of Michigan in the late 1600s. By 1700, the French had missions, trading posts and settlements at several spots on both Michigan peninsulas. In 1701 Antoine de la Mothe Cadillac established Fort Pontchartain, which later became Detroit.

Furs and Christian conversions were the objectives of the French. Furs also lured the British into the area. Great Britain fought a series of battles called the French and Indian Wars until 1763, when England took over most of the French interests in North America, including Michigan. In 1774 the British made Michigan a part of Quebec, sending white and Indian troops out of Detroit to harass American settlers during the Revolutionary War.

When the British lost the Revolution, Michigan's next transition was into the Northwest Territory, as ordained by Congress under the Articles of Confederation. (Those Articles are viewed by many historians as our first constitution. They were drafted by the Continental Congress ten years before the Constitution.) This Ordinance of 1787 created a territory embracing Ohio, Indiana, Illinois, Michigan and Wisconsin. It forbade slavery, encouraged education, and established the rights of trial by jury. Whenever an individual territory had 60,000 adult males, it could apply for statehood.

This 1935 stamp for 100 years of Michigan Statehood would seem to have the 1835 date wrong, since Michigan was not admitted to the Union until 1837. The text explains the anomaly.

The Territory of Michigan was formed in 1805. By 1835 Michigan voters ratified a state constitution and approved an application for statehood. The petition met with two setbacks. Michigan's admittance was opposed by southern legislators, since Michigan was a free state without slaves. In 1836 — when Arkansas was admitted — Michigan was to be "paired" with that state to keep free states and slave states in balance.

Another delay for Michigan arose because of its dispute with Ohio over the Toledo Strip, a 520-square mile area at Michigan's southern border. The U.S. Congress settled the argument by giving the Toledo Strip to Ohio and the entire upper peninsula to Michigan. Michigan finally became the 26th state on January 26, 1837.

When it came time to celebrate the centennial of Michigan statehood with a stamp, Michigan forces argued for a 1935 issue, because

1835 was the year Michigan voters had approved statehood. The new Michigan stamp marks 150 years since the actual admittance of Michigan as a state.

This 1955 stamp commemorated the 100th anniversary of the Soo Locks between lakes Huron and Superior. While Lake Michigan and Lake Huron flow into one another, Lake Superior is about 21 feet higher, necessitating the locks. Tonnage through the locks is 80 percent of that handled by the Panama Canal — even though the Soo Locks are icebound about five months out of the year.

Michigan's economy changed from agriculture and mining to manufacturing in the early 1900s. Detroit (an anglicized contraction of the French *La Ville d'Etroit* meaning "city of the strait") became far and away the nation's leading producer of automobiles, engines and parts. Michigan also leads the nation in producing conveyors, sporting equipment, refrigerators and hardware. Food products, lumber, chemicals and pharmaceuticals are also vital to the Michigan economy. Detroit is the sixth largest city in the United States, according to the 1980 census. Surprisingly, there is no other Michigan city in the top 75. Detroit is also the only city in the United States from which you travel south to get into Canada.

By population, Michigan is the eighth largest state with more than nine million persons. By size, it ranks 23rd with 56,800 square miles. Although it has no coastline, the surrounding Great Lakes give it more shoreline than any other state.

Michigan has never sired a president or vice-president of the United States. (Gerald Ford was born in Nebraska). It has never had a speaker of the House of Representatives. Michigan-born politicians have not had great impact upon the politics of this country. That, perhaps, is why it also boasts no major military installations.

Imprinted on the great seal of Michigan (seen on the 1935 stamp) are the words, "Se quaeris peninsulam amoenam, circumspice" ("If you seek a pleasant peninsula, look about you"). Tourists would seem to agree. They spend more than $4 billion annually in Michigan's 1,400 square miles of inland lakes, 19 million acres of wild forest and countless parks. Surprisingly, Michigan ranks ahead of Colorado as a tourist attraction.

From small cities to Detroit to the north woods of the upper peninsula, Michigan's 150th anniversary was to be a statewide, yearlong celebration. There were fishing contests, turkey shoots, wine festivals, a marigold fest and diving events to observe the scores of old ships sunken off the shores of Lake Huron. A July 17-26 Tour de Michigan Bicycle Race attracted some of the world's fastest cyclists, who pedaled from upper Michigan to Detroit.

The Design

While it is not a firm policy of the USPS to seek out a local artist for a statehood stamp, it does "add a bit to the stamp if a Michigan artist does one for his home state," says Jack Williams, program manager for stamp design. In the case of this stamp, a design coordinator of the Citizens' Stamp Advisory Committee suggested to Robert Wilbert, artist and professor at Detroit's Wayne State University, that he render a design for the Michigan issue. (Similar steps have taken place with 1986's Arkansas Statehood and Republic of Texas stamps.)

One of the first places a design coordinator will look is at the art department of a university within the state to be honored. This time Robert Wilbert's design was accepted. Wilbert worked in acrylic paint, stating that his design of a Michigan white pine — the state's official tree — against the background of a sunrise over Lake Huron suggested the importance of the lumber industry and water transportation to Michigan's early economic development. It was Wilbert's first stamp design.

First-Day Facts

First-day cancellations showed Michigan's state capital.

The stamp was released January 26, 1987, in Lansing, Michigan, the state capital. Taking place at the Lansing Radisson Hotel, the program featured Associate Postmaster General Fletcher Acord, speaking for the Postal Service, and Michigan Governor James J. Blanchard.

All post offices received their standard automatic distribution quantities. All Michigan stamps were shipped from the Bureau with this allocation. None remained for requisition at the BEP later.

Varieties

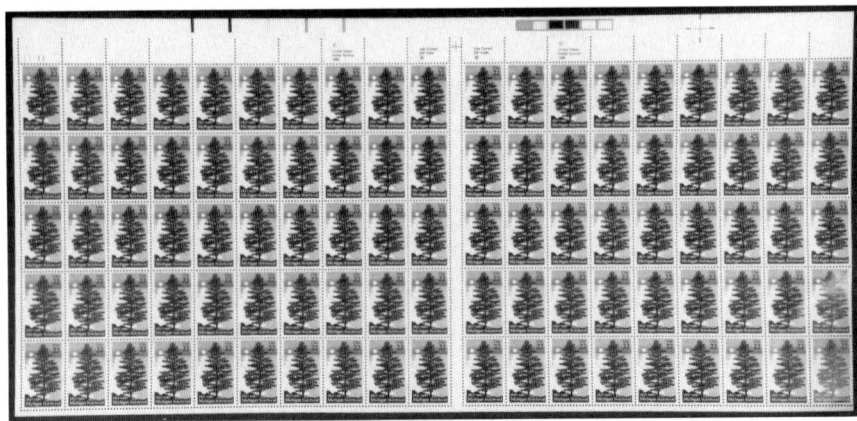

This block of 95 of the 22¢ Michigan Statehood stamps was found in a post office pad. Since it had been folded along the tenth row of vertical perforations, its presence went unnoticed. While foldovers in the cutting process occasionally result in a "guttersnipe" showing a full gutter and part of an adjoining stamp, very rarely do they create complete cross-gutter pairs. This piece has five of them.

22¢ PAN AMERICAN GAMES

Date of Issue: January 29, 1987

Catalog Numbers: Scott 2247   Minkus CM1211

Colors: special red, special blue, yellow, black, metallic silver

First-Day Cancel: Indianapolis, Indiana (Indiana War Memorial)

FDCs Canceled: 344,731

Format: Panes of 50, horizontal, 5 across, 10 down. Printing cylinders of 400.

Perf: 11.2 (Eureka off-press perforator)

Selvage Markings: U.S. Postal Service© 1986, Use Correct ZIP Code

Designer: Lon Busch

Art Director: Jack Williams (USPS)

Modeler: V. Jack Ruther (BEP)

Printing: Andreotti 7-color gravure press

Quantity Ordered: 150,000,000
Quantity Distributed: 166,555,000

Plate Block Detail: 5-digit number alongside corner stamps

Tagging: block over vignette

Plate Impressions: Special red: 1(961,159)
Special blue: 1(961,159)
Yellow: 1(961,159)
Black: 1(961,159)
Metallic silver: 1(961,159)

The Stamp

From the arched parallelograms and circular portraits of the 1893 Columbians through the computerized-grid hills and valleys of the 1983 Science and Industry issue, geometric shapes have played a vital role in the design of U.S. commemoratives. In the 1972 Olympic Games trio, simple geometrics represented bobsledders, runners and cyclists. But never before have geometric techniques been used to so accurately portray the human figure as on this stamp for the 1987 Pan American Games held in Indianapolis.

Accurate or not, the geometric man-in-motion was a design that collectors either admired or detested.

The stamp was unveiled December 10, 1985, by Indianapolis Postmaster Anthony Schiavone at the Indianapolis post office. Assisting Schiavone was Mark Miles, president of PAX/Indianapolis, a volunteer group of Indiana residents who would plan and implement the Pan Am Games, one of the world's largest sporting events.

Following the unveiling ceremony, the Indianapolis post office began the use of a special machine cancel, to be used on regular mail

The Pan American Games of 1959, held in Chicago, were honored by this less-complicated airmail stamp.

posted in Indianapolis until June 10, 1987. The cancellation read: "Pan American Games, Indianapolis, 7-23 August, 1987."

The Pan American Games are now 36 years old, having first been held in Buenos Aires, Argentina, in 1951. Their history, however, goes back to the 1932 Olympics, when the Mexican delegation proposed the establishment of a sports organization devoted to the showcasing of amateur athletes of the Western Hemispere. In 1940 the Olympic Committees of 16 nations of that hemisphere met in Buenos Aires to plan the first Pan American Games for 1942. World War II interrupted, so the games did not start until 1951. Since then, they have been held every four years under the aegis of the Pan American Sports Organization (PASO), which is sanctioned and supported by the International Olympics Committee.

The games attempt to increase goodwill among the countries of North and South America. Only amateur athletes from those lands may compete. The games adhere to rules set down by the IOC, and try to foster the Olympic ideals of friendship, cooperation and inter-American goodwill through sports.

The games have been held every four years since 1951. After the first Buenos Aires contests, game sites have been Mexico City (1955 and 1975); Chicago (1959); Sao Paulo (1964); Winnipeg (1967); Cali, Colombia (1971); San Juan, Puerto Rico (1979) and Caracas, Venezuela (1983). The United States issued a 10¢ airmail stamp in 1959 to honor the Chicago games.

Pan American events read like a roster of Olympic contests: track and field, swimming, basketball, boxing, cycling, fencing, gymnastics, weight lifting, shooting, rowing, wrestling, equestrian events, tennis, soccer, polo and a pentathalon. At the first 1951 games, the United States and Argentina dominated; between them, they fielded almost half the total competitors.

Since then, the United States has continued its domination, even though some top U.S. athletes do not enter. The Pan American Games precede the quadrennial Olympics by just a year; some athletes prefer to continue training for the tougher competition in the Olympics 12 months later. Although team scoring by country was eliminated in 1971, the United States reign goes on. At Winnipeg, for example, the United States won gold medals in 120 out of 171 events.

The 1987 games took place August 7-23 at 23 different sites throughout Indiana. More than 6,500 athletes and officials from 38 Western Hemisphere nations took part — the largest number of athletes and countries since the games began. The Postal Service assigned a nine-digit ZIP Code to each of the 38 nations to expedite mail sent to athletes, coaches, trainers and officials. The USPS also screened mail sent to the organizing committee's offices for hidden explosive or incendiary devices.

Trademarked symbol for the Indianapolis Tenth Pan American Games.

The Pan American Games were the biggest sporting event held anywhere in the world during 1987. They were also bigger than the 1984 Los Angeles Olympics, which had 65 fewer events than the Indianapolis happening. Cuba, which had boycotted the 1984 Olympics, came to Indianapolis in 1987. In the past decade, Indianapolis has built $136 million worth of athletic facilities — an indoor arena, a domed stadium, a velodrome (for bicycle racing), a natatorium, and a track and field stadium.

Much of the resurgence of Indianapolis, athletic and otherwise, has been due to Lilly Endowment, a fund established 50 years ago by Eli Lilly & Company, an Indianapolis pharmaceutical firm whose profits run to a half billion dollars per year. The fund provided $36 million in seed money to begin the construction of the Hoosier Dome and the Indiana University natatorium.

According to a PAX spokesman, Indianapolis almost lost out on the 1987 games. Sites in both Ecuador and Chile had been considered but were dropped when necessary plans went unfulfilled. The poor economies of the two countries were part of the reason for the switch to the United States and Indianapolis.

These were the first indoor games to be called a "world event." Only recently have records made indoors qualified for listing as world records. As with the Olympics, game officials do not keep team scores by participating country. These are kept only by the media. Olympic and Pan American committees feel that only individual results should be rewarded; thus, no medals or awards go to a winning nation.

The United States and Cuba were the dominant favorites, and off-track conflicts between the two countries started early. Cuba was the only country entered that had an established communist government. That caused the closing ceremonies to be moved from the American Legion Mall in downtown Indianapolis to the Hoosier Dome, when both the national and Indiana American Legions objected to a communist flag being flown over the mall.

Five of 35 special cancels available from the Pan American Games. These show canoeing, cycling, diving, equestrian events and fencing.

The U.S. State Department wanted some 400 Cuban athletes and coaches to come into the country through Miami. The Cubans refused, saying they feared problems with the large Cuban population in Miami. They wanted to fly directly to Indianapolis. After much bickering and discussion, the State Department relented. The Cubans flew directly to Indianapolis. Colombia was offended when a CBS announcer called that country, "unfortunately a major producer of cocaine." The passport status of a Chilean competitive shooter was in doubt until Olympic President Juan Samaranch asked Vice President George Bush to get him admitted for the Pan Am Games.

When the games had run their course, the United States won more medals than Canada and Cuba by a margin of about two-to-one. Brazil, Argentina, Mexico and Colombia came next, with Guatemala and Paraguay finishing last among 25 medal winners. With such continuing dominance by the United States, some reporters were asking how much longer the games could continue.

The Pan American Games stamp was announced by the USPS on September 24, 1985. Postmaster General Paul Carlin said the Postal Service would schedule the stamp for 1987, to mark the Tenth Pan American Games, "which will focus the world's attention on these momentous sporting events." Now, on both occasions in which these games have been held in the United States, they have been lauded with a special stamp.

The stamps were shipped from the Bureau based on automatic distribution quantities. All stamps were moved in this manner; none was left at the BEP for subsequent orders.

The Design

Designer Lon Busch also submitted these designs for swimming and bicycling. Similar in style to the final stamp, these were used on maximum cards issued in connection with the games.

Although the stamp was designed for five gravure colors by Lon Busch of St. Louis, the special red ink developed for this issue predominates. The image of the runner repeats in successively lighter shades from right to left. In this, his first stamp design, Busch wanted to depict one runner in motion — not several athletes. A special me-

Designers other than Busch were also asked for Pan American stamp designs. Some of these submissions concentrated on feet.

tallic silver ink was used for the value and lettering. Note that the word "Indianapolis" is in a different typeface from other lettering.

Busch's stamp design, as well as two of his other proposed designs, were made into maximum cards by the USPS (see Maximum Cards section). Busch operates Air Busch, a free-lance commercial illustration agency in St. Louis, Missouri.

First-Day Facts

Issuance of the Pan American stamp in January preceded the games by several months.

The indoor Indiana War Memorial for veterans of the Spanish-American War and World War I was the site for the first-day ceremony on January 29, 1987, in Indianapolis. Designer Busch came from St. Louis to attend. Central Region Postmaster General Jerry K. Lee spoke for the Postal Service and released the stamp.

During the August 8 to August 23 span of the games, 35 special cancels honoring the opening and closing ceremonies and all the events in between were available from the USPS Indianapolis Division. The stylized figures on the pictorial cancels depicted specific athletic competitions, while a circular postmark included the name of the city where each event took place.

22¢ JEAN BAPTISTE POINTE DU SABLE

Date of Issue: February 20, 1987

Catalog Numbers: Scott 2249   Minkus CM1213

Colors: magenta, cyan, yellow, black tone, black type

First-Day Cancel: Chicago, Illinois (Richard J. Daley Civic Center)

FDCs Canceled: 313,054

Format: Panes of 50, vertical, 10 across, 5 down. Printing cylinders of 400.

Perf: 11 (Eureka off-press perforator)

Selvage Markings: U.S. Postal Service© 1986, Use Correct ZIP Code

Designer: Thomas Blackshear

Art Director: Jerry Pinkney (CSAC)

Typographer: Bradbury Thompson (CSAC)

Modeler: Esther Porter (BEP)

Printing: Andreotti 7-color gravure press

Quantity Ordered: 138,000,000
Quantity Distributed: 142,905,000

Plate Block Detail: 5-digit number over/under corner stamps

Tagging: block over vignette

Plate Impressions: Magenta: 1(891,100)
Cyan: 1(891,100)
Yellow: 1(891,100)
Black tone: 1(891,100)
Black type: 1(891,100)

The Stamp

This 22¢ stamp in the Black Heritage series commemorates not only Jean Baptiste Pointe Du Sable, but also the sesquicentennial of the incorporation of the city of Chicago in 1837. It is another of those "hidden" anniversary commemoratives. Nothing of Chicago is mentioned on the stamp, perhaps because the 1985 U.S. Stamp Selection Criteria are ambivalent in this regard. The criteria allow marking of significant anniversary events every 50 years but, in another clause, forbid the honoring of cities, towns, municipalities and counties.

The stamp's selvage carries a 1986 copyright date. That's because the Bureau of Engraving and Printing received artwork on the stamp

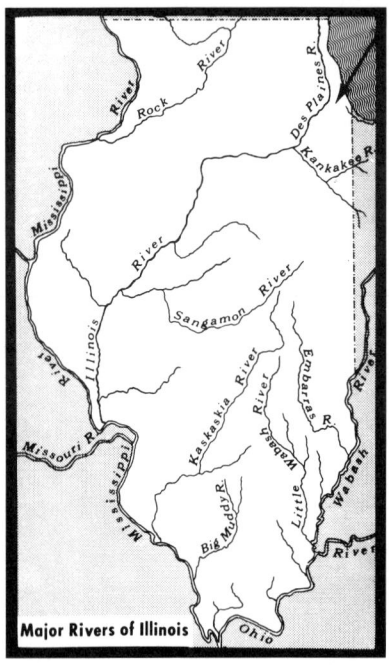

Arrow shows the approximate location of Du Sable's outpost at the mouth of the Chicago River. From there, the Chicago ran into the Des Plaines River, the Des Plaines into the Illinois River, and the Illinois into the Mississippi River. Traders and explorers used this route southward.

in late June 1986, sent the Du Sable issue to press in October 1986, and had it perfed, inspected, and delivered to the USPS by Christmas.

Du Sable is the tenth black in the Black Heritage series. Others have been Harriet Tubman (1978), Martin Luther King, Jr. (1979), Benjamin Banneker (1980), Whitney Moore Young (1981), Jackie Robinson (1982), Scott Joplin (1983), Carter Woodson (1984), Mary McLeod Bethune (1985) and Sojourner Truth (1986). Of these, Jean Baptiste Pointe Du Sable may be the most unknown and the most fascinating.

He was probably born in 1745, almost certainly in Santo Domingo (now Haiti), and undoubtedly of French and African parentage. At 20 he came to New Orleans, employed as an agent for a Santo Domingan mercantile firm. Later, when New Orleans came under Spanish domination, he traveled up the Mississippi River to St. Louis.

As the French boundaries in America constantly contracted northward, Du Sable consistently followed them. During the 1770s, he lived near the present site of Peoria, Illinois. No longer an employee, he was now his own businessman, trading furs with the French and Indians. As his trading flourished, he established a trading post (possibly as early as 1772) on Lake Michigan, at the mouth of what is now the Chicago River. He brought with him a woman of the Potawatomie tribe whom he had married in his Peoria sojourn.

The Chicago portage had attracted visitors long before Du Sable. Traders and Indians used the narrow waterway because it connected Lake Michigan with the Des Plaines River, thence the Illinois and Mississippi rivers. Du Sable was the first to settle there, however, and he found it a good choice.

There, in 1779, Du Sable was found by Colonel Arent Schuyler De Peyster, British commandant at Michilimackinac, a fortified trading post now known as Mackinac Island. In one of the few remaining written references to Du Sable, Peyster described him as "a handsome Negro, well educated and settled at Eschikagou, but much in the French interest." Later in 1779, Du Sable was arrested for spying for the French by British Lieutenant Thomas Bennett of the King's Regiment, then located near what is now Michigan City, Indiana.

Du Sable was taken to Mackinac, where Bennett later reported that he behaved "in every respect becoming to a man in his situation, and has many friends who give him good character." From 1780 to 1784, Du Sable was made superintendent of Lieutenant Governor Patrick Sinclair's business interests. Upon his release, he returned to Eschikagou (an Indian word said to mean "great," "skunk cabbage," "wild onion" or "garlic.")

In 1790 Hugh Heward from Detroit stopped at Du Sable's post, which was near the site of today's *Chicago Sun-Times* building. Heward wrote that he was provided with flour, bread and pork. Historians contend that Du Sable must have had his own flour mill, hogs, crops and even a baker.

Du Sable prospered during his approximate 20 years as Chicago's first settler. When he sold his property in 1800 to Jean Lalime, a French trader, the listed inventory for the sale included a house, 40 by 22 feet; a horse mill, 36 by 24; a bakehouse, 20 by 18; a barn, 40 by 48; a dairy; a poultry house; workshop and stable.

Du Sable's furnishings included a French cabinet with glass doors, a large feather bed, a couch, four tables, seven chairs, mirrors, paintings, dishes and a coffee mill. Undoubtedly, it was one of the most complete establishments owned by a frontiersman in the Middle West, outside of Detroit or St. Louis. To live on the edge of the frontier as Du Sable did, you had to be a jack-of-all-trades. He was a fur trader, probably a farmer, carpenter, cooper and miller — and perhaps even an early distiller.

Some historians have called John Kinzie, who bought Du Sable's old place from Lalime in 1804, the "first Chicagoan." Some, perhaps, dismiss Du Sable because he was not white and because he lived so closely with the Indians. Whatever his ancestry, Du Sable was able to prove he was an American citizen in 1783 when he obtained a government land grant.

Says an Illinois historian, the late Father Thomas A. Meehan: "The title and honor of 'first Chicagoan' belongs to Jean Baptiste Pointe Du Sable, a man whose claim can be substantiated by at least three contemporary documents. He resided in Chicago for almost 20 years, reared three children there, and even, in the last years of his residence, saw a grandchild born in almost the heart of the present-day city . . . From this ingenious, resourceful and seemingly well-educated Negro, Chicago draws her permanency."

After Du Sable left Chicago, he moved to St. Charles, Missouri, to the home of an old friend from Peoria. He died there in 1818.

The Design

The first nine stamps in the Black Heritage series were designed by one man: the Citizens' Stamp Advisory Committee's Jerry Pinkney. This stamp, though listing Pinkney as its art director, was designed by first-time stamp artist Thomas Blackshear of Novato, California.

Two items in the vignette are ficticious: Du Sable and the cabin. No contemporary portraits of Du Sable exist. His house is known to have been 40 by 22 feet from its sale papers, but no one knows precisely what it looked like.

Blackshear reviewed several artists' conceptions of Du Sable before rendering his design. These came primarily from Chicago's Du Sable Museum of African American History and from the Chicago Historical Society. The cabin is the artist's rendering.

First-Day Facts

The stamp was issued in Chicago on February 20, 1987, during Black History Month. The first-day ceremony took place in the Richard J. Daley Civic Center, with Central Region Postmaster General Jerry K. Lee as the USPS speaker.

The public ceremony in the lobby of the Daley Center in downtown Chicago drew a crowd of more than 1,000. Chicago Mayor Harold Washington spoke, recalling that Chicago has a local school named for each person pictured on all stamps in the Black Heritage series. The first-day event took place four days before a primary election was scheduled between Washington and his challenger, Jane Byrne.

22¢ ENRICO CARUSO

Date of Issue: February 27, 1987

Catalog Numbers: Scott 2250   Minkus CM1214

Colors: yellow, magenta, process black, line black

First-Day Cancel: New York, New York (Metropolitan Opera House)

FDCs Canceled: 389,834

Format: Panes of 50, vertical, 10 across, 5 down. Printing cylinders of 200.

Perf: 11 (L-style perforators)

Selvage Markings: U.S. Postal Service© 1987, Use Correct ZIP Code

Designer: Jim Sharpe

Art Director: Jack Williams (USPS)

Modeler: Richard C. Sennett (American Bank Note Company)

Printing: Printed by J.W. Fergusson and Sons on Champlain gravure press. Artwork, perfing, modeling and cutting by American Bank Note Co.

Quantity Ordered: 130,000,000
Quantity Distributed: 130,000,000

Plate Block Detail: Four-digit plate number over/under corner stamp, preceded by letter "A."

Tagging: block over vignette

Plate Impressions: A-1111 (736,172)

The Stamp

Although the 22¢ Caruso stamp was the first released in 1987 to be printed by J.W. Fergusson and Sons and the American Bank Note Company, it was actually produced in 1986. It was the last to be printed under the old ABNC contract with the Postal Service.

The stamp was the tenth in the Performing Arts series, begun in

1978. Caruso is the second operatic performer in the series, the first being John McCormack (1984). Others commemorated in the series are Jimmie Rodgers (1978), George M. Cohan (1978), Will Rogers (1979), W.C. Fields (1980), the Barrymores (1982), Douglas Fairbanks (1984), Jerome Kern (1985) and Duke Ellington (1986).

To millions, Enrico Caruso was grand opera. Struggling young tenors still strive to emulate him, and operatic impresarios continue to hope for his like to come again.

Errico Caruso (the "Enrico" did not emerge until years later) was born in Naples, Italy, on February 25, 1873. He was the 18th of 21 children, and the first to live past infancy. His father, Marcellino, was a hard-drinking mechanic who was all for putting Enrico to work as soon as possible. His mother, Anna, demanded that he go to school and take voice lessons. The young Caruso soon began singing in the churches of Naples.

His boyish contralto was the best in Naples; he became known as "Carusiello," or "little divo." Caruso was no sissy; he once drew blood from a deposed schoolmate champion who tried to wrest a medal from Caruso which he had won. Reprimanded by his principal for such violence, Caruso threw the medal at his pedagogue's feet and stalked off. From a fiesty child, he grew into an adult of great humor and compassion.

While doing some secular singing in 1891, he met his first mentor and discoverer, Eduardo Missiano. Caruso never forgot him. Years later, he saw to it that Eduardo's baritone was employed for small roles at the Metropolitan Opera.

All during Enrico's youth — over his father's objections — mother Anna was squeezing one dollar a month from the household budget for music lessons. Caruso made his operatic debut at 21 in Naples Teatro Nuovo. He sang in an opera called *L'Amico Francesco*, which lasted but two peformances and was never heard from again. His first standard opera appearance was in *Cavalleria Rusticana* at Casserta, Italy. He was good, but still learning.

At Salerno, in 1896, he first sang the role that was to belong to him forever: Canio, the tragic clown, in *Il Pagliacci*. Its "Vesti la giubba" aria became his trademark. His fame was spreading in Italy, but he suffered a disappointment when famed composer Puccini promised, and then withdrew from him, the tenor lead in *Tosca*. Caruso only said: "One's career is neither so brilliant nor so easy as may seem to the casual eye of the public." He and Puccini went on to become lifelong friends.

In 1898 Caruso was picked for the tenor lead in *Fedora*. After that performance, his name resounded throughout the operatic world. "The contracts descended on me like a heavy rainstorm," Caruso said. The highest-paid offer came from Russia, and Caruso triumphed at St. Petersburg in the role of Rodolfo in *La Boheme*. London, Paris,

Vienna, Buenos Aires, Rio de Janiero, Moscow and Lisbon soon followed. In Germany and Austria, seats for a Caruso performance were often so scarce they sold at auction.

On Monday evening, November 23, 1903, Enrico Caruso made his U.S. debut at the Metropolitan Opera in New York City as the Duke in *Rigoletto*. Though critics called his voice "a pure tenor of quality, range and power," the Met audience gave him no overwhelming ovation. Next came *Aida*, which found Caruso just recovered from tonsil-

Caruso was an expert caricaturist. Here are the great tenor's renditions of Woodrow Wilson, himself and conductor Arturo Toscanini.

litus. Singing the role of Radames, Caruso held back his voice until the final act, when he let it loose. The applause thundered at the curtain; critics were amazed. "His fire is unbounded. He hurls his heart at his listeners," said one.

Caruso was often called on to sing the National Anthem at various events. His English, at first, was very poor, so he carried the lyrics written in this form:

"O seiken iu sii bai dhi dons erli lait
huat so praudli ui heild
at dhi twailaits last glimmin
husis brod straips and
brait stars thru dhi perilos
fait — Or dhi ramparts ui
uact uere so gallontli strimmin."

Caruso captured New York. For 18 seasons, he returned every fall and winter to the Metropolitan, giving 607 performances in 37 different operas. During most of that time, he also made records for the Victor Talking Machine Company. Over his career, Victor paid him $1,825,000, about $130,000 more than he earned at the Metropolitan. Royalties from record sales paid to his estate now far exceed the worldwide fees Caruso earned in his lifetime.

Caruso called the critics "kind — except about my fat and my clothes." The contemporary critics conceded that Caruso's voice — big, brilliant, smooth and warm — was alone in its greatness, whether singing a simple song or a demanding aria. It was often advertised as "the most glorious voice of this generation." Opera fans or not, people loved Caruso for his outgoing mien, his mirth and his "innate kindness," as soprano Geraldine Farrar put it.

On Christmas Eve 1920, blood poured from his throat during an American performance of *LaJuive*. He had complained of pains in his side that often had him doubled over and screaming. Sailing for Naples after a mild recovery, Caruso was diagnosed by Italian doctors as having a purulent pleurisy, whose fluid caused the pain and threatened the heart.

Caruso died in his birthplace August 2, 1921, at age 48. The king of Italy himself opened a basilica for Caruso that had never been used for funerals. Mrs. Caruso was not impressed. "There have been many kings," she said, "but only one Caruso."

The Design

Artist Jim Sharpe made several changes in this early version of the Caruso stamp, although the image remained the same. Lines in the headdress and right shoulder of the cape were simplified and accentuated. More highlights were added to the face, buttons on the tunic were sharpened, and the linework in the pendant was improved.

The first eight stamps in the Performing Arts series bore the words "Performing Arts." With the ninth, the Duke Ellington issue in 1986, the series identification was eliminated. Neither does the designation appear on this stamp for Caruso. Smaller background and foreground designs have also disappeared.

Jim Sharpe of Westport, Connecticut, has designed all ten of the stamps in this series. His Caruso design is a composite of many photos of the tenor in his role of the Duke of Manua in *Rigoletto*. Some pictures show Caruso with a goatee and high, flounced collar as shown on this stamp. Others picture him in the same role with no beard and less flamboyant dress.

The role was one of Caruso's favorites. He performed it for his debuts in New York, London, Paris and Vienna.

Caruso was a noisy dresser — onstage and off. He had a particular penchant for odd hats and white suits.

First-Day Facts

The Metropolitan Opera at Lincoln Center in New York City, itself the subject of a 1983 centennial stamp, was the site for the Caruso first day on February 27, 1987. The public ceremony took place on the grand tier of the Metropolitan, with Postmaster General Preston R. Tisch speaking for the USPS. James A. Marcus, chairman of the Metropolitan Opera Association, and Enrico Caruso, Jr., the singer's son, also took part.

Varieties

Collectors may note color differences in the Caruso stamps, with selvage on some stamps exhibiting a yellowish hue and selvage on others tending toward the bluish side.

The reason for the color variations is that American Bank Note Company, producer of the Caruso issue, used two suppliers of standard gravure printing paper. Sixty rolls of paper were supplied by Henry & Leigh Slater, a British subsidiary of James River, an American firm. Seventy rolls were purchased from Champion Paper Company, a U.S. firm.

Although both papers are within USPS specifications, the Slater paper is yellowish, while the Champion paper is bluish in appearance. But such minor differences often occur in paper from a single production run from one supplier, said Don McDowell of the USPS Stamp Division. The Caruso issue was the last one produced under a contract between the USPS and ABNC that expired at the end of 1986. Permission was given by the USPS for ABNC to use up all remaining gravure paper stock.

Two right vertical rows on a pane of Caruso stamps were discovered with black gravure printing missing. Dealer William S. Langs reported the error.

22¢ GIRL SCOUTS

Date of Issue: March 12, 1987

Catalog Numbers: Scott 2251   Minkus CM1215

Colors: magenta, yellow, cyan, black, green (offset); black, red (intaglio)

First-Day Cancel: Washington, D.C. (Departmental Auditorium)

FDCs Canceled: 556,391

Format: Panes of 50, vertical, 10 across, 5 down. Printing cylinders of 400 (intaglio), 200 (offset).

Perf: 11 (Eureka off-press perforators)

Selvage Markings: U.S. Postal Service© 1987, Use Correct ZIP Code

Designer, Art Director and Typographer: Richard D. Sheaff (CSAC)

Engraver: Edward Archer (BEP)

Modeler: Ronald C. Sharpe (BEP)

Printing: 3-color intaglio, 6-color offset D Press

Quantity Ordered: 150,000,000
Quantity Distributed: 149,980,000

Plate Block Detail: Single-digit intaglio number over/under corner stamp; 5-digit offset number over/under adjacent stamp.

Tagging: block over vignette

Plate Impressions: Offset magenta: 1(1,064,104), 2(303,895)
Offset yellow: 1(1,064,104), 2(303,895)
Offset cyan: 1(1,064,104), 2(303,895)
Offset black: 1(1,064,104), 2(303,895)
Offset green: 1(95,871), 2(934,987), 3(337,140)
Intaglio black: 1(1,367,990)

The Stamp

According to the Postal Service's own stamp selection criteria, this 22¢ Girl Scout commemorative should never have been issued. The stamp rules state: "Events of historical significance will be marked only on anniversaries in multiples of 50 years." This stamp honors the 75th anniversary of the founding of the Girl Scouts of America. A 1962 issue had already highlighted the 50th anniversary.

The stamp also lauds the Girl Scouts organization. Here again, stamp selection rules forbid the honoring of any "fraternal, political, sectarian, service or charitable organizations." The USPS would only say that the Girl Scout stamp was a "long-standing commitment."

But it wasn't these technicalities that had the Girl Scout stamp in trouble long before its issue date. A February 2, 1987, letter from GSUSA New York national headquarters informed all cachetmakers that the Girl Scouts had entered into an exclusive agreement with Washington Press, makers of Artcraft covers. The contract forbade all other first-day cover servicers from picturing emblems, trademarks and uniforms of the Girl Scouts on their covers. That included the words, "Girl Scouts," and their 75th anniversary logo.

Several cachetmakers responded satirically and bitterly to the Girl Scouts' ban on using its name and symbols. One shows a new Merit Badge for Censorship, another a monetized version of its 75th anniversary logo, while a third avoids the forbidden Girl Scout uniform. Still another notes the 75th birthday of an anonymous "National Organization for Girls."

This letter, signed by Patricia A. Smith, assistant national executive director, said that any infringement would see the Girl Scouts "taking appropriate action under federal statutes and common law."

Cachetmakers were up in arms. Phone calls to GSUSA in New York went unanswered. Letters of protest from cachetmakers went to the Postal Service, the Girl Scouts and the philatelic press. One cachetmaker, who had already printed his covers, said he would block the design out by overprinting "Censored by a national organization." He also planned to change the name "Girl Scouts" to "Female Scouts." Postal Service action was almost immediate. They met with the GSUSA on February 13.

Rumor had it that the Postal Service was livid, that the USPS had threatened to cancel the stamp unless the Girl Scouts withdrew their cachet ban. That was unlikely, however, since the stamps were printed, perfed and ready to go as of mid-January. When questioned about the withdrawal threat, Don McDowell, general manager of the Stamps Division, said, "No comment." He suggested contacting the Girl Scouts, but the writer of the letter was not taking calls.

On February 17, a second letter went to cachetmakers stating that the first GSUSA letter was misunderstood. The second letter explained that "it was not the intention of the Girl Scouts to prevent cachet manufacturers from using the Girl Scout stamp." Officials said that cachetmakers were welcome to make generic cachets, but that anyone using the Girl Scouts logo, emblems or trademarked symbols had to get permission from national headquarters.

All of the furor recalled the W.C. Fields stamp of 1980 when Fields' heirs reminded the Postal Service that they had full control over the use of Fields' name, voice and likeness. The USPS negotiated a payment of $2,023 to rescue the commemorative stamp, but cachetmakers found that an advance payment of six percent of estimated cachet sales was expected if cachet designs used Fields' name or image.

With this stamp, the Girl Scouts went into the first-day cover business. The Artcraft licensed covers would be sold by National Equipment Service (the division of GSUSA that supplies Girl Scout badges and uniforms) for $1.25 each up to 100 covers, $1 each for 100 to 499, and 75¢ for quantities of more than 500.

The stamp design offers a fertile field for topical collectors. Pictured among the 14 merit badges are wagons, animals, space, medicine, weather vanes, traffic lights, numbers, anchors, buildings and national emblems. From top to bottom in the left column are badges for wildlife, computer fun, health and safety, individual sports, and the top half of a bicycling merit badge. The middle column features badges for active citizen, peoples of the United States, boating and popular arts. At the right are local lore, aerospace, wider opportunities, science around town and communications arts (partially obscured).

This 1948 stamp for Juliette Gordon Low, founder of the Girl Scouts, had no anniversary significance. Mrs. Low was born in 1860, died in 1927 and founded the Girl Scouts in 1912.

Girl Scouting was started in 1912 by Juliette Gordon Low, the daughter of a general and wife of a wealthy Englishman who lived in England, Scotland and the United States. While in England in 1911, she learned about the Girl Guide movement, organized along the lines of Sir Robert Baden-Powell's Boy Scouts. At her Scottish estate, she taught seven Guides to cook, raise chickens and spin wool.

On returning to the United States in 1912, she and a cousin, Nina

Use of this 75th anniversary logo — along with all other symbols, designations and uniforms — was forbidden by Girl Scouts to cachetmakers who did not secure permission.

Pape, enlisted 18 girls into the Girl Guides on March 12. One year later, their name changed to Girl Scouts.

From the first 18 who met on a Savannah, Georgia, tennis court, the Girl Scouts grew rapidly: 5,000 by 1915 and 40,000 by 1920. Since its inception, more than 52 million American girls and adults have participated in scouting.

Today, Girl Scouts have changed greatly from the beret-clad little scouts who came knocking at the door during cookie sale time. By the end of 1987, Girl Scouts will be dressed in urban blue. The girls will still be selling mints and cookies, but they are now learning to be far more than homemakers.

These are changing times for Girl Scouting. Several years ago, there was a general decline in membership all over the country. About two years ago, memberships began increasing again, as scouting widened its horizons. Programs for 5-year-olds, known as Daisy Scouts, brought in younger children. With more and more working women, older Girl Scouts are into career courses that may prepare them for traditional jobs or for police work, carpentry or computers.

Picturing an intermediate Girl Scout in uniform, this 1962 stamp marked the 50th anniversary of the founding of the Girl Scouts.

Local scouting units are now giving patches (not badges) for jujitsu, child abuse, suicide prevention, drugs and alcohol control, and emergency preparedness. While many Girl Scouts used to live in sheltered rural environments, most Scouts today live in urban settings where they are exposed to more people and ideas at an earlier age.

Girl Scouts of the U.S.A. is the largest voluntary organization for girls in the world. Open to all girls ages 5 through 17, Girl Scouts now offers five program levels: Daisy (ages 5-6), Brownies (ages 6-8), Junior (ages 8-11), Cadette (ages 11-14) and Senior Girl Scouts (ages 14-17). In Juliette Low's words, "A Girl Scout should be almost a grown-up woman, capable of bearing the responsibilities that come to her at home and in the community."

The Design

The Girl Scout stamp had progressed this far before careful research uncovered an error. The aerospace badge (second from top at right) had been rotated 180 degrees out of position.

The design was really a photographic creation by Richard D. Sheaff of Needham Heights, Massachusetts, one of the design coordinators for the Citizens' Stamp Advisory Committee. The green stamp background copies the color of the green sash upon which the badges are worn. The badges were selected to provide color contrast and note the wide range of Girl Scout training. It was Sheaff's first design since his award-winning Stamp Collecting booklet of 1986.

The stamp was printed on the intaglio/offset D Press. Prior stamps from that press have most often had their lettering and values in intaglio, the balance of the stamps in offset. This one uses reverse lettering for its legends, and scatters the intaglio throughout the stamp badges. Black intaglio made the ribs and shading of the Conestoga wagon, the black outlines of the Capitol dome, and the latitude/longitude lines on the globe. Red intaglio created the stripes on the running shoes and sock. Eveything else is printed in offset.

First-Day Facts

The stamp was released at ceremonies held on March 12, 1987, at the Departmental Auditorium in Washington, D.C. The auditorium, located at 1300 Constitution Avenue N.W., is one available for use by any government agency.

Senior Assistant Postmaster General David H. Charters spoke for the USPS. Betty S. Pilsbury, national president of the Girl Scouts of the United States of America, attended.

The Girl Scouts sold their official, unstamped cacheted envelopes for $1.25 each — a price that made most collectors blink. Stamped and postmarked first-day covers were $1.50 each. GSUSA workers said that 30,000 covers had been brought to the ceremony for sale.

22¢ UNITED WAY

Date of Issue: April 28, 1987

Catalog Numbers: Scott 2275   Minkus CM1226

Colors: magenta, yellow, cyan, purple, black (offset); purple (intaglio)

First-Day Cancel: Washington, D.C. (DAR Constitution Hall)

FDCs Canceled: 473,329

Format: Panes of 50, horizontal, 5 across, 10 down. Printing cylinders of 400 (intaglio), 200 (offset).

Perf: 11 (Eureka off-press perforator)

Selvage Markings: U.S. Postal Service© 1986, Use Correct ZIP Code

Designer: Jerry Pinkney

Art Director: Jack Williams (USPS)

Engraver: Kenneth Kipperman (BEP)

Modeler: Peter Cocci (BEP)

Printing: 3-color intaglio, 6-color offset D Press

Quantity Ordered: 157,000,000
Quantity Distributed: 156,995,000

Plate Block Detail: Single-digit intaglio number alongside corner stamp; 5-digit offset number alongside adjacent stamp.

Tagging: block over vignette

The Stamp

It was said of former Postmaster General William Bolger (only partly in jest) that "everytime he attended a cocktail party in Georgetown, the Postal Service got a new stamp." Despite the guideline rules of the Citizens' Stamp Advisory Committee, the postmaster general himself can direct, or can be influenced to direct, the issuance of a stamp. Members of the CSAC privately call these issues "directed verdicts." The United Way commemorative was such a stamp. It was ordered despite a rule against stamps for charitable organizations.

The United Way design was unveiled December 1, 1986, at the United Way national headquarters in Alexandria, Virginia, by Gordon C. Morison, assistant postmaster general for the Philatelic Affairs Department. Morison noted that the stamp honors volunteers who make the United Way work. He recalled an old Irish proverb that says: "Give cheerfully with one hand and you will gather well with two." While it is true that our country has been fortunate in many ways, it is also true that we have "gathered" as much as we have because so many men and women have been willing to share their time and good fortune with others, Morison said.

The United Way is 100 years old, and the stamp marks that anniversary. Though it has gone through many name changes — among them Community Chest and United Fund — the United Way counts its beginnings from the Denver of 1887, when a rabbi, a priest and two ministers created a community-wide effort to help the needy who had been left in the backwash of the gold and silver booms.

The former Community Chest organization, which appeared in 1913 in Cleveland, Ohio, also traced its roots to the Denver effort for a centralized fund-raising drive for community health and social welfare agencies. National coordination of Community Chests began in 1918 with the American Association for Community Organization.

During the 1940s and 1950s, business and labor leaders joined together in organizing and supporting community-wide campaigns to replace the multiple, time-wasting appeals in the workplace. The conglomerate came to charity as it had come to business. In 1970 the national organization became the United Way.

The United Way functions in more than 2,200 communities across the country, bringing together millions of volunteers from all walks of life to help with expanding needs for health and human services. In years ahead, the United Way of America sees family crises, unemployment and access to health care as future, crucial social needs.

That means more volunteers, and they are really the focus of the United Way's 100th celebration. The first-day ceremony for the stamp coincided with National Volunteer Week, April 26-May 2. While the United Way has salaried employees working in nearly every United Way community, they are there to administrate, train and guide volunteers.

Who sets local campaign goals from one year to the next? Local boards of United Way volunteers. Who serves on these local boards? Primarily local community leaders, who move from lower-level to greater responsibilities during their service to United Way. Who allots United Way donations to various agencies? Each agency must apply every year (except for a few multiple-year funding commitments in large cities). Which agency gets how much is again up to the local board of volunteer citizens.

The cost of full-time administration, training and audio-visual solicitation presentations runs from 10-11 percent of gifts received. As charitable expenses go, that is a very low figure. The United Way is a tightly budgeted business whose receipts go to the bottom line for the work that needs to be done.

This familiar symbol of the United Way was not used on the stamp. It has often appeared as a cancel marking, usually rendering the used stamp unfit for collecting purposes.

But all is not sweetness and light in the world of human help. In Washington, D.C., charities such as the American Cancer Society, American Heart Association, March of Dimes and others, have complained that the United Way is abusing its authority. The Combined Federal Campaign involves all charities, and its officials say that the United Way retains all funds not specifically designated to other charities. That's unfair to contributors who probably think that the CFC donations will be split evenly with the United Way and all other charities, say American Cancer Society representatives. Shakespeare notwithstanding, the quality of mercy does get strained occasionally.

The Design

Jerry Pinkney of Croton-on-Hudson, New York, intended that his United Way stamp design of six overlapping profiles of various ages and races represents the diversity of people giving to and receiving

These three lighthearted, whimsical approaches to a United Way stamp were considered by the Citizens' Stamp Advisory Committee. The CSAC opted, however, for the more serious design by Jerry Pinkney.

help from the United Way. Pinkney has also designed most of the stamps to date in the Black Heritage series, along with the macabre Help End Hunger stamp of 1985.

The profiles are all in purple. Their purple background was printed in offset, while facial details such as eyes, noses, mouths, ears and hair were highlighted by intaglio purple. All other colors on the stamp were applied via offset printing, including all lettering.

First-Day Facts

Postmaster General Preston R. Tisch released the stamp on the morning of April 28, 1987, in the Daughters of the American Revolution Hall in Washington, D.C. The first-day ceremony served as the final event of the United Way's special centennial conference on the efforts of America's volunteers. Thousands of those volunteers received "thank you" letters posted with the new United Way stamp.

Also taking part in the ceremony were James D. Robinson III, 1985-1986 chairman of the United Way's Board of Governors, and Richard J. Ferris, the 1987 chairman.

Backing up the "United Communities" lettering on the stamp, many U.S. post offices joined the United Way in saluting volunteers in their areas.

PMG Tisch, in his first-day remarks, compared the Postal Service and the United Way. "Like the United Way, the Postal Service is a huge network with a presence in every town and city. We both exist expressly to bring people closer together. And we succeed not because of technology or dollars. We succeed because of people."

22¢ WILDLIFE (PANE OF 50)

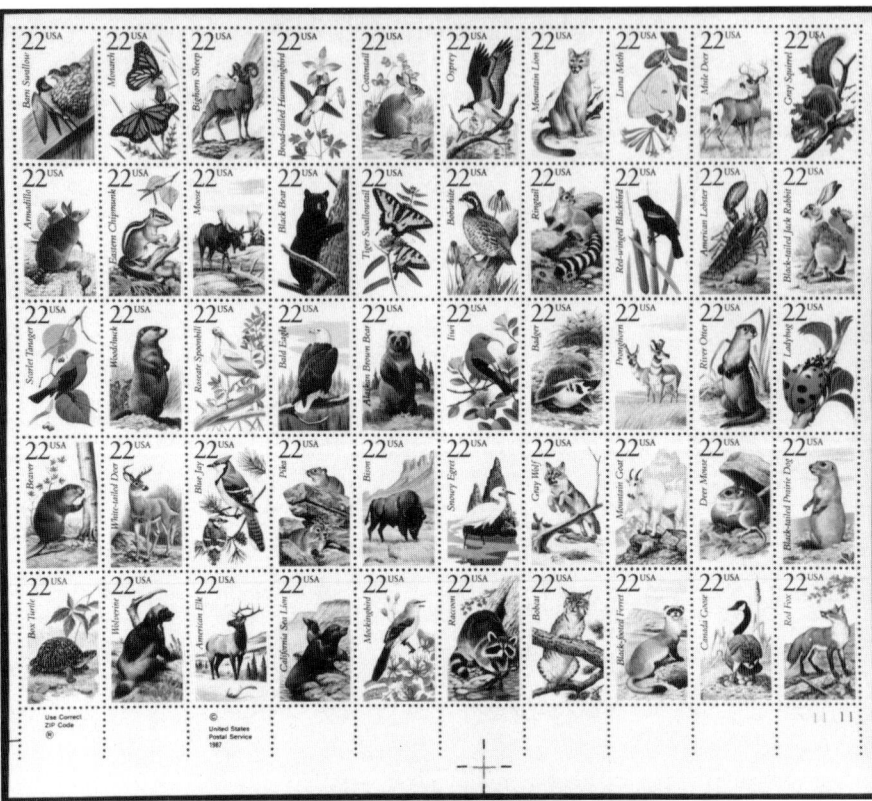

Date of Issue: June 13, 1987

Catalog Numbers: Scott 2286-2335 (pane of 50: 2335a)
Minkus CM1227-76

Colors: magenta, cyan, yellow, black tone, black type

First-Day Cancel: Toronto, Ontario, Canada (CAPEX 87 International Philatelic Exhibition)

FDCs Canceled: not available

Format: Panes of 50, vertical, 10 across, 5 down. Printing cylinders of 400.

Perf: 11 (Eureka off-press perforator)

Selvage Markings: U.S. Postal Service© 1987, Use Correct ZIP Code

Designer: Chuck Ripper

Art Director: Jack Williams, Program Manager Philatelic Design (USPS)

Modeler: Esther F. Porter (BEP)

Printing: Gravure Andreotti 7-color press

Quantity Ordered: 600,000,000
Quantity Distributed: 645,975,000

Plate Block Detail: 5-digit group over/under corner stamps

Tagging: block over vignette

Plate Impressions: Magenta: 1(3,433,500)
Cyan: 1(3,433,500)
Yellow: 1(3,433,500)
Black tone: 1(3,433,500)
Black type: 1(3,433,500)

The Stamps

Speaking before the Dallas Collectors Club on April 4, 1987, Senior Assistant Postmaster General Mitchell H. Gordon made this revealing statement: "The Postal Service has learned through marketing surveys that Americans favor wildlife themes above all other stamp subjects." Long before today's esoteric marketing techniques were born, however, the United States was picturing wildlife on stamps.

Since a horse and two eagles first appeared on the 1869 series, animals, birds, fish, crustaceans and insects have been seen almost 200 times on U.S. stamps. Most often, only one or two creatures are pictured. Occasionally, a single stamp may hold a menagerie, as did the 1984 Louisiana World Exposition commemorative. That stamp, also by Chuck Ripper, the designer of this Wildlife pane of 50, crowds in a turkey, a warbler, a heron, a crayfish, a goose, a turtle, a frog and three kinds of fish.

A 1967 5¢ U.S. stamp for the centennial of Canadian federation and a 1978 CAPEX sheet picturing wildlife along the U.S.-Canadian border were the only prior U.S. postal items to be released in a foreign country.

A catalog recap of wildlife on U.S. postage stamps shows this casual tally: 58 birds, 31 horses, 16 dogs, 14 fish, seven oxen and a half-dozen bears. Among the birds, the eagle has soared 13 times. The cardinal, meadowlark and mockingbird come next. At the bottom of the wildlife postal scale come snakes, elephants, dinosaurs and sheep. Ducks have appeared more often than cattle, and owls more frequently than cats.

This is the third time the USPS has issued a pane of 50 different stamps. The first was a 1976 pane of 50 State Flags for the Bicentennial Era; the second was a 1982 pane of 50 State Birds and Flowers stamps. The Postal Service got some hate mail on the State Flags, not because of the subjects or 50-stamp format, but because many people interpreted the words, "Bicentennial Era," as supporting the women's Equal Rights Amendment. The pane received the American Philatelic Society's "Black Blot" as an overextended issue, but went on to win the *Linn's* popularity poll for that year. More than 8,720,000 panes were printed.

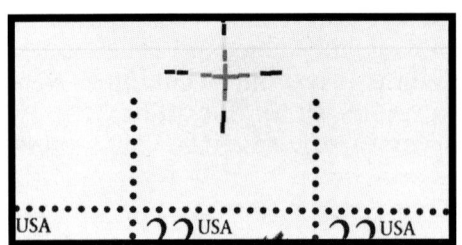

The registration cross on this pane of Wildlife stamps is slightly out of color alignment. Stamps from this pane appeared fuzzy, when compared to panes having more normal registration crosses.

When the 1982 State Birds and Flowers 50-stamp pane came along, the APS did not "Black Blot" the issue, saying that revised rules required a judgment on the overall stamp policies of a country — not on just one issue alone. The Birds and Flowers pane proved even more popular than the State Flags. More than 50,000 full panes of 50 were first-day canceled, over $500,000 worth of stamps. Since some states had duplicate state birds, the cardinal appeared seven times. There were multiple mockingbirds and robins, plus some repeated flowers.

Unlike these first two panes, the Wildlife stamps do not have a state name on each stamp. The stamps do not depict official state animals. Only 15 states have official state animals. Many of the animals, birds and insects shown in the Wildlife pane are found in more than one state. The USPS maintains that every area of the United States has at least one native animal shown.

From left to right, from top to bottom across the pane, these creatures appear. (Any identifiable flora on the stamps are in parentheses.)

The *Barn Swallow* is found almost everywhere in the United States. It spends summers as far north as Alaska, winters as far south as Brazil. Unlike other common swallows, it bears a deeply forked tail. It likes to nest — not only in barns — but almost any buildings.

Because it feeds on milkweed, the *Monarch Butterfly* has an unpleasant taste to birds, who leave it strictly alone. It migrates south in winter, either to the southern United States or Central America. Tagged Monarchs have been found and identified up to 1,800 miles away. (Field Thistle)

The *Bighorn Sheep* lives in the Rocky Mountains, where it is often sought by trophy hunters for its handsome, curling horns. Its superb sense of balance allows it to gallop down slopes that are almost vertical without losing its footing.

At four inches long, the *Broad-tailed Hummingbird* is the smallest inhabitant of mountainous country. When its wings move 60 to 70 times per second, they create the hum that gives it its name. It can hover in mid-air or dart upward, downward, forward or backward with great speed. (Colorado Columbine)

Wild *Cottontail* rabbits are found in the United States, Canada and Mexico. They live in shallow holes in the ground, often alone. In winter, they seek burrows made by badgers, skunks, prairie dogs and woodchucks. If forced to run, they are easily caught. Most survive little more than a year. (Red Clover)

The *Osprey*, a large bird of the hawk family, takes its name from a Latin word meaning "bonebreaker." Living near fresh and salt water in almost every temperate country in the world, it catches fish by diving feet first into the water and spiking its prey with sharp talons.

The *Mountain Lion*, which once had the widest distribution of any Western Hemisphere mammal, now exists primarily in the granite crags and isolated valleys of the Western Rocky Mountains. A few also inhabit the Florida Everglades and parts of New England. They are more common in Mexico and Central America than in the United States.

The *Luna Moth* belongs to the group of Giant Silkworm Moths, though it is not a silkmaker. With its pale green color and long tails, it has a graceful, fragile beauty not unlike a butterfly. It can grow up to four or five inches in length. (Trumpet Honeysuckle)

Mule Deer are much like the more common white-tailed deer, the most numerous large game animals of North America. The deer are named for their large, furry ears, resembling those of a mule. Like other deer, they are usually found near forests, where trees and grasses supply food, and bushes a place to sleep.

The *Gray Squirrel* is found throughout the United States. Common in cities and suburbs, they are often the first wild animal a child sees. Though largely vegetarian, they are known to eat eggs and small birds. One type of gray squirrel (having a skin fold attached at the wrist) is also a flying squirrel. (Red Oak)

The *Armadillo* likes a warm, moist climate. This nine-banded, bony plated mammal is found primarily in Texas, but also in Louisiana and parts of Florida. It feasts on insects, earthworms and spiders. Unable to run or fight, the armadillo curls into a ball when endangered. Few enemies can get a grip on him then with teeth or claws. (Texas Prickly Pear)

Shyer than the Gray Squirrel, the *Eastern Chipmunk* is usually found in wooded, less-settled areas. Smaller also, it measures about eight inches long, including tail. Chipmunks live in underground tunnels, where they store seeds and nuts for their winter's sleep. Their lifespan is just two to three years. (European White Birch)

Moose like forests with swamps and lakes. They want open areas without humans and development. The moose is the largest member of the deer family, often standing 7½ feet at the shoulder and weighing up to 1,800 pounds. In North America, they live from Maine to Alaska and in the Rockies south to Wyoming.

At about five feet long, the *Black Bear* is the smallest bear of North America. They can become troublesome around camps and cabins if food is left within their reach. They have been known to injure and kill people who feed them. About 75,000 of them inhabit the National Forests of the United States. Hunters kill about 25,000 per year.

The *Tiger Swallowtail* butterfly is so named because of the long, ribbon-like extensions on its rear wings. It is one of the largest butterflies in North America with wingspreads of about five inches. Like other butterflies, this one tastes a flower's sweetness with its feet. A long proboscis then uncurls to take the flower's nectar. (Orange Milkweed)

The *Bobwhite* is listed as a bird "that helps us." It can find and eat 5,000 to 15,000 weed seeds in one day. When bobwhites were killed off in some U.S. areas by man, efforts were often made to re-establish them because of their weed seed destruction. (Purple Coneflower)

The *Ringtail* is a speedy, slender member of the raccoon family, and has a black and white ringed tail that grows from 13 to 17 inches long. It lives in deserts and forests from Oregon to Mexico, and east into Colorado and Texas. It sleeps during the day and hunts at night, feeding on rodents, birds and insects. (Cape Marigold)

The *Redwinged Blackbird* is found all over North America. The red and yellow shoulder patch marks the male only. Their nests are found in marshes, cattails and bushes on the edge of water. Though they destroy weed seeds and insects, they also consume farmers' growing grain. (Common Cattail)

The *American Lobster* lives along the Atlantic Coast from Labrador to the Carolinas on the bottom of the ocean near the shore. From 12 to 24 inches long, it is larger than most European lobsters. Dark green or dark blue when alive, its shell turns bright red only when cooked. U.S. and Canadian fishermen catch about 80 million pounds of lobsters a year.

The *Black-tailed Jackrabbit* is not a rabbit. It's a hare. Hares are larger than rabbits, have longer ears and more powerful hind legs. Black-tailed jackrabbits are sometimes called "jackass hares" because their ears resemble those of a donkey. They inhabit the grasslands of the West and Southwest. (Beavertail)

The true *Scarlet Tanagers,* sometimes called "firebirds," are residents of the eastern United States. Males have bright red feathers with black wings and tails. A rosy-red summer tanager inhabits southern states. Tanagers are helpful to farmers since they are great eaters of insects. (American Basswood)

Woodchucks, better known as groundhogs, live in Canada and the eastern and midwestern parts of the United States. They build complex burrows containing several compartments, and hibernate through the winter months. How a woodchuck acts on Groundhog Day is supposed to predict when spring will arrive. (Common Dandelion)

Roseate Spoonbills are long-legged wading birds with large spoon-shaped bills. They live near estuaries, saltwater bayous and lakes, feeding by sweeping their spatulate bills from side to side, catching small fish and crustaceans. Roseate Spoonbills range from 24 to 32 inches tall. They are found in the Gulf Coast and warm areas of the southern United States. (Red Mangrove)

The *Bald Eagle,* for all its ferocious reputation, is a timid hunter that feeds mainly on fish and dead animals. It was chosen as the national bird of the United States in 1782. The bald eagle nests in tall trees or mountain cliffs. It is in danger of extinction, with only about 15,000 left in the United States, most of which are in Alaska.

Alaskan Brown Bears are the largest meat-eating animals living on land. They grow to nine feet long and weigh in at 1,500 pounds. Weak in sight and hearing, they have an excellent sense of smell. Like many bears, they can appear friendly and docile one minute, and attack the next. They are found in Alaska and its nearby islands.

The *Iiwi* is a Hawaiian songbird, named for its squeaky call, "ee-ee-ve-ee." A nectar-feeder with a long nose, the Iiwi is six inches long with a red body, black wings with small white patches and a black tail. Along with the Alaskan Brown Bear, it is the westernmost of the Wildlife stamp subjects. (Ohia Lehua)

Badgers are the champion diggers of the weasel family. Digging out gophers, ground squirrels and mice provides the meat in their diet. Badgers are named for the outline of a "badge" seen on their faces when viewed head on. Badgers are most at home in the plains, prairies and deserts of the West.

The *Pronghorn*, often called the American antelope, is not an antelope. It has no close relatives anywhere in the world. Standing from 35 to 42 inches high, the pronghorn is perhaps the fastest mammal in North America. Found from Iowa west to the Pacific Coast, the pronghorn sticks to open grasslands, where its superb vision and speed can protect it from enemies.

The *River Otter* lives close to water and spends most of its time in it. These members of the weasel family are expert swimmers, divers and fishers. They are awkward on land. The otter is found everywhere in the world except Australia. It is a playful, gregarious creature that often hunts in pairs and packs.

The United States has about 150 species of *Ladybugs*. The USPS chose to picture the convergent ladybug on this stamp. This specie gets its name from the habit of these colorful bugs to pass the winter months crowded in dense masses beneath overhanging ledges or other secluded locations. This bug is most prevalent in California. (Rose — no specific species)

The *Beaver*, equally at home in water or on land, is known as "nature's engineer." By cutting enough trees to dam up a stream, beavers create a pond deep enough to keep the bottom from freezing. The underwater entrance to the house and dam keeps them safe from predators. More beavers are found in the United States and Canada than anywhere in the world. (Maple and Quaking Aspen)

The *White-tailed Deer*, sometimes called Virginia deer, stands about 3½ feet tall and weighs roughly 200 pounds. Its white tail, for which it is named, grows about one foot long. It is brown on top, but white underneath. When the deer is frightened into running, the tail stands straight up, showing as white. It is found throughout the United States.

Blue Jays are large, bold, loud-voiced birds, relatives of the crows and magpies. They have adapted to civilization so well that they seem to prefer living near people. Throughout the eastern United States and Canada in fall and winter, they can be heard shrieking "Thief! Thief!" (Table Mountain Pine)

The *Pika*, a type of rabbit, lives among loose rock on mountain sides above timberline. It is called the "little haymaker of the mountains" because it spends most of its life collecting grasses and food for winter storage. About seven inches long, it resembles a guinea pig.

Bison are not buffalo. The United States has no buffalo, but it has some 40 thousand bison in fenced game preserves. In 1889 only 551 bison could be counted in the United States; millions had been slaughtered by white and Indian hunters. Three centuries ago, about 40 million roamed the North American continent.

The *Snowy Egret* is a heron, a group of large wading birds with slender bodies and long, broad wings. Although it was a common sight in the once-abundant wetlands of the East and South, the snowy egret barely escaped extinction when its airy, white feathers came into fashion for women's hats.

The *Gray Wolf,* looking much like a German shepherd dog, lives and hunts largely in Alaska, Canada and a few northern U.S. states. Wolves usually live in packs, with each member having its own dominant or subordinate rank. Packs establish private territories. Should an alien wolf venture into a territory, he might be killed.

The *Rocky Mountain Goat* looks like a goat, but is more closely related to the antelope. Dense, wooly underfur, covered with an overcoat of long, white hair, keeps it warm in its high, windy and cold home above timberline. Even more agile than the bighorn sheep, the mountain goat is found in the high Rockies from Alaska south through Washington, Idaho and Montana.

Deer Mice are found throughout North America from Mexico to Alaska. They live in mountains, plains, deserts and swamps. They build their nests in tunnels they dig, or in hollow logs, tree stumps or cracks in rocks. Sometimes they seek shelter in houses and barns. Their principal foods are fruits, leaves, nuts, seeds and insects.

The *Black-tailed Prairie Dog,* found throughout the western United States, is a type of squirrel. It got its name because it has a shrill bark, much like that of a dog. It burrows into the ground as deep as 12 to 15 feet. The prairie dog eats alfalfa and grain, and its burrow holes can break the legs of horses and cattle. For these reasons, millions have been gassed and poisoned.

The *Box Turtle*, like all turtles, is the only reptile with a shell. It is found east of the Mississippi River from the Carolinas north. The lower shell of this turtle is divided by a hinge, so that both front and rear sections may be brought up against the carapace (upper shell). So tight is the "box" thus formed that a straw cannot be inserted between the shells. (Virginia Creeper)

Pound for pound, the *Wolverine* is generally regarded as the most ferocious animal in North America. They once roamed from northern Canada through the northern tier of U.S. states. They can steal bait from hunters' traps, and seem to kill for the love of killing. The wolverine destroyed more animals than it could eat. They are rare today because they have been hunted ruthlessly for overkilling other animals.

In summer, the *American Elk* climbs to the highest alpine meadows of the Rocky Mountains to feed on grasses and escape insects. The antlers of a grown bull can spread more than 5 feet and have 12 points. The elk will come back down the mountains in winter, where the snow is not too deep. The largest herds live in Yellowstone Park, on Montana's Sun River, and in Washington's Olympic Mountains.

The *California Sea Lions* are the smallest sea lion species, a species that in turn belongs to the general classification of seals. Found off the California coast, this sea lion can turn its rear flippers forward and downward. It can walk on all four flippers or stand alone on its back flippers. That, plus its quickness to learn, makes the California Sea Lion a frequent and favorite performer in zoos and circuses.

So prevalent is the *Mockingbird* throughout the southern United States that five states — Arkansas, Florida, Mississippi, Tennessee and Texas — have named it their state bird. It can imitate the calls of other birds, hence the name "mockingbird." Southern or not, it has been seen as far north as Michigan and Massachusetts. (Royal Poinciana)

Raccoons enjoy a prolific diet: crabs, frogs, fish, acorns, birds' eggs, corn, fruit, nuts, seeds, grasshoppers, mice and insects. The raccoon is found throughout the United States because it is so adept at finding this wide-ranging diet. The raccoon is hunted and eaten, kept as a pet and often used for fur garments. A racoon's face resembles a mask.

The *Bobcat*, a North American wildcat closely related to Canada's lynx, is a furtive animal that is rarely seen by man. It lives primarily in the American West, in wooded areas and brushy ravines, living off rabbits, squirrels and gophers. Standing about 15 inches high, the bobcat usually weighs from 15 to 25 pounds.

The *Black-footed Ferret* is a small, feisty animal that may be the rarest mammal in North America. It lives in the Great Plains, the abode of the prairie dog, which was the principal food item in the ferret's diet. As settlers poisoned the prairie dogs' burrows, the ferrets ate the poisoned animals and died in great numbers.

All geese living in the United States — including the *Canada Goose* — are migratory birds that fly south in the winter and north in the summer. In the case of the Canada goose, it can be found from the Arctic Ocean to Mexico. The best known goose of North America, it is distinguished by a broad white band across its throat and cheeks.

The *Red Fox* is a bushy-tailed, sharp-nosed member of the dog family. It can easily catch a dodging rabbit, or stalk silently toward a bird and pounce upon it before the bird can fly away. A fox's den may be underground, in a cave, among rocks, or in a hollow log or tree. Foxes help farmers by eating mice and rats, but they also frequently attack chickens left uncaged. (Red Maple)

The Designs

Chuck Ripper, the virtuoso wildlife designer who selected, researched and drew the 50 Wildlife stamps.

Almost the entire story of this pane of 50 stamps can be attributed to Chuck Ripper of Huntington, West Virginia. He is the premier wildlife artist for the modern-day Postal Service.

Encouraged by his art-teacher mother, and his landscape-painter father, Ripper developed a passion for art and nature at an early age, spending his free time exploring the woods of western Pennsylvania with his Irish setter. Ripper drew and painted throughout his school years, taking up his career as an artist after graduating from high school. He honed his skills as a staff artist for the Carnegie Museum in Pittsburgh. His wildlife stamps now number 60, which include the 1981 Wildlife Habitats block of four, the 1984 Louisiana Expo stamp and the 1986 booklet of five Fish commemoratives. He also did the 1980 Coral Reefs block of four, which included fish as secondary subjects.

Artist Chuck Ripper pencil sketched each creature in the Wildlife pane before submitting final, colored art. He asked the USPS to withdraw this moose sketch because he wasn't pleased with it.

Who did the research? How were the 50 animals chosen? Let the art director for the Wildlife pane, Jack Williams, program manager for philatelic design for the USPS, tell the tale:

"Chuck Ripper, at our request, did all of the initial research about the creatures to be depicted and where they roamed. As a noted wildlife artist with considerable experience and a well-stocked reference library, he was well-equipped for the job. After Ripper's list had been reviewed by the CSAC, the artist prepared pencil sketches which the Postal Service checked with expert sources, such as the Smithsonian and *National Geographic* magazine, for anatomical accuracy and proper locale. Subsequently, each piece of Ripper's final art was reviewed with the same experts for color accuracy." And that, says Williams, is how the Wildlife stamps were selected and developed.

Because the 50 creatures on this pane come from all parts of the United States, the USPS decided to offer pictorial cancellations from ten U.S. National Parks. These cancels, also designed by Chuck Ripper, show scenes ranging from Florida's Everglades to California's Yosemite to Wyoming's Yellowstone. The ten Ripper cancels were available from individual parks or the Philatelic Sales Division, which applied them only on 14¢ Flag postal cards.

Chuck Ripper also entered the contests for the Migratory Bird Hunting and Conservation (Duck) stamps in 1974 and 1975. He came in second both times.

First-Day Facts

The Wildlife pane was the third U.S. postal item to be first-day canceled on foreign soil. All three have been canceled in Canada. A 1967 U.S. 5¢ stamp for the 100th anniversary of Canadian federation was first canceled on May 25, 1967, in the U.S. Pavilion at EXPO '67 in Montreal. The 1978 CAPEX sheet of eight 13¢ stamps was released by the USPS on June 9, 1978, at the Canadian International Philatelic Exhibition in Toronto. Four of the creatures from that CAPEX sheet — the blue jay, Canada goose, chipmunk and moose — are repeated on this Wildlife pane.

As the 1987 CAPEX show approached, criticism was heard about the lack of data, promotion and publicity for the show. Many details were not available on a timely basis — as exemplified by the first-day program for the Wildlife pane. The USPS printed an attractive, eight-page program, complete with multicolor covers and high grade printing stock. Unlike most first-day programs, however, no schedule of first-day ceremonial events was listed. The eight pages had two strips of five Wildlife stamps affixed to the third page, with indicated spaces for 40 more. No master of ceremonies, no speakers, no guests were included in the program. The USPS would only say that such details were missing because the information could not be confirmed by CAPEX officials in time.

The first-day release of the Wildlife stamps was actually a part of the CAPEX opening ceremonies. A color guard, fifer and drummer escorted postal and philatelic dignitaries to the podium where Jim Stanton, director of communications for Canada Post's York Division, served as master of ceremonies. CAPEX Chairman Vincent G. Greene welcomed guests.

The USPS was ready with a blowup of the pane of 50 Wildlife stamps, unveiled by Mitchell Gordon, senior assistant postmaster general, USPS Marketing and Communications Group, and stamp designer Chuck Ripper. Gordon made the principal speech releasing the stamps.

Canada Post unveiled its CAPEX 87 stamps and souvenir sheet at the ceremony, even though both had been issued a day earlier. Canada and Mainland China (People's Republic) announced a joint issue for Dr. Norman Bethune in 1990. All of this took place at the Metro Toronto Convention Centre before CAPEX 87 was officially opened.

The Postal Service promoted and advertised the Wildlife stamps in a manner not seen since the 1983 Summer Olympics issues. Television spots invited customers to buy the stamps. A five-page foldout ad in *Reader's Digest* lured new and old collectors with stamps shown in full color. The USPS offered a 56-page Wildlife book, a sheet of the 50 stamps and a mount at $16.95. Available free was a booklet entitled, *The Wonderful World of Stamps*. Though CAPEX planners had been accused of ineptness, no one could say the USPS was not pushing every promotional button to entice new collectors and make its Wildlife pane the top seller in Postal Service history.

The Postal Service would not honor requests for specific stamps, either at post offices or the Philatelic Sales Division. Stamps sold in less than quantities of 50 were removed randomly from panes. The USPS supplied only full panes of 50 first-day canceled on a large, free uncacheted envelope from its PSD at $11 per cover.

FDC customers who applied their own stamps could get first-day cancellations from the Buffalo, New York, post office. Such stamp-affixed covers could be submitted with single stamps or any multiple of stamps. In anticipation of heavy FDC requests, the Postal Service extended its usual grace period for first-day covers from 30 days to 60 days after the stamps were issued.

Two different varieties of machine-applied first-day cancellations were inadvertently used by the Postal Service. One style read "USPS CAPEX STA/JUNE 13"; a second read "USPS CAPEX STA./JUN 13." The differences are the period after the "STA" abbreviation for station and the "E" in June. Since the differences were discovered after most cancels had already been applied, there was no way to determine how many of each type exist. The USPS said it believes the numbers to be roughly equal.

22¢ DELAWARE STATEHOOD

Date of Issue: July 4, 1987

Catalog Numbers: Scott 2336   Minkus CM1277

Colors: yellow, magenta, cyan, black (offset); red, black (intaglio)

First-Day Cancel: Dover, Delaware (Legislative Hall)

FDCs Canceled: 505,770

Format: Panes of 50, vertical, 10 across, 5 down. Printing cylinders of 400 (intaglio), 200 (offset).

Perf: 11 (Eureka off-press perforator)

Selvage Markings: U.S. Postal Service© 1987, Use Correct ZIP Code

Designer, Art Director and Typographer: Richard Sheaff (CSAC)

Engraver: Inscriptions: Robert G. Culin, Sr. (BEP)

Modeler: no modeling credit

Printing: 3-color intaglio, 6-color offset D Press

Quantity Ordered: 170,000,000
Quantity Distributed: 166,725,000

Plate Block Detail: Single-digit intaglio number on corner stamp; 4-digit offset number on adjacent stamp.

Tagging: block over vignette

The Stamp

A good case could be made that Delaware has been the most neglected of all U.S. states throughout the 140 years that this country has been issuing postage stamps. Except for the State Flags, and State Birds and Flowers 50-stamp panes that postally noted every state, only one other U.S. issue could be remotely connected with Delaware — but you won't find the state's name anywhere on the stamp.

A 1938 stamp celebrating 300 years since the landing of the Swedes and Finns at a site near present-day Wilmington, Delaware, comes close to state recognition. But since Delaware did not exist at that time, it may be stretching credulity to call that a "Delaware" stamp. There was a later 1976 five-stamp souvenir sheet that pictured "Washington Crossing the Delaware." The state got its name on that postal piece, but Washington was actually sailing from Pennsylvania into New Jersey to attack the British. Delaware was involved, but only as a river, not a state.

Much of the reason that Delaware has been so anonymous on stamps is that no U.S. president has ever come from Delaware. Indeed, no vice president has ever been born there. Only one of Delaware's three signers of the Declaration of Independence — Caesar Rodney — has ever appeared postally. But he was on a 1976 postal card, not a stamp. None of Delaware's five signers of the Constitution has ever appeared on a stamp.

Until 1976, this was as close as the state of Delaware had come to having a stamp issued for it.

Although Delaware was the first state to ratify the Constitution on December 7, 1787, the ensuing 200 years have never brought forth a statehood anniversary stamp. (Meanwhile, we have had two such stamps for both Arkansas and Colorado.) As the 1986 *Yearbook* explained under the Arkansas Statehood chapter, the 13 states missing statehood anniversary recognition are the original 13 colonies. The Postal Service is setting out to correct that horrendous oversight with this one for Delaware, followed in 1987 by Pennsylvania and New Jersey Statehood commemoratives.

The Bureau of Engraving and Printing produced the stamp on its combination intaglio/offset D Press. The red and black intaglio colors printed the word "Delaware," the "Dec 7, 1787" date, and the denomination. All colors in the seal vignette are offset.

Henry Hudson, an English explorer, was probably the first white person to visit the Delaware area, sailing into Delaware Bay in 1609. A year later, Samuel Argall of Virginia sailed into the bay, seeking shelter from a storm. He named the bay De La Warr Bay, for Lord De La Warr, governor of Virginia. The Dutch established the first settlement at present-day Lewes in 1631, but the Indians drove them out within a year. Swedish settlers came in 1638, building Fort Christina at what is now Wilmington. Peter Minuit was appointed first governor of New Sweden. He and his settlers built what are thought to be the first log cabins in America.

The 1976 State Flags pane of 50 had its stamps arranged according to each state's admission date to the Union. First in the upper left corner was Delaware.

The Dutch, under Peter Stuyvesant, recaptured New Sweden in 1655, only to lose it in a decade when the British took over all New Netherland. When the English Duke of York gave the Delaware region to William Penn, as part of his Pennsylvania colony, Penn established representative government for both his colony and his new territory. Pennsylvania governors continued to govern the Delaware territory until the Revolutionary War. In 1776, after voting for independence at the Second Continental Congress, the region became the state of Delaware, and its people adopted their first state constitution.

Delaware now ranks 49th among the 50 states in area (only Rhode Island is smaller). It is 47th in population with an estimated 622,000 (only Alaska, Vermont and Wyoming are less populated). More than 95 percent of Delaware is coastal plain, with the remainder of the state, about 100 square miles in the extreme north, consisting of the rolling hills of the Piedmont plateau. It is this area that contains the state's largest city, Wilmington. Nearly 70 percent of the state's population resides in Wilmington's metropolitan area. Dover, the capital of Delaware, has just 23,500 people. Only 12 cities throughout the state contain 5,000 or more residents.

Some of the largest corporations in the United States have home offices and/or are incorporated in Delaware. A state law allows them to incorporate in Delaware, even though most of their business is done elsewhere. It is easier and cheaper to be incorporated in Delaware than in most other states. Franchise state income taxes from such companies provide about 16 percent of the state income.

The Design

Designer, art director and typographer for the stamp was Richard Sheaff of Needham, Massachusetts, one of the design coordinators of the Citizens' Stamp Advisory Committee. Sheaff is a relative newcomer to U.S. stamp designing, bursting on the scene in 1985 with designs for AMERIPEX 86, Korean War Veterans, Social Security and World War I Veterans commemoratives, plus the 21.1¢ Letters definitive. In 1986 he crafted three of the four designs used in the Stamp Collecting booklet. His prior design in 1987 was for the 22¢ Girl Scouts issue. In many of these works, Sheaff acted as designer, art director and typographer, as he does for this stamp. His forte would seem to be working up whole designs from already-existing elements and photographs.

The colonial farmer at left has a scythe in his right hand and holds aloft a model of a sailing ship with his left hand, to mark the importance of farming, shipbuilding and coastal commerce to early Delaware. The man at right is a Revolutionary militiaman, ready with rifle in hand to defend American liberties.

As mentioned in the commemoratives introduction, this was the first commemorative to have a slightly smaller image area. The size of the entire stamp will remain the same. Reducing the vignette by just 3/100 of an inch vertically on vertical stamps and horizontally on horizontal stamps is an attempt to get equal amounts of white space around the image, thus making all stamps appear better centered.

First-Day Facts

This stamp denoting the 200th anniversary of the first state's admission to the Union was released July 4, 1987, at Dover, the state capital. The actual admission date, "Dec 7, 1787," is printed on the stamp. The ceremony was held in Legislative Hall with Gordon C. Morison, assistant postmaster general for philatelic affairs, speaking for the Postal Service.

22¢ FRIENDSHIP WITH MOROCCO

Date of Issue: July 17, 1987

Catalog Numbers: Scott 2349   Minkus CM1278

Colors: red (offset); black (intaglio)

First-Day Cancel: Washington, D.C. (Smithsonian Institution); Rabat, Morocco

FDCs Canceled: 372,814

Format: Panes of 50, vertical, 10 across, 5 down. Printing cylinders of 400 subjects intaglio, 200 subjects offset.

Perf: 11.2 (Eureka off-press perforator)

Selvage Markings: U.S. Postal Service© 1987, Use Correct ZIP Code

Designer: Howard E. Paine (CSAC)

Art Director: Jack Williams (USPS)

Engraver: Inscriptions: Robert G. Culin, Sr. (BEP)

Modeler: Clarence Holbert (BEP)

Printing: 3-color intaglio, 6-color offset D Press

Quantity Ordered: 157,000,000
Quantity Distributed: 157,475,000

Plate Block Detail: Single-digit offset number on corner stamp; single-digit intaglio number on adjacent stamp.

Tagging: block over vignette

The Stamp

No listing of a joint stamp issue with Morocco was made in the first 1987 USPS stamp program. Its surprise announcement came at the AMERIPEX international stamp show in Chicago on May 26, 1986. Assistant Postmaster General Gordon C. Morison revealed this stamp, the 18th joint postal issue for the United States since 1959. Its first joint issue, with Canada, honored the St. Lawrence Seaway. Including this new one with Morocco, the United States has now joined with 11 other nations in postal commemoration of a historic event or personage. Such joint issues are often released on the same day in the two countries, and usually (but not always) have similar designs. They must, however, denote the same theme.

After much vacillation about the lettering, denomination, vignette size and background color, Morocco finally issued this stamp on July 17 — a date that had also been changed at the Moroccans' request.

USPS releases said, "The stamps would mark the 200th anniversary of the signing of the Treaty of Peace and Friendship between the two nations. The treaty forms the cornerstone of diplomatic relations between the U.S. and Morocco and predates any other pact still in force." That was simply not true. Just four years ago the USPS issued a 1983 stamp with Sweden, marking the bicentennial of the Treaty of Amity and Commerce signed by Ben Franklin and the Swedish French ambassador in Paris on April 3, 1873.

It is unlikely that any ground swell of public opinion had asked for a stamp marking the anniversary of the U.S.-Morocco treaty. It is equally unlikely that Citizens' Stamp Advisory Committee members — so hip-deep in a year of Constitutional and statehood commemorations that they forgot the bicentennial of the Northwest Ordinance, which begat Michigan, Ohio, Indiana, Wisconsin and part of Minnesota — would initiate a postal memento of U.S.-Moroccan 1787 occurrences. The push and shove for this joint issue came from the Department of State, perhaps trying to restore some ties with Morocco that had come loose in 1984 when King Hassan II of Morocco shocked the U.S. diplomats by signing a treaty of union with Colonel Muammar Qaddafi of Libya.

Hassan said he signed the treaty to gain Libyan support against his eastern neighbor, Algeria, which in turn was aiding a guerrilla movement against Morocco in the Western Sahara. King Hassan later described his treaty as an exercise in the balance of power in African politics, stating that "My China is Libya and my Russia is Algeria."

The Postal Service appeared to be having problems in getting Moroccan details finalized. At first, Morocco's stamp was going to have a white background like the U.S. version. Two weeks before issue that was changed to blue. Late in the game, the Morrocan denomination of value switched from 2 dirhams to 1 dirham. First-day ceremonial details were not complete until little more than a week before the event.

Few Americans are probably aware that Morocco was one of the first foreign powers that stepped forth to shake the hand of the new America, born in 1776. Prior to the Revolutionary War, Great Britain's maritime umbrella protected U.S. shipping in the Mediterranean. When the colonists rebelled, England ended its protection and tried to enlist the help of the corsair states of North Africa against the Americans. On December 20, 1777, the ruler of Morocco, Sultan Mohammed III of the Alawy dynasty, penned a letter to "the consuls in Tangier, including those of the Russian Empire, the Knights of Malta, the kingdoms of Sardinia, Prussia, Naples, the German States and the Republics of Leghorn, Genoa and of the Americans."

The imperial order commanded the sultan's ships to "let pass freely all of their ships." The order also permitted the ships of these nations "to provision in any ports" of his realm, and to have the same privileges as other nations "with whom His Majesty is at peace." For that letter, the sultan received a note of thanks from George Washington, who was still fighting the British.

In response to the sultan's overtures, the U.S. Congress appointed a committee to pursue an agreement. Negotiations were conducted by John Adams and Thomas Jefferson, whose proposals formed the basis for the Treaty of Peace and Friendship, also known as the Treaty of Marrakesh. It was the first comprehensive diplomatic agreement between the United States and an Arab, Muslim or African state. It was ratified by Congress on July 18, 1787.

Throughout history Morocco has been fought over and occupied by many forces. In ancient times, it was a part of Carthage. Rome ruled it for a few centuries, only to be followed by Byzantines, Arabs, Moors, Spanish, Portuguese, French and Germans. The Germans held Morocco after the French capitulated to Hitler in World War II. U.S. troops landed in Morocco in November 1942 as part of an Allied campaign to take all of North Africa from Axis control. Serious fighting occurred only in Casablanca, and it ended in only a few days when Morocco's Vichy bosses stopped the resistance.

Morocco is now a constitutional monarchy, with a prime minister, Council of Ministers and Chamber of Representatives (elected by the people) to assist the king. It has a population of more than 20 million, one-third of whom speak Berber dialects. The rest of the people speak Arabic. Most of the land is covered by the Atlas Mountains, the source of Morocco's mineral exports. The coastal areas have a nearly ideal climate, averaging 72 degrees in summer and 60 degrees in winter. If Humphrey Bogart could return to Casablanca — Morocco's largest city— he would now find it to be a metropolis of more than 1.5 million persons.

The Design

These designs were considered for the Morocco joint issue before another was chosen. At left is a different arabesque than seen on the stamp. At right is the American Legation Building in Tangier, Morocco — the only registered U.S. historic landmark outside this country.

The central arabesque design for both the U.S. and Moroccan issues was created by Howard Paine, a design coordinator for the Citizens' Stamp Advisory Committee. Paine took his design from an arabesque on an ornate painted door of the Dar Batha Palace in Fez, Morocco. (An arabesque is the name given to the ornate, lacy decorations found on Moorish and Arabian buildings. Such ornamentation has graceful, interlocking lines that frequently include leaves, branches, star shapes, triangles and octagons. This one is a 12-pointed star, formed by one continuous, unbroken line.)

The design of the U.S. stamp, once announced, stayed constant. But the Moroccan stamp, as finally issued, was greatly different from the one unveiled at USPS headquarters on March 17, 1987. The small Arabic "Kingdom of Morocco" inscription at the bottom of the original design was moved to the top of the stamp and the lettering enlarged. Below it, in Arabic, is "Morocco and the United States — Uninterrupted Friendship — 1787-1987."

The inscription, "Kingdom of Morocco," in French, dropped to the bottom of the stamp with the "Two Centuries of Friendship with the United States," also in French, just above it. The central arabesque is smaller than on the first design, and the denomination changed from the 2-dirham basic airmail rate to the 1-dirham domestic letter rate.

When Morocco Post finally had its stamp finalized, they ordered one million of them, printed via gravure and intaglio.

First-Day Facts

Original first-day ceremonies in both Washington and Rabat were scheduled for July 18, 1987, which would have marked 200 years to the day since the U.S. Congress ratified the U.S.-Morocco treaty. For reasons undisclosed, the Moroccans wanted the ceremonies changed to July 17 — one day earlier.

The USPS changed the Washington site for the ceremonies from the Smithsonian Institution's Art and Industries Building to Anderson House at 2118 Massachusetts Avenue. The switch was made because the Smithsonian could not satisfy security requirements for the ceremony, which had Secretary of State George Shultz, Postmaster General Preston Tisch and Morocco's U.S. Ambassador M'hamed Bargach attending. This change came so late that some of the philatelic press did not have time to alert collectors.

Shown, left to right, at the first-day ceremony for the U.S.-Moroccan joint issue are M'hamed Bargach, ambassador from the Kingdom of Morocco to the United States; U.S. Secretary of State George Schultz; and Postmaster General Preston Tisch.

The 7 p.m. ceremony was by invitation only because of the size of Anderson House. However, local collectors were told they could secure an invitation by calling the USPS — until the site was filled up.

Associate Postmaster General Fletcher F. Acord represented the United States on the Rabat first-day program. M'hamad Laenser, minister of posts and telecommunications for Morocco, released the Moroccan stamp.

The Philatelic Sales Division offered mint Moroccan stamps for sale at 12¢ each until December 31, 1987, along with a first-day cover produced by Moroccan Post for 15¢, and bearing a Moroccan stamp and circular cancel.

The PSD also made combination covers available, bearing the U.S. and Moroccan stamps. Collectors could get the covers canceled with both countries' cancellations or with either a U.S. or Moroccan cancel applied to both stamps.

Varieties

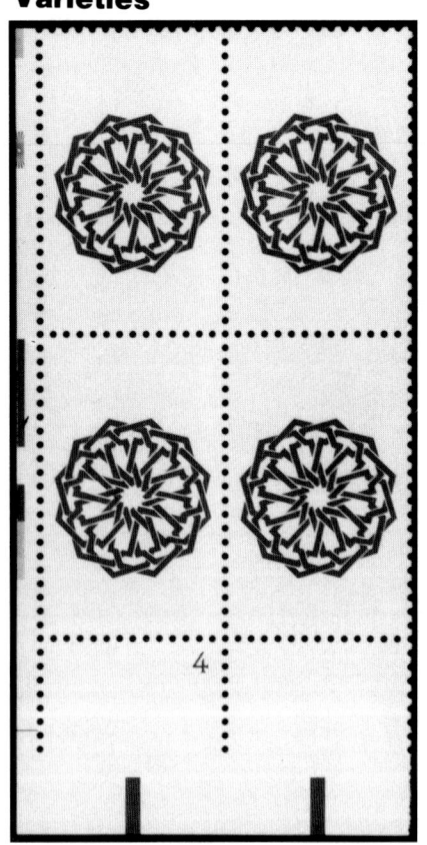

The Morocco stamp was discovered with all black intaglio printing missing. The plate block illustrated here came from a pane of 50, purchased by a collector from a post office in southeastern Massachusetts. Another pane in the same purchase showed partial black inking.

22¢ WILLIAM FAULKNER

Date of Issue: August 3, 1987

Catalog Numbers: Scott 2350   Minkus CM1279

Color: dark green

First-Day Cancel: Oxford, Mississippi (University of Mississippi)

FDCs Canceled: 480,024

Format: Panes of 50, vertical, 10 across, 5 down. Printing cylinders of 400.

Perf: 11 (Eureka off-press perforator)

Selvage Markings: U.S. Postal Service© 1987, Use Correct ZIP Code

Designer, Art Director and Typographer: Bradbury Thompson (CSAC)

Engravers: Vignette: Thomas Hipschen (BEP)
            Inscriptions: Gary J. Slaght (BEP)

Modeler: Esther Porter (BEP)

Printing: intaglio portion only of intaglio/gravure A Press

Quantity Ordered: 156,000,000
Quantity Distributed: 156,225,000

Plate Block Detail: single-digit intaglio number over/under corner stamp.

Tagging: block over vignette

The Stamp

William Faulkner, one of the most respected writers of the 20th century, became the sixth U.S. author to be honored in the Postal Service's Literary Arts commemorative series, joining John Steinbeck (1979), Edith Wharton (1980), Nathaniel Hawthorne (1983), Herman Melville (1984) and T.S. Eliot (1986). The design for the Faulkner stamp had been approved by Postmaster General William Bolger in February 1984, but it never reached press until three years later.

It is not unusual for commemoratives to be designed and approved a year or more ahead of time, then snatched from reserve status when the time for issue seems appropriate. In Faulkner's case, his stamp was listed for 1987 release in late 1986, but without a firm date. In January 1987, it was scheduled for release on September 25, the 90th anniversary of Faulkner's birth.

In March the USPS advanced the release date to August 3, ostensibly to coincide with the Faulkner Yoknapatawpha Conference to be held August 2-7 at the University of Mississippi. At the time, late July and early August were wide open for the USPS. No first days were planned for that time, while late September and early October were filled with six new postal releases. For both reasons, Faulkner was a legitimate candidate for first-day advancement.

Like a few of his predecessors in the Literary Arts series, Faulkner rewrote his own name. Nathaniel Hathorne had added a "w" to his, and Herman Melvill tacked on a final "e." Faulkner's parents were Murray and Maud Falkner. Son William added the "u."

To the postal inspector who fired him, William Faulkner gave a book inscribed: "To whose friendship I owe extrication from a very unpleasant situation."

Born in New Albany, Mississippi, the young Faulkner — like the young Jack London — was an avoracious reader who never took to schooling. Faulkner was raised in Oxford, Mississippi, where he attended school only sporadically after the fifth grade. After his sophomore year in high school, he quit entirely. In the summer of 1918, he enlisted in the Canadian Royal Air Force as a cadet pilot. The war ended before his training did, so Faulkner returned to his Oxford childhood home.

He enrolled as a special student at the University of Mississippi, but only for one year. In December 1921, Faulkner received word that he had been named acting postmaster at the university post office at $1,500 per year. It was a fourth-class post office, and Faulkner would later claim, with straightforward accuracy, that he had been "a fourth-class postmaster."

Faulkner infuriated his postal customers with his arrogance and devil-may-care attitude. He left incoming mailbags unopened while he chatted with his pals. His main interest was in weekend travels to New Orleans, where he hobnobbed with literary lights such as Sherwood Anderson. Having also spent some time in New York City, he felt too experienced and worldly for the boredom of being responsible for a small post office.

As packages piled up, Faulkner often refused to open his post office window. When this came to the attention of a postal official, Faulkner was fired. He told friends that he was glad to be no longer at the mercy of "any SOB who had two cents."

At least one other fired postal employee has been seen on U.S. stamps. Abraham Lincoln was appointed postmaster of New Salem, Illinois, in 1833 by President Andrew Jackson. Lincoln's sloppy record keeping and failure to file required reports lost him the job in short order.

Faulkner's first book, a volume of poems entitled *The Marble Faun*, was published while he was still postmaster. He gave a copy of the book to postal inspector Mark Webster, who had investigated his performance. Faulkner inscribed it, "To whose friendship I owe extrication from a very unpleasant situation."

Faulkner's greatest fame as an author derives from a series of books known as the Yoknapatawpha cycle, tales about the mythical county of Yoknapatawpha and its county seat, Jefferson. Patterning his fictional area around his own hometown of Oxford, Faulkner explored his mythical county's history, economy, social life and mores. He vividly described the decadence of its aristocratic families and their inability to adjust to changing times.

His novels and short stories frame a wide range of style, tone and theme. In *The Sound and the Fury* and *As I Lay Dying*, he used the stream-of-conciousness technique. In *Requiem For a Nun*, he alternated prose with sections of a stage play. In *A Fable*, he let the experiences of a World War I soldier symbolize the passion of Christ. By creating characters who gave different versions of the same person or situation, he made readers cognizant of the difficulties of arriving at true judgments.

Faulkner not only won fame as a writer but also as what he called "a motion picture doctor," patching and reworking scripts for Hollywood studios. In 1949 he was awarded the Nobel Prize for Literature. He won two Pulitzer Prizes: one in 1955 for what experts have termed one of his least impressive works, *A Fable*, and one in 1963 for his last novel, *The Reivers*. Shortly before his death on July 6, 1962, Faulkner penned this letter to the editor of an Oxford newspaper about the tearing down of an old village church:

"It was here in 1861; it was the only building on the square still standing in 1865. It was tougher than war, tougher than artillery and dynamite and crowbars and cans of kerosene. But it wasn't tougher than the ringing of a cash register bell. It had to go — obliterated, effaced, no trace left — so that a sprawling octopus covering the country from Maine to Oregon can dispense in cut-rate bargain lots, bananas and toilet paper. They call this progress. But they don't say where it's going. Also there are some of us who would like the chance to say whether or not we want the ride."

Like his own Yoknapatawpha characters, an aging William Faulkner seemed to be having trouble adjusting to changing times.

The Design

The CSAC looked at several typographic approaches to the Faulkner stamp. The committee opted for "William Faulkner," and changed the denomination to the new format without the "¢" sign. (The 20¢ value on these shows that the Faulkner stamp was in the planning stage for more than two years.)

This Faulkner stamp, like the previous five in the Literary Arts series, was designed by Bradbury Thompson of Riverside, Connecticut, a design coordinator for the Citizens' Stamp Advisory Committee. He also served as art director and typographer for the stamp.

First-Day Facts

The first-day ceremony was held August 3, 1987, in the University of Mississippi's Education Building auditorium in Oxford, Mississippi, Faulkner's hometown. It coincided with the Faulkner and Yoknapatawpha Conference, which took place at the university August 2-7. Faulkner scholars from around the world attended.

Speaking for the USPS was Harry C. Pentalla, regional postmaster general for the Southern Region.

22¢ LACEMAKING (BLOCK OF FOUR)

Date of Issue: August 14, 1987

Catalog Numbers: Scott 2351-54   Minkus CM1280-83

Colors: First and second blue (PMS 286U) offset; third blue (PMS 288U) offset; white (intaglio).

First-Day Cancel: Ypsilanti, Michigan (Eastern Michigan University)

FDCs Canceled: not available

Format: Panes of 40, horizontal, 5 across, 8 down. Printing cylinders of 320 (intaglio), 160 (offset).

Perf: 11 by 10.9 (Eureka off-press perforator)

Selvage Markings: U.S. Postal Service© 1986, Use Correct ZIP Code

Designer: Libby Thiel

Art Director and Typographer: Derry Noyes (CSAC)

Engraver: Inscriptions: Gary J. Slaght (BEP)
          Vignettes: Edward P. Archer (BEP upper left)
                    John Wallace, Jr. (BEP upper right)
                    Gary Chaconas (BEP lower left)
                    Thomas Hipschen (BEP lower right)

Modeler: V. Jack Ruther (BEP)

Printing: 6-color offset, 3-color intaglio D Press

Quantity Ordered: 155,000,000
Quantity Distributed: 163,980,000

Plate Block Detail: Single-digit white intaglio number in blue box on corner stamps; 3-digit blue number on adjacent stamps.

Tagging: block over vignette

Plate Impressions: Offset: first blue: 1(914,500)
80 percent blue: 2(914,500)
100 percent blue: 2(914,500)
Intaglio white: 1(506,000), 2(408,000)

The Stamps

For approximately ten years, Washington postal officials had been thanking 77-year-old Mary McPeek of Ann Arbor, Michigan, for suggesting that the USPS issue a stamp for lacemaking. They had been thanking her often and regularly, telling her that the proposal would be considered. (The postal people say this perhaps a thousand times a year or more; what it almost always means is, "No.")

But few proponents of stamp ideas have had the staying power of Mary McPeek. "I became a famous nagger," she says. From Joan Mondale on down, she petitioned anyone who would listen to her cause. Finally, last year, the USPS announced a stamp for lacemaking — or, rather, four stamps. Mary McPeek and her Great Lakes Lacers Group of Ypsilanti, Michigan, had been consulted by artist Libby Thiel of Baltimore, who had been selected to design a Lace stamp.

As Mrs. Thiel looked at examples of the group's lacework, she finally narrowed the design choices down to four. She could not decide between them and submitted all four to the Postal Service. At that point the single stamp for lacemaking became a block of four stamps for lacemaking.

 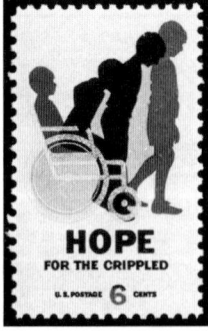

White engraving over darker colors was tried on the 1968 HemisFair stamp (denomination and radiating lines), and on the 1969 Hope For The Crippled stamp (wheelchair frame). The BEP was satisfied with neither. It determined to do better for the Lacemaking issue.

Originally, the block was to have been issued May 2, 1986. When the Postal Service's Ann Robinson journeyed to Ypsilanti, all she had were designs for an unveiling. There were no stamps because the USPS and Bureau of Engraving and Printing had run into production problems in printing the intricate lines and swirls produced by the ladies of the Great Lakes Lacers Group. Said Robinson, "Because we want everyone to appreciate the detailed artistry involved in these lace designs, we have postponed the issuance of the stamps until we can be assured of producing a quality product."

Fine bobbin lace is being crafted by this lacemaker in Bruges, Belgium. Such handmade lace is usually sold to tourists as a souvenir.

The BEP had tried to make the stamps in 1986 but had trouble producing the lace designs. They tried embossing the paper to raise the lace from the background. They tried printing the stamps via the gravure method, with the lace being formed by the stamp paper showing through unprinted areas — the "dropout" technique.

Prior stamps that have used white intaglio (engraved) printing have not satisfied the Bureau or the Postal Service. The HemisFair '68 stamp had white lines radiating from San Antonio and a white numeral of value in intaglio printing. Both were printed over blue and red offset colors, but often the white ink did not have enough opacity to block out the colors underneath. In the 1969 Hope For Crippled stamp, the engraved white wheelchair was printed in white intaglio. It, too, failed to cover. Printing white over colors is like painting a dark house in white paint. Adequate coverage is hard to obtain.

The BEP and USPS worked for four years to get an opaque intaglio white that would be satisfactory for printing on dark colors. Part of the formula for such an ink finally involved titanium, a metallic element used in alloys and coatings. It worked, but its abrasiveness forced the printing sleeves to be rechromed.

After much experimenting, the Bureau produced the stamps on D Press, by the offset/intaglio method. The offset stations on this press precede the intaglio printing station. A light offset blue was laid down for the lettering and numeral of value. A second station printed an 80-percent blue over the entire vignette background area. This was followed by another printing of the same blue at a 100-percent intensity over the entire vignette background. By applying the ink twice, through two different screen patterns, an unusually even color tone was achieved. The last printing also created the blue block on the selvage upon which the white intaglio plate number was printed.

By using screens to apply the blue ink, a slightly rough surface was achieved on the solid background blue. This was necessary to keep the white intaglio ink from flaking off the preprinted offset inks, another problem that had arisen. The white ink, said the Postal Service, was able to "grab" the two coatings of blue. It no longer chipped off.

(The PMS color numbers used on the specification page are from the Pantone Matching System, a standard reference used by the printing industry to designate colors.)

The final intaglio station on D Press printed the white lacy patterns on the block of stamps. This resulted in two groups of plate numbers: a three-digit blue number for the various colors and intensities of the blue offset, and a white engraved number 1 or 2 on the blue block of the adjacent stamp. (This was the first time that an engraved plate number other than 1 has ever appeared on an offset/engraved stamp.)

The Great Lakes Lacers Group is the largest and most active such organization in the United States. Its 300 members combine a variety of centuries-old techniques to produce innovative new designs. Each of the stamps is a replica of a pattern created by a Michigan member.

The upper left stamp comes from a squash blossoms design by Ruth Maxwell of Dearborn. Her lace is characteristic of Bucks Point style, with design and background worked in one piece. The lower left stamp, by Leslie K. Saari of Cadillac, features a mixed technique that blends bobbin lace with needle and tatting applique. Mary McPeek of Ann Arbor, who brought many members into the Great Lakes Group, created the floral design at upper right. Trenna Ruffner of Grosse Pointe Park rendered dogwood blossoms (lower right) that typify "sprig" bobbin lace, and incorporate methods found in the Honiton and Duchesse traditions.

Lace — which comes from Latin meaning "noose" or "snare" — is believed to have originated from a form of cutwork that involved the removal of squares from woven linen to create a meshwork. The two principal types are bobbin and needlepoint. Other types are crocheting (done with a needle) and tatting (made by knotting threads).

Bobbin lace is sometimes called pillow lace because the design is drawn on parchment fastened to a pillow. Small pegs are stuck into the pillow along the lines of the design, and many small bobbins of thread are worked around the pegs to produce the lace. The lacemaker then pulls the pegs or pins out and removes the lace from the pillow.

In making needlepoint lace, the lacemaker first draws the design on parchment and stitches it to a backing of stout linen. The lace is made by filling in the pattern with button-hole stitches. It should not be confused with a kind of embroidery that is also called needlepoint.

In the 16th and 17th centuries, the lace that was heretofore only ornamental became the fabric of luxury. Great quantities of lace were worn by both men and women. Most of it was produced in Italy, Flanders and France. Machine-made lace took over after 1800. Men stopped wearing it, but women still demanded it. Cotton replaced linen; it was cheaper, but less satisfactory. Late in the 1800s, China began to make lace in competition with the machine-made variety. About 1920, lace seemed to disappear from fashion and the industry was dying everywhere. It is now a craft, but no longer an industry.

These stamps honoring that lacemaking craft are the eighth issue in the Postal Service's American Folk Art series, but represent the 29th, 30th, 31st and 32nd Folk Art stamps. All issues in the series so far have been in blocks of four: four pieces of Pueblo Indian pottery (1977), four American quilts (1978), four examples of Pennsylvania toleware (1979), four Indian masks of the Pacific Northwest (1980), four duck decoys (1985), four styles of Navajo Indian blankets, (1986), and four woodcarved figurines (1986).

The Design

Lace stamp designer Libby Thiel also proposed these designs to the CSAC. Much more intricate than the lace patterns finally selected, they would have been more difficult to print. Note that the name of the stamps changed from "American Lace" to "Lacemaking."

Libby Thiel, the Bryans Road, Maryland, artist who designed the Lacemaking stamps, began her research on American lace at the Smithsonian Institution, but says she made the greatest progress after consulting the Great Lakes Lacers Group in Michigan.

This is Thiel's first stamp design. She studied at the Corcoran Gallery in Washington where she met her husband, Bruce, a silk-screen artist. Together, they have a studio southeast of Washington that overlooks the Potomac River. Thiel knew that she would receive far less for designing a stamp than for designing the cover of a record album, but she says that an accepted stamp design is impressive in an artist's portfolio.

First-Day Facts

The USPS returned to Ypsilanti, Michigan, site of the designs' unveiling in 1986, for the first-day release of the Lacemaking block of four. The McKenny Union of Eastern Michigan University, venue for the 11th convention for the Michigan lacemaking group, was host to first-day ceremonies on August 14, 1987. Central Regional Postmaster General Jerry K. Lee was featured speaker for the Postal Service.

Varieties

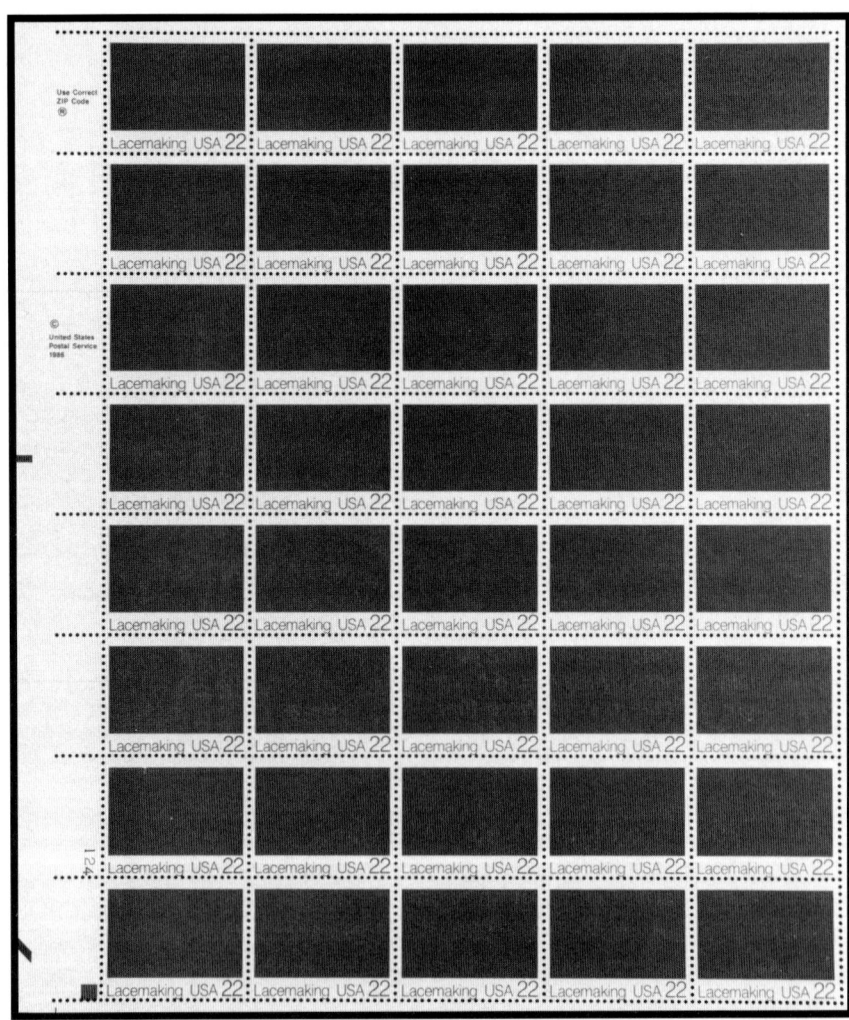

Two full panes of Lacemaking stamps with the white intaglio lace missing were found by a woman at the Des Moines, Iowa, post office. She sold them to a local dealer. Another full pane of 40 showing partial lace images was discovered later.

22¢ PENNSYLVANIA STATEHOOD

Date of Issue:	August 26, 1987
Catalog Numbers:	Scott 2337 Minkus CM1284
Colors:	yellow, magenta, blue, black, line red
First-Day Cancel:	Harrisburg, Pennsylvania (State Capitol)
FDCs Canceled:	367,184
Format:	Panes of 50, vertical, 10 across, 5 down. Printing plates of 200.
Perf:	11 (L-style perforator)
Selvage Markings:	U.S. Postal Service© 1987, Use Correct ZIP Code
Designer, Art Director and Typographer:	Richard Sheaff (CSAC)
Modeler:	Richard C. Sennett (American Bank Note Company)
Printing:	Printed by J.W. Fergusson and Sons on Champlain gravure press. Artwork, perfing, modeling and cutting by American Bank Note Company
Quantity Ordered:	186,575,000
Quantity Distributed:	186,575,000
Plate Block Detail:	5-digit plate number over/under corner stamp, preceded by letter "A."
Tagging:	block over vignette
Plate Impressions:	A11111 (1,095,958)

The Stamp

At least for 1987, the USPS was releasing Statehood stamps for the 13 original colonies in exactly the order those colonies ratified the Constitution and officially became states. Delaware had been the first; this stamp for Pennsylvania marked the second U.S. state; a subsequent 1987 issue for New Jersey would commemorate the third state to join the Union.

The Delaware stamp represented the first postal issue for that state beyond the State Flags, and State Birds and Flowers panes. If Delaware had been ignored on U.S. stamps, the opposite was true for Pennsylvania. If you eliminated all of Pennsylvania's famous men and favorite sons, that state would still rank high on the "most stamps" listing.

Three of the most popular Pennsylvania subjects for stamps have been Independence Hall, Valley Forge and the Liberty Bell.

The first Pennsylvania-related stamp is the 24¢ 1869 pictorial that shows the signing of the Declaration of Independence at the State House in Philadelphia — later renamed Independence Hall. That Pennsylvania site has since been commemorated nine additional times. Washington at Valley Forge has made seven stamps over the years, while the Liberty Bell has been seen three times and Carpenters' Hall twice. There have been Pennsylvania stamps for the Battle of Braddock's Field, the Penn Academy of Fine Arts, Penn State, President James Buchanan's Wheatland home, Fort Duquesne, Gettysburg and Pennsylvania toleware. In total, the stamps associated with Pennsylvania run to nearly 40 — not counting those for favorite sons such as James Buchanan, Daniel Boone, Stephen Foster, Betsy Ross, George C. Marshall and the like.

And if you consider those for Benjamin Franklin, the Pennsylvania numbers would be astronomical. Franklin, admittedly, was born in Boston, but his careers in science, education, publishing and statesmanship associate him for most Americans with Pennsylvania — most especially Philadelphia.

Pennsylvania would not exist had it not been for an English religious renegade named William Penn, born in London, England, on October 14, 1644. His father, Admiral Sir William Penn, sent his 23-year-old son to manage an estate for him in Ireland. Here Penn fell under the influence of Thomas Loe of Oxford, an early disciple of George Fox, who founded the Society of Friends. Imprisoned in Cork, Ireland, for his new faith, Penn told the court that he had "a lifelong commitment to the principle of freedom in things relating to conscience." His father threatened to disinherit Penn, but they became reconciled on the elder Penn's deathbed three years later.

Back in England in 1668, Penn advocated the simplicity of the

Quaker message against the ritualism and dogmatism of the Roman Catholics and the complicated Trinity doctrine of Catholics and Protestants. For this he was imprisoned in the Tower of London, where he wrote his most famous book, *No Cross, No Crown.* Penn condemned the worldliness of Restoration England, its pride, luxury and greed. He challenged Englishmen to take up the cross of self-denial and to work for social justice.

When his father died in 1670, young Penn inherited more than the admiral's estates in England and Ireland. He also assumed his father's standing at court and the personal friendship of King Charles II and James, the duke of York. Penn continued his religious battles in the pamphlet wars of the times, and he became involved with the new American colonies in 1675 when he was appointed a Quaker Proprietor of West New Jersey.

King Charles II owed a debt to Penn's father. It was an obligation the king proposed to cancel by granting Penn a large tract of land in the New World. The royal charter covered three degrees of latitude between New York and Maryland, and five degrees of westward longitude from the Delaware River. Penn saw it as a chance to found a colony based on Quaker principles. He wrote to a friend, "There may be room there, but not here, for such a holy experiment."

This chalk portrait of Quaker William Penn was drawn by an English artist when Penn was in his mid-fifties.

In 1681 Penn became proprietor of Pennsylvania. The king granted him almost unlimited power over it, and in return, Penn canceled the debt of some $80,000 owed his father. The name *Sylvania*, meaning Woods, was suggested. To that, the king's council added *Penn*, in honor of the late Admiral Sir William Penn. Pennsylvania thus means Penn's Woods.

Penn was an infrequent visitor to his new colony. He came first in 1682, more than a year after he had been granted the charter. He made peace treaties with the Indians, saw the colony started, and returned to England in 1684.

Back in England again in 1701, Penn's health was ruined by a prison term for false claims of debts. He lay paralyzed for six years before his death in 1718. Penn left his interests to four sons. Two of his grandsons, John and Richard, later became lieutenant governors of the state of Pennsylvania.

Today's Pennsylvanians are Englishmen, Italians, Polish, Russians, Germans, Austrians, Irish and Slavs. Early in the 18th century, a large number of Germans, whose descendants are often erroneously called Pennsylvania Dutch, settled here. The state population is now reckoned at about 12 million, ranking it fourth among all states. Only California, New York and Texas are larger.

Pennsylvania's largest city, Philadelphia — in addition to having the first bank (1781), the first circulating library (1731), and the first daily newspaper (1784) — is literally the birthplace of the United States. It was the seat of the federal government almost continuously from 1776 to 1800. Here the Declaration of Independence was signed in 1776, and the U.S. Constitution drawn up in 1787.

During this country's formative years, Philadelphia climbed to an importance in culture, government and society that no U.S. city can now claim. Within a century of its founding, William Penn's "green country towne" had become the most cosmopolitan, progressive and affluent city in the British colonies and, after London, the second-largest English-speaking city in the world.

The Design

Richard Sheaff, a design coordinator for the CSAC, based his design on a National Park Service photograph of Philadelphia's Independence Hall, formerly the State House of Pennsylvania.

The photo was computer edited to remove a tree limb and its shadow on the building. This was done at the Acme Printing Company in Boston, Massachusetts. The original photo was also computer enhanced by a scanner. Since the NPS photo was taken in this century, it shows the tower on Independence Hall, which did not exist in 1787. Only a spire sat atop the roof on the smaller, central section.

First-Day Facts

The August 26, 1987, first-day ceremony took place at noon on the steps of Pennsylvania State Capitol in Harrisburg. Among those taking part were Governor Robert P. Casey and Gordon C. Morison, assistant postmaster for philatelic affairs.

Morison noted that Pennsylvania "provided the backbone of our infant nation's economy." He said the state spawned the retail industry, dominated North American trade and supported growth to the West. "Pennsylvania lumber built our expanding nation," Morison said, "and it was Pennsylvania oil that gushed through the first commercial oil well near Titusville in 1859."

22¢ DRAFTING THE CONSTITUTION BOOKLET

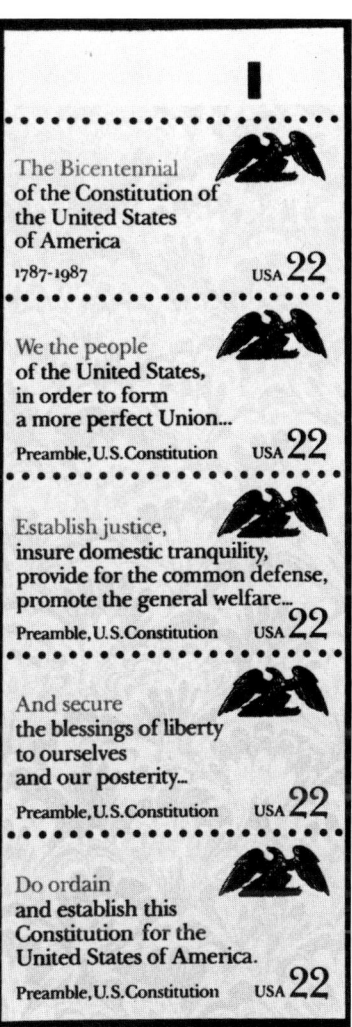

Date of Issue: August 28, 1987

Catalog Numbers: Scott 2355-2359 (pane of five 2359a); Minkus CM1285-89

Colors: black, red, light blue, yellow

First-Day Cancel: Washington, D.C. (rotunda of National Archives Building)

FDCs Canceled: 1,008,799

Format: Four booklet panes of five different horizontal stamps. Printing cylinders of 120.

Perf: 10 (Goebel booklet machine)

Selvage Markings: Plate number and registration mark on tabs. USPS copyright and Universal Product Code (UPC) on covers.

Designer: Bradbury Thompson (CSAC)

Art Director: Joe Brockert (USPS)

Typographer: Bradbury Thompson (CSAC)

Modeler: Clarence Holbert (BEP)

Printing: Andreotti 7-color gravure press and Goebel booklet-forming machine.

Quantity Ordered: 540,000,000
Quantity Distributed: 584,340,000

Plate Block Detail: 4-digit plate number on each pane tab.

Tagging: Phosphor band over vignette

The Booklet

This booklet, containing four panes of five stamps each, was the first commemorative booklet to have four panes. To find a booklet with more, you would have to go back to the five-pane $4 booklet of 1974, which carried five panes of eight 10¢ Jefferson Memorial definitive stamps. The first two commemorative booklets issued in 1986 — the Stamp Collecting and Fish booklets — each carried only two panes of stamps.

The top stamp in the panes of this 1987 booklet specifically notes the bicentennial of the Constitution, and is the only stamp to bear the dates 1787-1987. The remaining four stamps in each pane contain quotations from the Preamble to the Constitution, a 52-word masterful summary that outlines the intents of the 55 Constitutional Convention delegates.

In its original form, the preamble began, "We the undersigned citizens of the States of New Hampshire, Massachusetts Bay . . . " and so on down the list of the 13 states under the Articles of Confederation. It had been written by the Committee on Style and Arrangement. Rhode Island was named, even though it had not participated in the convention. Pennsylvania's Gouverneur Morris — perhaps determined to make the preamble shorter than that of the Declaration of Independence — changed it when he boldly wrote, "We the People of the United States . . ."

The change roused the bitter oratory of Patrick Henry. To him, the Constitution was written for the states, not for the people as a whole. Henry argued that "We the People" would permit the national government to ride roughshod over the states and their rights. He was, of course, voted down.

This best-known painting of the adoption of the Constitution by J.B. Stearns — the basis for this 1937 stamp — molts away at the Virginia Museum of Fine Arts. Some of the paint is flaking off, preventing it from being exhibited in this bicentennial year.

Morris, who with 173 speeches had outdone all others at the convention, wrote on: "We the People of the United States in order to form a more perfect union (second stamp); establish justice, insure domestic tranquility, provide for the common defense, promote the general welfare (third stamp); and secure the blessings of liberty to ourselves and our posterity (fourth stamp); do ordain and establish this Constitution for the United States of America (fifth stamp)."

Morris believed that the preamble and the entire document should be plain, brief and intentionally vague in places to allow for the flexibility to handle future circumstances. Many years later, Morris, in writing to Timothy Pickering, said the Consititution "was written by the fingers which write this letter." Said James Madison, "The finish given to the style and arrangement belongs to the pen of Mr. Morris."

Aside from the small, stylized eagle that appears in the upper right corner of each stamp, the booklet is entirely made up of letters and numerals on stamps. But postage stamps in which text and numbers dominate the vignette designs are nothing new to this country.

A 1902 14-stamp definitive series bore small portraits of presidents, generals, statesmen and admirals. Their likenesses were overwhelmed by "United States of America," "Series 1902," and "postage." Denominations were in both numbers and words, the person pictured was named, and the dates of birth and death were on each stamp.

Commemoratives, beginning in 1925 with the 5¢ Lexington-Concord stamp and running through the 2¢ Carolina-Charleston issue of 1930, often show more billboard lettering than pictorial design. The same holds true for the 1940 3¢ Wyoming Statehood stamp and the 1943 1¢ Four Freedoms issue. Getting ever closer to nothing but pure text were the designs of the 5¢ United Nations stamp of 1945 (only a tiny spray of laurel leaves interrupts the letters and digits), the 6¢ Blood Donor stamp of 1971 (only one drop of blood intrudes), and the 18¢ Alcoholism issue of 1981 (in which a caduceus-like key helps form the letter "o").

Gouverneur Morris of Pennsylvania is given credit for writing most of the Preamble to the Constitution. He lost the leg in a carriage accident.

Then, from 1960 to 1961, came the American Credo series — perhaps the stamps most similar to the designs of this Constitution booklet. Although they were released as single stamps, the Credo issues also bore only writing and numbers, save for a symbolic device for each person honored.

Have there ever been U.S. stamps with only letters, numbers or manuscript — minus any seals, logos, trademarks, emblems, backgrounds of stars and suns, or flora and fauna? The United States has issued at least six such stamps: the 5¢ Salvation Army stamp (1965), the 6¢ U.S. Servicemen commemorative (1970), the 8¢ Parent Teachers Association stamp (1972), the 8¢ Love special stamp (1973), and two 10¢ stamps in the 1974 Continental Congress block of four.

A new "stripe" style of tagging was used for the Constitution booklet stamps. The lacquer containing the phosphor tagging was applied in continuous wide bands over the stamp design. The stripes intentionally missed the perforation areas at the top and bottom of each design, so as to not corrode perfing pins.

New water-based gravure inks were introduced with this booklet. Earlier water-based inks (OSHA has long forbidden solvent-based inks at the Bureau of Engraving and Printing) have sometimes resulted in "snowflaking," the appearance of small white spots where there should be ink, or in stamps with a mottled look. Collectors may not notice much improvement, however, since the tagging lacquer covers up the brilliance of the new inks. The brightness of the new inks will become apparent in future stamps made on prephosphored paper that needs no lacquer overcoat.

The Assembly Room at Independence Hall. With windows closed to keep deliberations secret, 55 delegates spent the steamy summer here drafting the Constitution.

(The gravure stamps made by American Bank Note Company on the presses of J.W. Fergusson & Sons in Richmond, Virginia, still use solvent-based inks. The environmental restriction against the BEP doing so is a localized edict. This explains why some gravure ABNC-produced stamps appear more colorful than BEP-made issues.)

The booklets were perforated, cut into panes, assembled and sealed shut on the BEP's Goebel booklet-forming machines. Booklet covers are also printed, cut and applied by the machines. The covers for this $4.40 Constitution booklet were printed in red and blue, and include a larger eagle, a Universal Product Code (UPC) lineal code and an advertisement for the USPS Commemorative Stamp Club on the fronts. Inside the cover are more details on the club.

The Designs

In the early stages of the Constitution booklet, the phrase "A More Perfect Union" was to have been the unifying theme. It was planned for use with patriotic objects, such as the drum and eagle in the above essays.

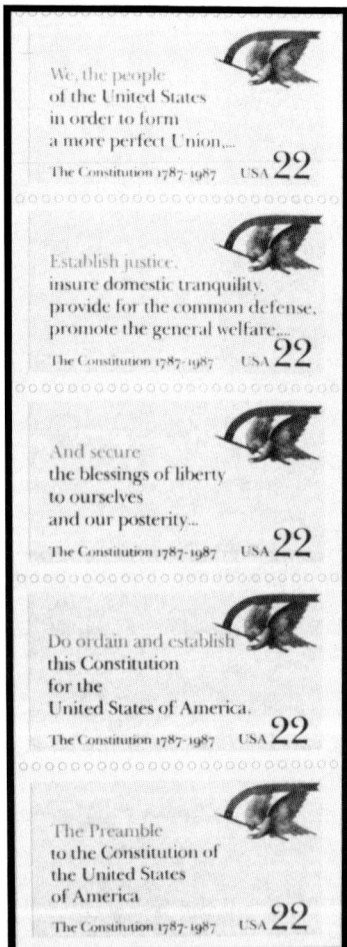

Designer Bradbury Thompson then decided that the full Preamble might be more apt, and devised a way for it to be printed on four stamps — with the fifth reserved for the thematic inscription. A wood eagle was placed at upper right.

As the design progressed, a different wooden eagle appeared and a background of handmade marbleized paper was used. (The eagle shown here was later photographically elongated and made smaller for the stamps.)

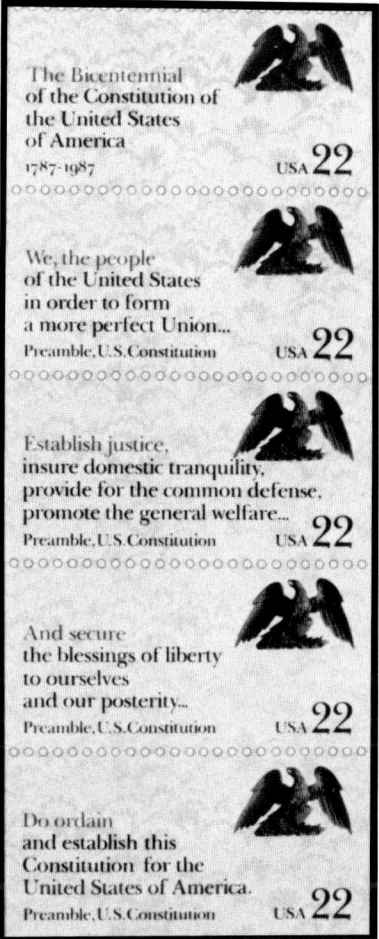

Several changes were made in this original booklet cover design. "$2.20" became "$4.40." "Ten, twenty-two cent stamps" was shortened to "Twenty 22-cent stamps." The eagle became smaller and more elongated, as it had on the stamps.

Designer Bradbury Thompson, a design coordinator for the Citizens' Stamp Advisory Committee, created the stamps and the booklet cover art. The stamps have a printed light blue background that gives the effect of marbleized paper. This design is constant from one pane to another, and was finalized by an outside contractor on computers to assure consistency. The marble effect covers the entire stamp, extending through the perforations.

The type on the stamp is Baskerville, a typeface created by English printer John Baskerville in the 1750s. The yellow and black stylized eagle was based on a photo of an original woodcarving, believed to be the work of William Rush, who worked in the 18th and 19th centuries. He is considered the first native American to have devoted himself seriously and successfully to sculpture.

First-Day Facts

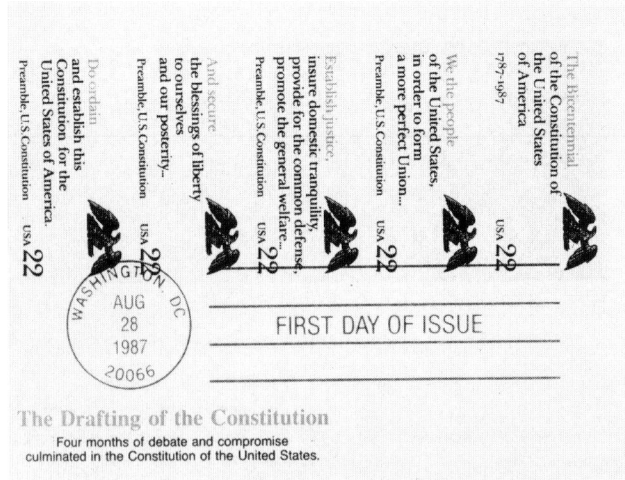

Even when the Constitution booklet was placed sideways, it almost overlapped many first-day cover cachets.

The Drafting of the Constitution booklet was released in an August 28, 1987, first-day ceremony held in the rotunda of the National Archives Building in Washington, D.C., where the original document is on display. The building is also the repository of the Declaration of Independence, the Bill of Rights, and millions of records that delineate the history of the United States.

Postmaster General Preston R. Tisch and Frank G. Burke, acting archivist of the United States, spoke at the first-day ceremony.

22¢ NEW JERSEY STATEHOOD

Date of Issue: September 11, 1987

Catalog Numbers: Scott 2338   Minkus CM1290

Colors: beige, yellow, red, blue, black

First-Day Cancel: Trenton, New Jersey (State Museum Auditorium)

FDCs Canceled: 432,899

Format: Panes of 50, vertical, 10 across, 5 down. Printing plates of 200.

Perf: 11 (L-style perforator)

Selvage Markings: U.S. Postal Service© 1987, Use Correct ZIP Code

Designer: Jim Lamb

Art Director: Richard Sheaff (CSAC)

Typographer: Richard Sheaff (CSAC)

Modeler: Richard C. Sennett (American Bank Note Company)

Printing: Printed by J.W. Fergusson and Sons on Champlain gravure press. Artwork, perfing, modeling and cutting by American Bank Note Co.

Quantity Ordered: 184,000,000
Quantity Distributed: 184,325,000

Plate Block Detail: 5-digit plate number over/under corner stamp, preceded by letter "A."

Tagging: block over vignette

Plate Impressions: A-11111 (1,058,214)

The Stamp

The New Jersey Statehood stamp is the third and last commemorative of 1987 to note the entrance into the Union of the first three states: Delaware, Pennsylvania and New Jersey. Eight more of the first 13 states are to be honored on their anniversaries in 1988. North

Carolina's 200th year of statehood is to come in 1989. Rhode Island — last of the original 13 colonies to achieve statehood, and the only one that refused to send delegates to the Constitutional Convention — is due for commemoration in 1990.

The first three stamps have been called a "series" of issues, since their overall design and layout is almost (but not quite) alike. All have been issued in vertical commemorative size; all have been printed in multicolor; all have carried the state name in red at lower left; all have borne, under the vignette, the month, day and year of each state's admittance. The Delaware and New Jersey stamps have had "USA 22" printed at lower right, but the Pennsylvania stamp (because of name length) has it in dropout lettering at upper right. The Delaware stamp was printed by the Bureau of Engraving and Printing in offset and intaglio on D Press, while the Pennsylvania and New Jersey issues were produced entirely in gravure by the outside team of American Bank Note Company and J.W. Fergusson and Sons.

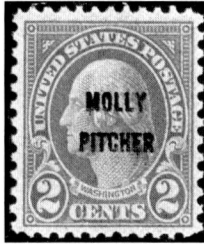 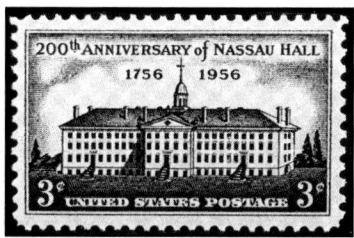 

All three of these stamps have a connection with New Jersey.

Aside from those issued for all states in the 50-stamp panes for State Flags and State Birds and Flowers, only three prior postage stamps have pictured New Jersey. The first was the 3¢ Nassau Hall commemorative of 1956, issued for the 200th anniversary of that first building on what is now the Princeton University campus in Princeton, New Jersey. But the stamp carries no mention of either Princeton or New Jersey.

The second was a 1964 5¢ commemorative to celebrate the 300th anniversary of the arrival of English colonists in New Jersey. It was inscribed New Jersey and pictured colonists landing at Elizabethtown against a background map of New Jersey. The third stamp may be the most anonymous of the three. The 1978 29¢ value in the Americana series bears the words, "Lonely beacon protecting those upon the sea," and pictures a lighthouse. The lighthouse shown is the one at Sandy Hook, New Jersey, which watches over the entrance to lower New York Bay.

But New Jersey does hold one philatelic distinction among all the stamps issued that related to the first 13 states. It is the only state to get an overprinted stamp — the 1928 Molly Pitcher overprint on a regular 2¢ Washington definitive. Molly Pitcher was the heroine of the Battle of Monmouth, New Jersey.

New Jersey was first claimed by the Dutch as a part of New Netherland. Between 1614 and 1621, the Dutch established settlements in what is now Hudson County. The Swedes settled on the New Jersey side of the Delaware River in 1643, but in 1644, Charles II of England granted the entire region to his brother, James, the Duke of York. James then gave the land between the Hudson and Delaware rivers to John Berkeley and Sir George Carteret. The state received its name from the Isle of Jersey, of which Carteret was then governor.

In 1674 Berkeley sold his interest to two English Quakers who settled in the western part of the territory. William Penn and some of his Quaker associates later purchased the area, which was then called West Jersey. Two years later, the colony was divided into two sections: West Jersey and East Jersey. In the very late 1600s, the colonists in both sections rebelled against the owners over rent and property titles. When the owners gave up East and West Jersey in 1702, England united the two sections into one royal colony.

As a strong supporter of the Revolutionary War, and with deep cultural and economic ties to neighboring Philadelphia and New York City, New Jersey saw almost 100 battles and skirmishes fought on its land — including the important Revolutionary War victories at Trenton and Princeton.

During the Constitutional Convention, New Jersey was aligned with the smaller states who were concerned about protecting their rights against the richer and more populous entities. New Jersey started with five delegates, four of whom finally signed the new constitution. Among them was William Paterson, their spokesman for the New Jersey Plan.

The New Jersey Plan did not seek the creation of a national government, as suggested by Madison's Virginia Plan. It instead proposed that "The Articles of Confederation be revised so as to render the federal Constitution adequate to the exigencies of government and the preservation of the Union." Paterson sustained the sovereignty of the states, while the Virginia Plan advocated the total superiority of the national government.

New Jersey delegate William Paterson was a Princeton graduate and lawyer who was born in Ireland. His New Jersey Plan called for equal votes for all states in the new Congress.

The New Jersey Plan proposed a congress with a single legislative chamber, where states voted equally without regard to population or wealth. The final bicameral compromise created the Senate (equal votes by state) and the House of Representatives (proportional vote by population). Virginia's plan derived the legislative powers from the people; New Jersey's plan derived them from the states. The compromise between the two became the Constitution.

In its early years, New Jersey was known for its vegetables and fruits. It became known as the "Garden State." New Jersey farmland, said the U.S. Department of Agriculture in 1986, was valued at $3,913 per acre — higher than any other state and seven times as much as the national average. A wide assortment of industrial manufacturing, research, government, public services and retail trade supports a strong economic base in New Jersey.

Despite this stamp's vignette and the nickname of "Garden State," New Jersey no longer relies on agriculture. Manufactured products now account for 97 percent of all goods produced, agriculture less than 2 percent. Today, only one New Jerseyite in 300 is a farmer.

The Design

First-time designer Jim Lamb used himself as the model for the colonial New Jersey farmer on the stamp. Lamb's wife, Cathy, took this photo.

Designer Jim Lamb also drew pencil sketches of a hats-in-the-air celebration and a political discussion outside a pub for the New Jersey Statehood stamp. Both were passed over in favor of the agrarian theme.

Jim Lamb, a first-time stamp designer from Issaquah, Washington, pictured a colonial farmer in a tricorn hat carrying a basket of fresh produce from his New Jersey fields. The flock of ducks flying overhead connote the marshes that make the state of New Jersey a major flyway for waterfowl.

Lamb says that he was contacted in 1986 by Richard Sheaff, a design coordinator on the Citizens' Stamp Advisory Committee. Sheaff asked Lamb to submit three designs showing politicians talking in pubs, a depiction of the celebration of New Jersey's statehood, and a third with an agrarian theme. After about a month, Lamb submitted the two pencil sketches shown here along with one of a farmer holding a basket that finally became the New Jersey Statehood stamp.

Four to six weeks later Lamb heard from the CSAC. They liked the agrarian work best and asked him to proceed with that. Lamb completed the painting in two or three days. The only revisions requested by the CSAC were that the farmer's hair change from black to red, and that the geese in the sky be made darker so as not to be lost when the painting was reduced to stamp size.

While Jim Lamb was signing autographs at the first-day ceremony in Trenton, a reporter asked if he was aware that the stamp had been criticized for having tomatoes in the basket, a vegetable thought to be poison before the 1800s. Lamb told her he had discovered that fact while researching elements of his design, but that New Jersey had long been famous for its "Jersey tomatoes." Because of their reputation — and also because Lamb needed some strong reds for added color — the tomatoes stayed in.

First-Day Facts

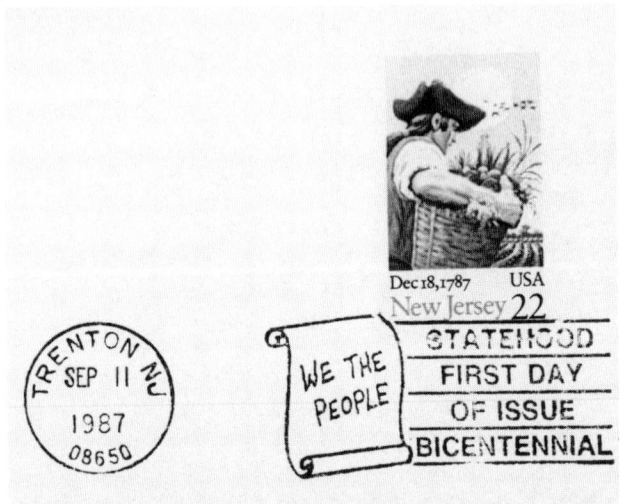

This pictorial cancel appeared on many first-day covers.

The stamp honoring 200 years of New Jersey statehood was released September 11, 1987, in Trenton, the capital of New Jersey. Governor Thomas H. Kean and Senior Assistant Postmaster General Mitchell H. Gordon took part in the first-day ceremony in the State Museum Auditorium.

Gordon called stamps "snapshots of certain places in certain times." He told the audience that "tomorrow at 30,000 post offices across the nation, millions of Americans will begin finding a snapshot of New Jersey on their mail."

22¢ SIGNING OF CONSTITUTION

Date of Issue: September 17, 1987

Catalog Numbers: Scott 2360   Minkus CM1291

Colors: yellow, magenta, cyan, black, dark blue (offset); black (intaglio)

First-Day Cancel: Philadelphia, Pennsylvania ("We, the People 200" celebration)

FDCs Canceled: 719,975

Format: Panes of 50, vertical, 10 across, 5 down. Printing cylinders of 400 intaglio and 200 offset.

Perf: 11 (Eureka off-press perforator)

Selvage Markings: U.S. Postal Service© 1987, Use Correct ZIP Code

Designer: Howard Koslow

Art Director and Typographer: Howard Paine (CSAC)

Engraver: Inscriptions: Robert G. Culin, Sr. (BEP)

Modeler: Esther Porter (BEP)

Printing: 3-color intaglio, 6-color offset D Press

Quantity Ordered: 169,000,000
Quantity Distributed: 168,995,000

Plate Block Detail: 5-digit offset number (magenta, cyan, black, dark blue, yellow) on corner stamps. Single-digit black intaglio number on adjacent stamps.

Tagging: block over vignette

Plate Impressions: Offset yellow: 1(362,000), 2(22,000), 4(658,000)
Offset magenta: 1(11,000), 2(679,000), 3(363,000)
Offset cyan: 1(569,000), 2(473,000)
Offset black: 1(448,000), 2(594,000)
Intaglio black: 1(1,042,000)

The Stamp

The U.S. Postal Service had planned to release this stamp's design on July 17, 1987. They had to advance the announcement of the stamp to May 19, however, after a mass marketer of first-day covers guessed at what the stamp would look like in its April-May advertising mailers. The Franklin Mint of Franklin Center, Pennsylvania, printed its own "We the People" design in its color brochures.

A cachetmaker's close concept of the stamp forced the Postal Service to speed the unveiling of the actual 22¢ Signing of the Constitution stamp.

The Franklin creation was similar to the real stamp. The words "We the People" were highlighted, and a quill pen ran diagonally from lower left to upper right. Although the Franklin ads said the design shown was "for purposes of illustration only," collectors might have easily been misled into thinking the Franklin version was the real stamp. (Large cachetmakers are often given advance descriptions of U.S. stamps so their cachet designs can be appropriate. The cachetmakers are forbidden, however, from publicizing the designs until they have been announced by the USPS.)

The Postal Service reacted quickly by releasing all details about the stamp, complete with design photos, on May 19 — almost two months ahead of time. This was the last 1987 stamp in the Postal Service's recognition of the Constitution.

The stamp was printed on the BEP's offset/intaglio D Press. Offset colors account for everything seen on the stamp except the manuscript duplicating the actual Constitution. Black intaglio printed the handwriting, a miniscule reproduction that BEP engraver Robert G. Culin, Sr., executed. It is some of the tiniest, finest engraving seen on U.S. stamps in recent years.

Eleven years before the 55 delegates to the Constitutional Convention met in the Assembly Room of the Philadelphia State House, the Declaration of Independence had been debated and signed there. It was a meeting place for the Continental Congress in the early 1770s. The State House Yard was surrounded by a wall seven feet high that typified the privacy of what was going on inside. On the first day, the delegates agreed that their proceedings should be kept secret. Throughout the summer, no delegate leaked any news to the press.

The men inside at work on liberty's charter were in no way typical or representative of the "We the People" they labored for. They were all white males, largely Protestant, with two Catholics and a few Quakers mixed in. America in 1870 was 90 percent a farming nation, yet only two of the 55 delegates were small farmers. More than half were lawyers, with another 25 percent being owners of large commercial farms and plantations. All had held public office. Three were governors of their states; four others had served as governors. Eight were judges, 42 had been congressmen. They were about as typical of their constituents as Babe Ruth was of other ball players.

The official secretary of the convention was 28-year-old William Jackson. James Madison did not trust him to keep notes, so set about to record everything on his own. Madison was right about Jackson; all he recorded were the official votes. Madison did not permit publication of his notes until the last delegate had died. Fittingly, that was James Madison.

Elbridge Gerry of Massachusetts did not sign the Constitution and fought its ratification — but still was elected to Congress and ultimately became vice president under James Madison.

The delegates were of all various tempers and temperaments. Some were quick to anger and bombastic. Others were almost shy, afraid to speak out as they may have wanted. Ben Franklin, the 10th son of a soap and candlemaker, was not afraid to speak, but throughout the summer had to rely on a fellow Pennsylvanian, James Wilson, to read his longer speeches. Franklin was suffering from respiratory problems, gout and other ailments. He had to be carried daily to the hall in a sedan chair borne by inmates of Walnut Street Prison. He admonished others that "We are here to consult, not to contend."

The James Wilson who read Franklin's speeches (and delivered many of his own) was astute in legal knowledge and political savvy. He advocated mandatory voting by all citizens; if one did not vote, he would lose his citizenship. An expert on finance, Wilson died a pauper while serving as a Supreme Court justice.

Gouverneur Morris, also from Pennsylvania, lived in high style in his bachelor quarters in Philadelphia. He had magnificent bearing, in spite of a wooden peg leg that replaced one lost in a carriage accident. Well known for his prowess with the ladies, Morris was also a serious literary craftsman who gave the Constitution its final polish.

The convention even had its own drunk: Luther Martin of Maryland. It was said that at no time during the deliberations did he show up sober. Always at odds with the majority view, he would espouse his ideas nightly as he gathered delegates in his rooms to drink and discuss the day's events.

George Mason of Virginia authored Virginia's Declaration of Rights — later the basis for the Bill of Rights. He refused to sign the Constitution because it contained no guarantees of civil liberties.

The biggest faux pas of the convention might be attributed to Elbridge Gerry of Massachusetts. He proposed a Constitutional clause limiting the peacetime U.S. Army to 3,000 men. Even George Washington, who rarely broke his silence, could not let that go by. In a sarcastic and loud stage whisper, Washington said he also hoped they would insert a clause making it unconstitutional to invade America with more than 3,000 men.

September 17, 1787, a Monday, dawned clear and cool in Philadelphia. In final assembly were 38 of the 55 delegates who had attended the convention at one time or another. The Constitution, now copied onto parchment in a flowing script, was read aloud before the signing ceremony. Ben Franklin spoke to Washington and the others: "I consent, Sir, to this Constitution because I expect no better and because I am not sure that it is not the best. The opinions I have had of its errors, I sacrifice to the public good. I have never whispered a syllable of them abroad. Within these walls they were born, and here they shall die." Franklin asked that every member who had objections to the Constitution "would, with me, on this occasion doubt a little of his own infallibility — and put his name to this instrument."

Then Franklin offered a motion that contained a calculated trick of language to woo dissenters. The motion suggested that the Constitution be signed in the following form: "Done in Convention, by the unanimous consent of *the States* present." This meant that the delegates were not individually committed to the Constitution.

Forty-one of the 55 delegates were in Philadelphia. Three dissenters did not attend the signing ceremony, but there are 39 signatures on the Constitution. George Read, a delegate from Delaware, also signed for his colleague, John Dickinson, who had gone home ill.

The trio who refused to sign consisted of George Mason and Edmund Randolph of Virginia, and Elbridge Gerry of Massachusetts. Mason, although a slave owner himself, opposed the continuation of slave trade and refused to sign. Randolph objected to the Great Compromise on congressional representation, but he later voted for ratification. Gerry withheld his signature because he feared the document gave too much potential power to as yet unborn Western states.

James Madison made a last note. "The Constitution, being signed by all the members except Mr. Randolph, Mr. Mason and Mr. Gerry, the convention dissolved itself by an adjournment *sine die*." The delegates left the State House for the last time about four o'clock. A farewell dinner had been arranged at the Philadelphia City Tavern, and here, said Washington in his diary, "the delegates took a cordial leave of one another."

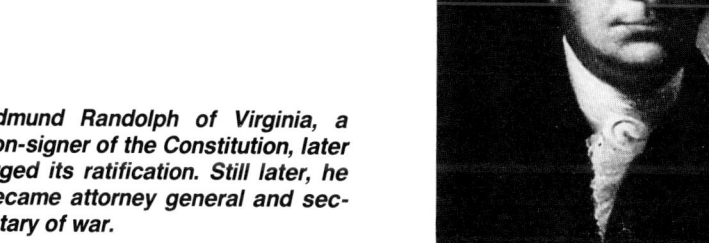

Edmund Randolph of Virginia, a non-signer of the Constitution, later urged its ratification. Still later, he became attorney general and secretary of war.

The U.S. Constitution was signed and sealed — but not yet delivered. Nine states had to ratify it. New Hampshire became the ninth state to do so on June 21, 1788.

The Design

This early sketch of a design possibility for the Signing of the Constitution stamp was made by Art Director Howard Paine.

Designer Koslow created these variations: vertical, horizontal, one using the Constitution, one showing a silver inkstand from Independence Hall.

This was almost the final design, but one more correction had to be made. The document pictured was based on a facsimile of the Constitution in which the articles were one-half actual size, while the Preamble was full size. The issued stamp pictures an authentic replica of the real document.

Howard Koslow of East Norwich, New York, submitted five sketches to the USPS and Citizens' Stamp Advisory Committee in the fall of 1986. Said Koslow, "They went for something that's fast to read, and that's where my poster style comes in. It's a very simple design in concept, but striking." Koslow is a graphic artist, and he gave the stamp graphic treatment — a hand holding a quill pen is superimposed on the front page of the Constitution.

First-Day Facts

The first-day ceremonies for the Signing of the Constitution stamp were just a tiny portion of a three-day-long Philadelphia extravaganza.

In 1887 Philadelphia held a three-day gala to celebrate 100 years of the Constitution. In 1987, to honor the 200th birthday of the document, Philadelphia threw a party called, "We the People 200." The first-day release of this stamp was a small part of those activities on September 17, 1987.

Philadelphia's "We the People 200" parade on September 17 was a five-hour, $3.5 million extravaganza that featured 30 floats, the *Stars and Stripes* America's Cup yacht, celebrities, Pony Express riders and 20,000 participants.

Because the first-day ceremonies were squeezed into a full program of events, Postmaster General Preston Tisch's remarks set a record for brevity. In a first-day speech that was just 103 words in length and took less than a minute to deliver, Tisch called the Constitution stamp "a small but powerful symbol for the world, transforming millions of letters into fliers for freedom."

22¢ CERTIFIED PUBLIC ACCOUNTANTS

Date of Issue: September 21, 1987

Catalog Numbers: Scott 2361   Minkus CM1292

Colors: brown, red, green, black (offset); black (intaglio)

First-Day Cancel: New York, New York (Radio City Music Hall)

FDCs Canceled: 362,099

Format: Panes of 50, vertical, 10 across, 5 down. Printing cylinders of 400 (intaglio), 200 (offset).

Perf: 11 (Eureka off-press perforator)

Selvage Markings: U.S. Postal Service© 1987, Use Correct ZIP Code

Designer: Lou Nolan

Art Director: Derry Noyes (CSAC)

Typographer: Bradbury Thompson (CSAC)

Modeler: Esther Porter (BEP)

Printing: 6-color offset, 3-color intaglio D Press

Quantity Ordered: 165,500,000
Quantity Distributed: 163,120,000

Plate Block Detail: 4-digit offset number over/under corner stamp; single-digit intaglio number on adjacent stamps.

Tagging: block over vignette

The Stamp

U.S. stamps of prior years have been used to highlight many trades, businesses and professions. Those stamps have included doctors, newspaper carriers, firemen, bankers, lawyers, architects, teachers, pharmacists and others. This new stamp reinforces a philatelic truism:

When it comes to choosing stamp subjects, sometimes there is no accounting for taste.

As was true for 1987's Girl Scouts, United Way and Morocco stamps, the Citizens' Stamp Advisory Committee had nothing to do with initiating this stamp for Certified Public Accountants. This CPA stamp was mandated by the postmaster general's office, and since the CPA stamp design had been in the works for more than 18 months, its origins trace back to Bolger-Carlin days. The CSAC gets to comment on various designs for such mandatory stamps, but the choice of subject is dictated from on high.

Washington talk had it that the prime mover for the CPA stamp was John R. McKean, the former chairman of the Board of Governors for the Postal Service. A California friend and worker for Ronald Reagan, McKean became chairman in 1984. McKean is himself a CPA and president of John R. McKean Accountants, an accounting and tax planning firm he founded in San Francisco in 1958. McKean had the influence, contacts and motivation to push for the CPA stamp . . . and get it.

The stamp design was unveiled May 18, 1987, before a meeting of the American Institute of Certified Public Accountants (AICPA) in Phoenix, Arizona. The 248,000-member AICPA traces its beginnings to the founding of the American Association of Public Accountants in 1887. The CPA stamp thus marks the 100th anniversary of the U.S. accounting profession.

Since the design went to press using both offset and intaglio black colors, collectors should know that the intaglio (engraved) black consists of the letters CPA and USA, plus the "22" denomination. All other design elements were printed in brown, red, green and black via the offset method.

Accounting has been called the "language of business." The need for accurate record keeping dates back 5,000 years when records of receipts and disbursements were kept on clay tablets. With the almost simultaneous discovery of papyrus (paper) and calamus (a pen) in Egypt about 400 B.C., a far easier method of keeping records evolved. Modern day accounting had its origins in 15th-century Italy when the Medici family began a complex set of records consisting of a cash book, a stock book, a wage book and a book of income and outgo. Approximately 100 years later, Luca Pacioli, a Franciscan monk, espoused the first rudiments of double-entry bookkeeping in his *Summa de Arithmetica.*

Originally, the terms "accounting" and "bookkeeping" were used interchangeably. Now, however, bookkeeping is generally restricted to the keeping of the books of a business enterprise. Accounting now means the development of methods by which records are to be kept, the analysis of those records, and the judgments as to the condition and conduct of any business. Accounting now demands a wide knowledge of business in general, as well as an understanding of relations between business and such fields as finance and law.

If an accountant aspires to public accounting, he will want to take the CPA examination to qualify as a certified public accountant. Although much industrial and governmental accounting does not require a CPA, accountants in these fields also take the CPA examination for the added prestige of the designation.

The Design

Lou Nolan of McLean, Virginia, was designer of the stamp, his third in three years. Nolan has also created the 3.4¢ School Bus of 1985 and the 17¢ Dog Sled stamp of 1986, both coils in the Transportation series.

Some in the USPS's Stamps Division thought this was the finest stamp design in years. The simplicity of design and the striking dominance of the steel pen point made it "the best poster art style stamp we have printed in years," said one. With Postmaster General Preston Tisch's appointments of three graphic artists to the Citizens' Stamp Advisory Committee in June 1987, poster-like stamps may grow in number. What exactly is "poster art?"

Initially, it was a simple, bold advertisement — a poster to be mounted where people could see it, promoting a product, name, service or cause. Since most viewers of a poster would be walking or riding by it, it had to be simple, dynamic and easily grasped. One word or one simple picture was often relied on to send a message.

In the 17th and 18th centuries, posters were commonly used in France and Italy to advertise theater performances and display government decrees. Many great artists have since specialized in poster art: Toulouse-Lautrec, Pierre Bonnard, Howard Chandler Christy, James Montgomery Flagg, Charles Dana Gibson and Norman Rockwell. Since stamps, like posters, are usually seen only for an instant, the USPS obviously plans on many more poster-art designs.

First-Day Facts

The CPA stamp for the 100th anniversary of the accounting profession was issued September 21, 1987, in Radio City Music Hall, New York City. Since the first-day ceremony was held during a membership meeting of the American Institute of Certified Public Accountants, it was not open to collectors or the general public. Collectors were able to get handback first-day cancellations at the Rockefeller Center Station of the New York Post Office and at the Main Post Office of the city.

The Postal Service's top accountant, Comer S. Coppie, senior assistant postmaster general for finance and planning, released the stamp. Coppie told the CPAs, "Your profession has many things in common with the postal business. The smallest financial transactions are im-

First-day ceremonies at Radio City Music Hall in New York City were closed to all but accountants.

possible without us. And yet, the people who deliver the nation's mail — and audit its books — will have a long wait if we expect great public recognition."

Varieties

The CPA stamp was found in a Chicago-area post office with the black engraved portion — "C.P.A." and "22 USA" — completely missing. Two panes of 50 were discovered, which means that at least two more should exist somewhere.

22¢ LOCOMOTIVES BOOKLET

Date of Issue: October 1, 1987

Catalog Numbers: Scott 2362-66   Minkus CM1293-97

Colors: green, blue, brown, yellow, red, black (offset); black (intaglio)

First-Day Cancel: Baltimore, Maryland (Baltimore & Ohio Railroad Museum)

FDCs Canceled: 976,694

Format: Four booklet panes of five different horizontal stamps

Perf: 10 (Goebel booklet machine)

Selvage Markings: Plate number and registration mark on pane tabs. Copyright slogan on inside of booklet cover.

Designer: Richard Leech

Art Director and Typographer: Howard Paine (CSAC)

Engraver: Robert G. Culin, Sr. (BEP)

Modeler: Clarence Holbert (BEP)

Printing: 3-color intaglio, 6-color offset D Press

Quantity Ordered: 642,040,000
Quantity Distributed: 394,776,000

Plate Block Detail: Single intaglio black plate number on pane tab

Tagging: block over vignette

The Stamps

In 1987 the USPS issued six Locomotive stamps — this booklet of five and the 2¢ re-engraved Locomotive coil stamp in the Transportation series. In fact, the unveiling of this booklet of Locomotive stamp designs took place in Milwaukee March 6, 1987, at first-day ceremonies for the re-engraved B Press 2¢ Locomotive stamp.

These six Locomotive stamps of 1987 represent almost one-third of all stamps picturing locomotives issued by the United States since 1847. U.S. postal paper has featured a locomotive just 21 times: 14 times on commemoratives and definitives, six times on stamped envelopes and once on a parcel post stamp. The Postal Service had selected this new Locomotives booklet to herald its seventh annual National Stamp Collecting Month, "Steaming Along With Stamp Collecting. All Aboard!"

Rail fans will find no steam behemoths or giant diesels on these stamps. The Postal Service shows, instead, five early locomotives from 1829 to 1839, all distinctively different and all forerunners of the steam-powered engines that helped settle the American continent. The Post Office Department first climbed on board railroads in 1831, when the small iron horses moved at only 15 miles per hour. As tracks spread throughout the United States and locomotives grew faster and more powerful, the Railway Post Office was born. Here men worked day and night sorting mail on trains as they sped from city to city.

In the 1930s, more than 10,000 trains were moving mail all over the United States. In the 1960s, postal use of the rails began to decline. Trucks and airplanes latched on to the bulk of U.S. mail, and by 1970, the Railway Post Office was gradually phased out. That's not to say that trains do not still handle U.S. mail. The USPS's annual budget for moving mail by rail is still more than $200 million.

The Stourbridge Lion

This first steam locomotive to operate commercially in America was actually a British-made engine. The *Lion's* initial run was in 1829 for the Delaware & Hudson Canal Company. Built by Foster, Rastrick and Company of Stourbridge, England, the little seven-ton *Stourbridge Lion* was floated up a canal to Honesdale, Pennsylvania. The coal to be moved to Honesdale by rail lay 16 miles to the west, behind formidable Mt. Moosic.

The man who made the first trip with the *Stourbridge Lion* denied that he went the entire 16 miles to Carbondale. Horatio Allen wrote, "I started with considerable velocity, passed the curves over the creek safely, and was soon out of hearing of the cheering of the vast assemblage. At the end of two or three miles I reversed the valve, and returned without incident to the place of starting, having made the first locomotive trip in the western hemisphere."

Ironically, a stamp for the 150th anniversary of the *Lion's* initial run was turned down in 1979 by the Citizens' Stamp Advisory Committee. Suggested by members of the Wayne County, Pennsylvania, Historical Society, the request was denied because "the Postal Service could not honor something that was not of U.S. origin."

The locomotive proved too heavy for the track. Its seven tons of unsprung weight caused derailments, so it was stored in a shed at Honesdale. Its boiler and cylinders were cannibalized in 1849 for service in a foundry. Years later, the parts were shipped to the Smithsonian, where the restored locomotive may be seen today.

It should be noted that the *Stourbridge Lion* was not the first steam locomotive to run in the United States. That honor belongs to a small cog-rail engine that was demonstrated on the estate of Colonel John Stevens of Hoboken, New Jersey, in 1825. It failed to impress several executives who were already heavily invested in canal construction.

The Best Friend of Charleston

In the summer of 1830, New York City's West Point Foundry, a firm principally known for manufacturing ship fittings, built a five-ton steam locomotive called the *Best Friend of Charleston*. In December of that year, over the Charleston & Hamburg Railroad in South Carolina, the locomotive hauled a string of cars full of nearly 200 passengers at up to 21 miles per hour on an excursion run. As the engine pulled the first passengers on a U.S. railroad, a trio of artillerymen fired salutes from a cannon strapped to the deck of a flag-draped flatcar ahead of the engine.

Just a few months later, a stuck or tied-down valve lever caused the *Best Friend* to explode with great violence. The railroad announced that a "barrier car" would be placed between the engine and coaches of all future passenger trains. "Loaded with six bales of cotton," said an advertisement, "it will protect travelers when the engine explodes."

The John Bull

The first *John Bull* locomotive was officially named the *Stevens*. Like many other locomotives imported from England in the 1830s, it was usually called the *John Bull* because its full boiler and profile resembled the gentleman who personified England. Thus, there were many *John Bulls*.

The original *John Bull* was delivered in pieces to the Camden & Amboy Railroad from England's Stephenson Company. When finally assembled from unlabeled parts, the *John Bull* carried its New Jersey passengers at speeds up to 35 mph. It was often improved and modified over the years.

A restored version of the locomotive ran from New York to Chicago in 1893. The original *John Bull* engine was presented to the Smithsonian in 1885.

The Brother Jonathan

John B. Jervis made the greatest single improvement in locomotives of the 1830s when he incorporated a swiveling guiding truck of small wheels at the front of the engine. His first engine, *Brother Jonathan*, smoothly adapted itself to every dip and rise in the wavering tracks of those times. It went around dogleg curves easily and fast. Running on the Mohawk & Hudson Railroad, it was for years the world's fastest steam locomotive. Rightly or wrongly, it was often credited with speeds of 60 mph.

The Gowan & Marx

Made by the firm of Eastwick & Harrison in 1839, the *Gowan & Marx* eight-wheeler went to work on the Philadelphia and Reading Railroad. Its four guiding wheels, or lead trucks, and four drivers made it the largest, most powerful of the five locomotives shown in the booklet of stamps. Its firebox was directly above the rear drivers, an added weight that increased the traction of the driving wheels.

The *Gowan & Marx* proved that on February 20, 1840, when it pulled 101 loaded cars for 60 miles. No engine had ever handled such a load. Less than a decade earlier, sales contracts for locomotives specified that they should pull no more than three times their weight. The *Gowan & Marx* was a 22,000-pound locomotive that toted 412 tons — 40 times its own weight.

The booklet cover — printed on the same Goebel machine that perforates stamps, inserts the sliced panes into booklets and seals them shut — features a symbolic locomotive design in multicolor. On the reverse is a notice about the USPS Commemorative Stamp Club and a Universal Product Code (UPC) marking. Inside the booklet is a form for joining the USPS Commemorative Stamp Club.

The initials "SBL" in the lower right corner of the application for joining the commemorative stamp club on the inside of the booklet cover are something new. They are a source key meaning "Stamp Booklet Locomotive," and indicate to the USPS Marketing Division which postal product was responsible for the return of the application.

The stamps were printed on the BEP's offset/intaglio D Press. Inscriptions on the stamps are in black engraving; all else is printed by the offset method.

The Design

The Citizens' Stamp Advisory Committee often identifies stamp subjects years in advance of their appropriate issue time. Artist Richard Leech was placed under contract in 1979 and submitted these locomotive sketches. Because of a rush to get stamps for a rate change in 1981, the CSAC did not see Leech's work until 1982. Leech originally drew the Locomotive stamps as a block of four, but the committee later recommended a booklet of five.

Richard Leech of Orinda, California, designed the stamps and the booklet cover. Leech originally drew a block of four se-tenant designs, but the Citizens' Stamp Advisory Committee decided on a booklet pane of five stamps. Leech's first four locomotives were the *Stourbridge Lion*, the *Best Friend of Charleston*, the *Gowan & Marx* and the *Jupiter*. When the stamps were adapted to booklet format, the *Jupiter* was dropped, and the *John Bull* and *Brother Jonathan* engines were added.

Leech's other stamp designs were the 1983 Streetcars block of four.

The only U.S. stamp to honor a commercial business operation, this 1952 issue marked the 125th anniversary of the Baltimore & Ohio Railroad.

First-Day Facts

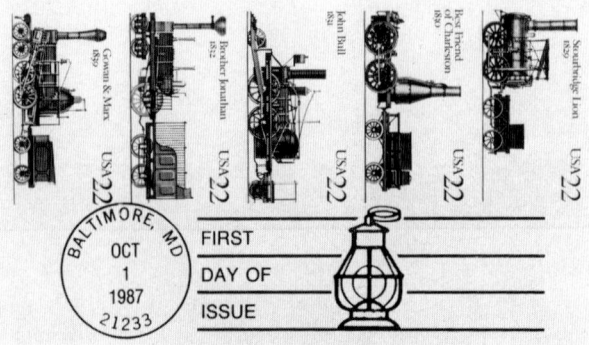

A full pane of five Locomotives stamps gets the signal for the start of its first-day journey.

The Baltimore & Ohio Railroad Museum in Baltimore, Maryland, was the first-day-of-issue site on October 1, 1987. Speaking for the USPS was Mitchell H. Gordon, senior assistant postmaster general for marketing and communications, who noted that the Postal Service has had a key role in aiding almost every form of transportation. "Mail has been walked, trotted, rolled, floated, trucked and flown to its destinations," he said.

Since the booklet panes were nearly 4½ inches deep, collectors had to affix the panes on their sides to either the Number 6¾ or large Number 10 envelopes.

SPECIAL STAMPS

Special stamps are those that are on sale for longer periods of time than the limited-sale commemoratives. Unlike commemoratives, special stamps may go back to press again and again. Unlike definitive stamps, however, special stamps do not remain on sale for years or until the next rate change.

When the *Yearbook* first started to separate special stamps from normal commemorative issues in 1984, the new category consisted of only three stamps: the two Christmas issues and the Love stamp. A special stamp for Christmas dates back to 1962. Since then, one or more have appeared each Christmas season.

The Love stamp has a more sporadic history and took much longer to achieve an annual appearance. The first Love stamp was issued in January 1973. The USPS ordered 150 million printed, but demand soon exceeded that figure. The stamp went back to press for another 50 million. By August 1973 the orders had reached 233 million, and a third printing was necessary. When the Postal Service finally removed the first Love stamp from sale on January 31, 1975, more than 330 million had been sold.

Nine years passed before the second Love stamp was released on February 1, 1982. During the nine-year interval, the USPS was receiving many requests for an additional Love stamp. About 1980, Postmaster General William Bolger made up his mind that such a stamp should be constantly available, possibly with a new one issued every year. A postal release of December 13, 1983, announced the 1984 Love stamp, emphasizing that it would be available throughout the year. With two Love stamps in a row for the first time in 1984 and 1985, the USPS embarked on its now annual tribute to love.

Love and Christmas stamps are joined this year by a Special Occasions booklet consisting of one pane of ten stamps bearing eight different messages. Using four horizontal commemorative-size stamps, two stamps of vertical commemorative size, and four definitive-size stamps, the booklet holds messages of Get Well, Thank You, Love You Dad, Best Wishes, Love You Mother and Keep In Touch. Two stamps duplicate messages of Congratulations and Happy Birthday.

They appear here as special stamps because Deputy Postmaster General Jackie Strange told the Greeting Card Association that the "Postal Service has classified them as special stamps, because they would remain on sale longer than commemorative stamps." Local postmasters were instructed to have this booklet on sale throughout 1987. The BEP was told to make them available for the entire year. With those instructions, the Special Occasions booklet became the first "special" stamp booklet.

22¢ LOVE

Date of Issue: January 30, 1987

Catalog Numbers: Scott 2248   Minkus CM1212

Colors: yellow, orange, blue, green, blue type

First-Day Cancel: San Francisco, California (Fairmont Hotel)

FDCs Canceled: 333,329

Format: Panes of 100, vertical, 10 across, 10 down. Printing cylinders of 800

Perf: 11.2 (Eureka off-press perforator)

Selvage Markings: U.S. Postal Service© 1986, Use Correct ZIP Code

Designer: John Alcorn

Art Director: Derry Noyes (CSAC)

Modeler: V. Jack Ruther

Printing: Andreotti 7-color gravure press

Quantity Ordered: 1,020,000,000
Quantity Distributed: 811,560,000

Plate Block Detail: 5-digit number alongside corner stamps

Tagging: block over vignette

The Stamp

This smallest of the six Love stamps issued to date carries the series' biggest heart.

The stamp was the first Love issue produced in definitive size for a less-than-idealistic reason: money. Like the Christmas stamps of 1986 that preceded it, 1987's Love stamp fell victim to an earlier postal edict to cut costs. Downsizing the commemorative-sized Love and Christmas stamps was the most effective way to save money. With all three accounting for about three billion stamp sales annually (and Love responsible for almost half that total), getting 100 stamps for the price of 50 larger Loves brought more savings into postal coffers than could have been possible with a dozen smaller commemoratives.

Copies of this Love panel could be sent from San Francisco via Intelpost to friends and collectors anywhere in the world.

The first 800 million Love stamps for 1987 were produced in roughly half the time it would have taken to make them in the large, former size. Possibilities are good that they will have to go back to press for more stamps before 1988's Love issue makes its appearance, creating more bottom-line savings for the Postal Service.

The symbolic drawing of the heart (as seen in Bradbury Thompson's five-heart 1984 Love stamp and on this one) is just that: symbolic. Yet, it has some relationship to an actual human heart. The left and right ventricles make up the lower and larger part of the heart. Atop them sit the atria. Together, they approximate the two curved parts of the traditional Valentine heart candy box. The heart sits on a slant in the chest and, when viewed that way, can be presumed to look somewhat like the pointed bottom of the symbolic heart drawing.

The human heart is a masterful machine, a constantly beating muscle that pumps oxygen-carrying blood over some 100,000 miles of venous pipelines. Without oxygen, the brain, lungs, kidneys and other vital organs would quickly perish. The average man's heart weighs about 11 ounces; a woman's about 9 ounces. To visualize how big your heart is, advises noted heart specialist Dr. Michael DeBakey, look at your closed fist. Your heart and your fist grow at approximately the same rate.

The heart beats about 70 times per minute — more than 100,000 times in a single day. It pumps five quarts of blood through its chambers every 60 seconds. The heart works hard enough in one hour to lift a weight of 1½ short tons more than a foot off the ground. About the only thing modern medicine doesn't know about it is why it evolved into the symbol of love.

It may stop beating because of an accident, a heart attack or surgical shock — never because of love. It beats faster when you are angry, frightened or excited. Perhaps that last word holds a clue as to why the heart has come to stand for love. Physicians, however, attribute any quivering or fluttering of the heart to fibrillation of heart muscles — not to love.

Cor is the Latin word for heart. The English language is full of derivations: core, cordial, courage and coronary. Aristotle may have come closest to a definition of the heart, when he termed it "the seat of the soul."

For the fourth straight year, the new Love stamp had a towering unveiling that signaled the beginning of a new year for America. At 11:59 p.m., December 31, 1986, a giant reproduction of the new Love issue slowly descended from the Old Post Office Pavilion's clock tower, touching ground precisely at midnight. The unveiling kicked off the annual New Year's Eve official civic party for Washingtonians.

Beams of laser lights illuminated the design colors of yellow, orange, blue and green, as tower bells rang in another year. The outdoor Old Post Office party is becoming a tradition in Washington — and the newest Love stamp is a part of it. Television stations around the country carry the event. No other U.S. stamp gets the promotion and publicity accorded each Love stamp.

The Design

Love stamp designer John Alcorn also submitted these two designs. The CSAC found the ornate calligraphy on the stamp at left too hard to read, while the colors on the stamp at right were too pale.

John Alcorn, a graphic artist from Lyme, Connecticut, created his first stamp design with his hearts and flowers rendition of love. The pastel hues and quilted appearance are intended to represent Pennsylvania Dutch folk art, where such images are found frequently.

With the release of this sixth Love issue (others have occurred in 1973, 1982, 1984, 1985 and 1986), the Postal Service noted that the stamps have been issued annually since 1984. They confirmed that Love stamps will continue to appear each year in the years ahead. Sales show a strong customer demand for them, especially for use with wedding invitations, Valentines, greeting cards and personal correspondence.

First-Day Facts

The Love stamp was serenaded by Tony Bennett in San Francisco on its January 30 release.

The stamp was released January 30, 1987, in indoor and outdoor ceremonies at San Francisco's Fairmont Hotel. Singer Tony Bennett, a frequent performer at the Fairmont, arrived by cable car at the hotel — as did others taking part in the first-day ritual. Accompanied by his trio, Bennett sang his biggest hit, "I Left My Heart In San Francisco," to those crowded outside the hotel.

Moving inside, the rest of the occasion featured remarks by Gordon C. Morison, assistant postmaster general for philatelic affairs. Mary A. Brown, San Francisco's divisional general manager and postmaster, presided over the ceremony.

A special Love panel, consisting of a facsimile of the stamp and first-day postmark, a legend "From San Francisco to the world with love," and autographs of officials in attendance, was available to those at the ceremony. They could send copies of the panel and a personal message anywhere in the world via Intelpost, the USPS service for electronic international facsimile transmission.

Though first intended only for first-day attendees, the San Francisco post office made a similar service available to any collectors who requested and paid for it by February 28.

Varieties

A North Carolina collector found a half pane of this Love variety. The red and yellow are registered properly on each other, but too low versus the blue and green. The green color is slightly to the right of its proper position.

22¢ SPECIAL OCCASIONS BOOKLET

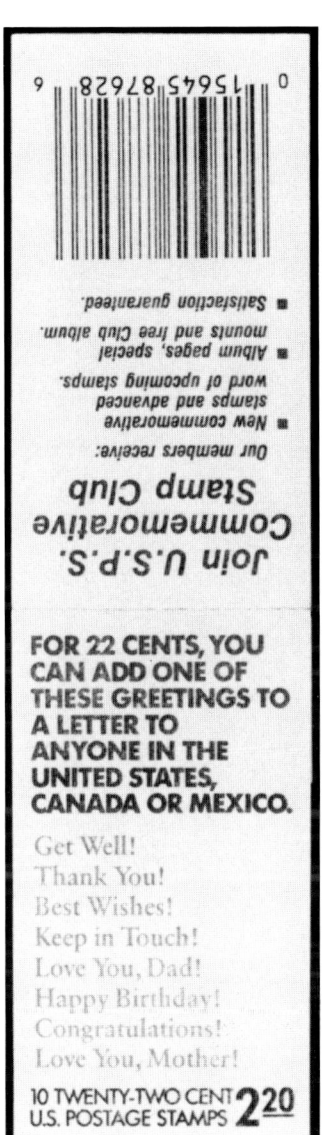

Date of Issue: April 20, 1987

Catalog Numbers: Scott 2267-74   Minkus CM1216-25

Colors: lavender, red, blue, yellow, black, special blue

First-Day Cancel: Atlanta, Georgia (Atlanta Historical Society)

FDCs Canceled: 1,588,129

Format: One booklet pane of four horizontal commemorative, two vertical commemorative, and four regular size stamps. Eight varieties.

Perf: 10 (Goebel booklet machine)

Designer: Oren Sherman

Art Director: Richard D. Sheaff (CSAC)

Typographer: Richard D. Sheaff (CSAC)

Modeler: Frank J. Waslick (BEP)

Printing: Andreotti 7-color gravure press (booklet covers printed inside and out by Goebel booklet machine)

Quantity Ordered: 640,530,000
Quantity Distributed: 610,425,000

Plate Number Detail: Group of six cylinder numbers (one for each color) appears on pane tab.

Tagging: block over vignette

The Booklet

The 22¢ Special Occasions booklet was a long time coming. When it finally arrived, it had gone through many changes and set several new records for USPS booklet stamps.

For years, says the Postal Service, it has had requests for stamps that could be used on special occasions: Mother's Day, Father's Day, weddings, graduations, birthdays and the like. But the stamps requested were not so much for holidays as for special feelings — love, gratitude, congratulations, good wishes and health. In partial response to those requests, the Special Occasions booklet began as one stamp. This stamp was announced and unveiled in 1985 to coincide with the 50th anniversary of American Mothers, Inc. The stamp was to be issued in 1986.

Mothers were to be saluted by a stamp depicting flowers, but the idea grew from a matriarchal issue to a Messages booklet of seven different designs. For many months this project was referred to as the Messages booklet. When it finally emerged in 1987, it had changed to a Special Occasions booklet of ten stamps to a pane, with eight different designs.

This was the first U.S. issue of a stamp, or stamps, to be specifically targeted to a specialized group of retailers, who were courted, surveyed and market tested before the stamps were ever issued.

This was the first U.S. booklet to contain stamps in three different configurations.

This also was the first U.S. booklet to have the familiar Universal Product Code bar code on its cover — a practice the USPS said may be followed for future booklets.

To track the changes in the booklet — and to observe the marketing moods of the Postal Service — it is necessary to follow each on a chronological basis.

August 19, 1985: Deputy Postmaster General Jackie Strange reveals the design of a "Get Well!" stamp, saying that it will be one of seven in a special Messages booklet to be released in September 1986. The stamp featured flowers. The USPS had wiggled its way onto the 75th anniversary program of FTD (Florists' Transworld Delivery Association) in Detroit, Michigan.

December 1985: A release from the USPS confirms the progress of the Messages booklet. It says all designs — except one — are still unknown, but the booklet will have seven different stamps per pane.

February 15, 1986: Stamps Division Manager Don McDowell says that the issuance of the booklet will be postponed from September 1986 till a date in May 1987. The greeting card industry has joined the florists as a possible outlet for the sale of the booklet in stationery stores, card shops, large supermarkets and other locales. The Postal Service envisions non-postal outlets that could turn this booklet into something as big as Love and Christmas stamps.

The USPS begins to rationalize how they will supply the booklets. If Muncie, Indiana, has three stationery stores and two florists, the USPS can take orders and make sure that the quantities shipped to post offices in Muncie include enough booklets to fill the orders. Other sugarplums fill postal heads. The USPS decides to go after the florists and greeting card people — seeking their advice as to the possible scope of this new idea. The industries are encouraged to poll their associations to find out what interest exists in selling stamps in their shops. Every year a Stationers' Trade Show takes place in New York City. Why not consider that as a May 1987 first-day site?

August 11, 1986: "Love You, Mother!," the second stamp from the renamed Special Occasions booklet, is unveiled in San Diego, California, at the annual convention of the FTD — the second year in a row that the Postal Service has attended this convention of florists. (Florists' Transworld Delivery is the oldest and largest of the flowers-by-wire organizations. Originally Florists Telegraph Delivery, it was founded in 1910 by 15 florists attending an industry meeting in Rochester, New York. Today it has some 21,000 members and more than two-thirds of the market.) At this time, the booklet was still planned for two panes of the 22¢ stamps, to sell for $4.40. The number of different stamp designs now moved from seven to eight.

September 30, 1986: All eight stamp designs are unveiled at a Greeting Card Association meeting at the Silverado Country Club in Napa, California. Deputy Postmaster General Jackie Strange says the stamps will be issued in 1987 in New York City, and that the Postal Service has classified them as "special" stamps because they will remain on sale longer than commemorative stamps.

On October 1, 1986, a day after Strange's speech, a USPS release specifies for the first time that the booklet will have just one pane. The Postal Service decides, after considering all marketing aspects, that two panes of ten at $4.40 per booklet would inhibit sales. Twenty Special Occasions stamps might take the average mailer too long to use. Ten messages at $2.20 would sell the booklet faster, and perhaps create a better selling environment for a second purchase.

Designs and messages on each stamp are:
- Fireworks, "Congratulations," horizontal commemorative format (two in each pane).
- Iris flowers, "Get Well!" vertical commemorative format.
- Balloons, "Thank You!" vertical commemorative format.
- Coffee, eyeglasses and crossword puzzle, "Love You, Dad!" horizontal commemorative format.
- Four-leaf clover, "Best Wishes!" small format.
- Cake and candle, "Happy Birthday!" small format (two in each pane).
- Gerber daisies, "Love You, Mother!" horizontal commemorative format.
- Stationery, pen and clover, "Keep In Touch!" small format.

The four small stamps are the same size as those in the Seashells booklet (22.09 by 24.43 millimeters). The horizontal commemorative-like stamps are twice as wide as the small stamps. The two vertical stamps are one and one-half times as tall as the small stamps.

The outside of the booklet lists the stamp subjects and urges people to join the USPS Commemorative Stamp Club. It also carries the UPC (Universal Product Code) lines and numbers most often seen on food items. The spacing and thickness of these lines can be scanned by built-in or handheld pencil scanners, which feed price and stock information to cash registers and computers. Inside the cover is an application form for joining the USPS club. The outside of the cover was printed via offset, the inside by letterpress on the Goebel booklet machine. Stamp perfing was also done on the Goebel machine.

For the past few years, the Postal Service has been selling stamp booklets to Giant stores under its Sales By Consignment program. The USPS consigns booklets to the retailers for sale to customers at face value. A float period is allowed before Giant has to pay the USPS for the full cost of the booklets.

A more complicated marketing scheme has been arranged between the USPS and Community Marketing Concepts Limited of Hicksville, New York. The firm purchases stamp booklets from the Hicksville post office, with 30 days to pay. The firm then repackages the booklets with advertising, plus local, regional and national merchandising coupons, in a pocket-size package called the Stamp Pack.

The advertisers pay Community Marketing Concepts to place their ads into the pack containing the booklet. The firm then sells the Stamp Packs to retail stores at less than face value. The retailers, in turn, sell Stamp Packs to customers at the booklet's normal cost. The customers buy the stamps at face, and get a packet of coupons and ads in the bargain.

The Stamp Pack brought booklets to supermarket shoppers at face value — courtesy of the ads and coupons tucked inside.

No advertising is affixed to the stamps. The Postal Service pays nothing to Community Marketing Concepts. The only agreement between the firm and the USPS is to sell the stamps to the firm on a 30-day consignment basis.

Collectors had many reactions to the idea behind the Special Occasions booklet. Many felt the messages would be unreadable after being canceled. If you want only a "Get Well!" or "Thank You!" stamp, you have to buy nine others. A Maryland collector said, "Instead of the ridiculous price I pay for greeting cards, I can now simply send the appropriate stamp on an envelope." A divorced collector claimed that these stamps would make his life more difficult: "Before, when I sent my alimony check, I had only to be careful not to grab a Love stamp. Now, I'm going to have to stay away from 'Thank You,' 'Love you, Mother,' 'Best Wishes,' and 'Keep In Touch.' "

Many such comments were made tongue-in-cheek. Far more collectors were looking forward to these stamps — and the special occasions that would prompt their use.

Postmasters were told to make this booklet available to their customers throughout calendar year 1987. They were assured by the Postal Service that the Bureau of Engraving and Printing and Stamp Distribution Offices would have them available for the entire year. With that edict, there was no longer any doubt that this booklet had become the first "special" stamp booklet.

The Designs

Three early concepts of stamps that appear in the Special Occasions booklet. The "Love You, Mom!" and "Get Well!" early versions changed markedly. The "Keep In Touch!" design originally showed a profile stamp affixed to the envelope. That became a shamrock to match the "Best Wishes!" stamp.

Oren Sherman of Boston, Massachusetts, was commissioned by the CSAC to do the designs for the Special Occasions booklet — his first attempt at stamp designing. The messages on the stamps were selected by the CSAC and USPS, with Sherman working his designs to fit each stamp theme. He rendered a few at first and filled out the ten-stamp pane as the number of designs changed and expanded over a two-year development period.

First-Day Facts

As has already been noted, two postal officials remarked early in the booklet's development that an annual May New York City trade show of a stationers' group would provide the ideal springboard for the new stamps. When the April 20, 1987, first day rolled around, however, the ceremony was shifted to Atlanta, Georgia. Instead of a professional trade show background, the setting was the scenic grounds of the Atlanta Historical Society. What changed the plans?

The New York trade show was locked into a date after Mother's Day. That would never do because one of the stamps ("Love You, Mother!") was a natural for sales prior to Mother's Day. With New York City out of the running, the USPS sought another site — one that would be large enough to provide good media exposure and also help spread first days evenly among the five postal regions. Atlanta and the Southern Region offered both opportunities.

Gordon C. Morison, assistant postmaster general for philatelic affairs, was the USPS speaker at the first-day ceremony. He was joined on the platform by Martha Burke, National American Mother of the Year. The Postal Service emphasized that it would affix and cancel only full panes of the booklet, applied horizontally to an envelope at least nine inches long.

22¢ CHRISTMAS MADONNA AND CHILD

Date of Issue: October 23, 1987

Catalog Numbers: Scott 2367   Minkus 881

Colors: gray, red, cyan, yellow, black, green

First-Day Cancel: Washington, D.C. (National Gallery of Art)

FDCs Canceled: unavailable

Format: Panes of 100, vertical, 10 across, 10 down. Printing cylinders of 800.

Perf: 11.2 (Eureka off-press perforator)

Selvage Markings: U.S. Postal Service© 1987, Use Correct ZIP Code

Designer: Bradbury Thompson (CSAC)

Art Director: Jack Williams (USPS)

Modeler: Frank J. Waslick (BEP)

Printing: Andreotti 7-color gravure press

Quantity Ordered: 525,000,000
Quantity Distributed: 4,650,000

Plate Block Detail: 6-digit plate number on corner stamps

Tagging: random overall

The Stamp

The traditional, or religious, Christmas stamp might be said to have begun with the 1965 5¢ stamp portraying an angel-with-trumpet weather vane from the People's Methodist Church in Newburyport, Massachusetts. Three prior Christmas stamps from 1962 through 1964 had dealt with secular subjects: a wreath, candles, holly, mistletoe, poinsettias, conifers and a White House Christmas tree.

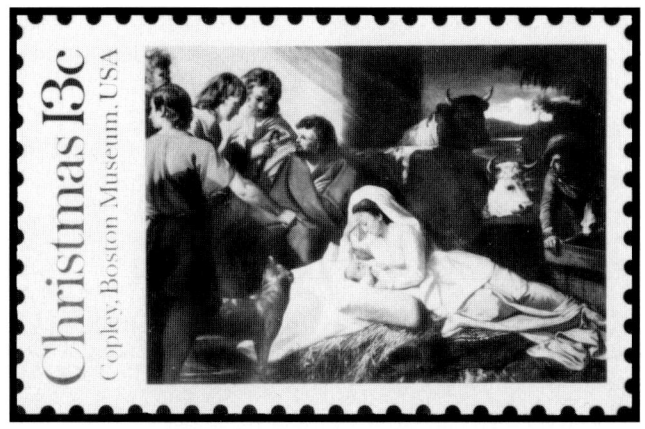

John Singleton Copley's Nativity *was a natural choice for the 1976 Madonna stamp. He was a native-born American who painted the work in 1776. Copley's Madonna is the only one by an American artist in the Christmas series to date.*

Other angels appeared on the traditional holiday stamp in 1968, 1972 and 1974, but in the 22 years since the first Madonna and Child stamp of 1966, the Madonna theme has been used 17 times — overwhelming three angel designs, a Sunday in Maine pictorial and a 1977 stamp showing George Washington at prayer.

When it comes to artists of the Madonna and Child on Christmas stamps, the Italian school predominates. In 12 out of 17 years, the Christmas traditional issues have carried the work of Italian artists and sculptors. That is true with the 1987 stamp as well, whose vignette shows a detail from a larger painting by Italian artist, Giovanni Battista Moroni.

Moroni was an artist unique among those of the Italian Renaissance for confining his work almost entirely to portraits. His paintings were principally of the petty aristocracy and bourgeoisie around his birthplace of Bergamo, Italy. Born in 1525, Moroni created likenesses that emphasize the sitter's individuality and personality.

Because of their order quantities — usually five to six times as large as commemoratives — Christmas stamps have to be scheduled far ahead of time. In 1987 they went to press in June. As they have been for the last several years, both Christmas issues were produced on the seven-color gravure Andreotti press. The gravure section of A Press prints only five colors, one color shy of the needs for both 1987 Christmas stamps. The Andreotti also runs at faster speeds than any other BEP gravure press, and possesses more types of color and registration controls.

For the second year in a row, both Christmas stamps were made in definitive size to reduce costs of paper, press time, ink and other factors. With prospects of more than a billion and a half to be sold, the USPS could save almost as much money as they would had they printed all commemoratives in definitive size except for the American Wildlife issue.

The Design

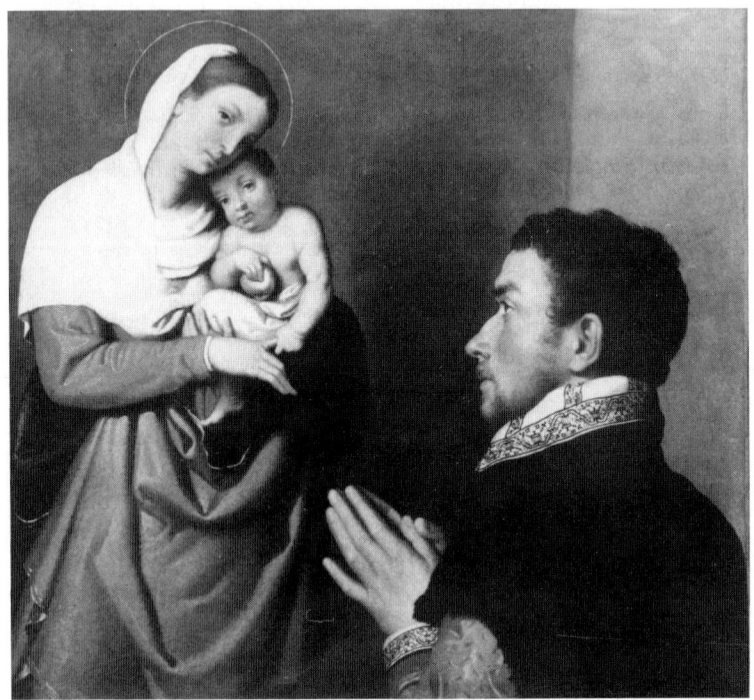

This is the entire painting of A Gentleman in Adoration Before the Madonna. *Only the upper left portion was used for the stamp.*

For Bradbury Thompson, a design coordinator for the Citizens' Stamp Advisory Committee, this was his 13th Madonna and Child design. Thompson's first design for the Postal Service was the 1958 3¢ Brussels Exhibition stamp; since then he has created more than five dozen U.S. stamp designs, exclusive of the Christmas Madonnas.

First-Day Facts

The Madonna and Child stamp was issued in Washington, D.C., October 23, 1987. The first-day ceremony was held in the auditorium of the East Building at the National Gallery of Art, the 14th such

This special pictorial cancel was used in Washington on the traditional stamp, and in Holiday, California, on the contemporary issue.

ceremony to be held at the National Gallery for the 14 works of art for Christmas stamps provided to the Postal Service.

USPS speaker was Assistant Postmaster General Gordon C. Morison, who remarked, "At Christmas time, people mail everything from ties to trees, from live creatures to major appliances, from tons of Florida fruit to truckloads of Wisconsin cheese." He predicted that in December 1987 the Postal Service would deliver a billion more pieces of mail than they do in a normal month.

22¢ CHRISTMAS GREETINGS

Date of Issue: October 23, 1987

Catalog Numbers: Scott 2368   Minkus 882

Colors: magenta, cyan, yellow, green, bright green, black

First-Day Cancel: Anaheim, California (Disneyland)

FDCs Canceled: unavailable

Format: Panes of 100, horizontal, 10 across, 10 down. Printing cylinders of 800.

Perf: 11.2 (Eureka off-press perforator)

Selvage Markings: U.S. Postal Service© 1987, Use Correct ZIP Code

Designer: Jim Dean (CSAC)

Art Director: Jack Williams (USPS)

Typographer: Howard Paine (CSAC)

Modeler: Peter Cocci (BEP)

Printing: Andreotti 7-color gravure press

Quantity Ordered: 975,000,000
Quantity Distributed: 4,650,000

Plate Block Detail: 6-digit plate number on corner stamps

Tagging: block over vignette

The Stamp

Prior to the two issued in 1987, the Postal Service had released either 52 or 53 Christmas stamps since the holiday stamps debuted in 1962. Putting the total in question is a 1982 13¢ Kitten and Puppy stamp. Although it was released after the five acknowledged Christmas stamps of that year, the USPS says it was issued in response to requests for a stamp to use on a postcard for holiday greetings.

But whether the total is 52 or 53, stamps of the contemporary or non-religious style have accounted for 31 issues — about 60 percent of all Christmas stamps. Though the Madonna and Child theme dominates the traditional or religious Christmas stamps, no such dominance of one subject occurs in the contemporary issues. Toys have appeared five times, Santa Claus and children at play four times each. Other pictorial choices have been wreaths, candles, Christmas trees, village snow scenes, sleighs and a rural mailbox.

This 1987 contemporary Christmas stamp greets us with an ornament, and pieces thereof. Ornaments have appeared only once before, when designer Eskil Ohlsson portrayed one shaped like Santa Claus on the 1979 Christmas stamp. The 1987 stamp is the eighth consecutive contemporary Christmas stamp to bear the word "greetings."

Produced by Disney artists, the cover of this first-day program for the Christmas Greetings stamp has a cartoon mouse gradually changing into Santa Claus as he strides from left to right.

As the Madonna and Child images dominate the Christmas stamps, so does the press that produces them. The seven-color gravure Andreotti press of the Bureau has printed 30 holiday stamps, a record that goes back to the 8¢ Christmas issues of 1971. The first four Christmas issues (1962 through 1965) were produced by the Giori intaglio press. It could print no more than three colors, however, so in 1966 it was used with offset presses to produce a multicolor stamp.

The intaglio Huck press made just two Christmas stamps, in 1968 and 1969. Then, in 1970, gravure printing took over the Christmas stamp production — never to this day to relinquish it. The BEP had no gravure press that could do the five Christmas stamps released in 1970, so the USPS went outside to Guilford Gravure, Inc., of Guilford, Connecticut.

Crews from the Bureau went to Guilford to actually run a gravure press, an Andreotti similar to the one soon to be placed in the BEP. In 1971 the Bureau's Andreotti began a 17-year production of Christmas stamps, interrupted only now and then when the gravure section of A Press stepped in to help with production or to take over one of the two annual Christmas stamps.

This contemporary stamp with the sparkling ornaments will outsell the traditional Madonna and Child stamp by 54 percent to 46 percent, if sales of the last three years are any indication.

The Design

James Dean, an Annandale, Virginia, artist, created the ornamental Christmas design that pictures three red, blue and gold glass balls hanging from a Christmas tree. Dean had created a watercolor painting of the sky and background of the Statue of Liberty from which Howard Paine had designed the 1985 22¢ Frederic Bartholdi stamp. He was also the designer of the 1985 22¢ Christmas Poinsettias stamp.

Dean, like Bradbury Thompson who designed the 1987 Madonna and Child stamp, is a design coordinator of the Citizens' Stamp Advisory Committee. Like their four fellow coordinators — Howard Paine, Derry Noyes, Richard Sheaff and Jerry Pinkney — they often design stamps, usually seek out other designers, and render opinions of work placed before the committee. None of them, however, is allowed to vote on a stamp design.

First-Day Facts

Holiday, California, is the station of the Anaheim post office closest to Disneyland.

In what was a first for both Disneyland and the U.S. Postal Service, this 1987 Christmas Greetings stamp had its first-day-of-issue ceremony at the Anaheim, California, theme park on October 23, 1987. Western Region Postmaster General Joseph Caraveo presided before more than 200 specially invited guests, including state, city and county political leaders. The ceremonies were closed to the public.

The usual first-day USPS protocol was enhanced by Mickey Mouse and other Disneyland characters performing a Christmas mailing skit. Present at the festivities were Michael Eisner, president of the Walt Disney Company; the U.S. Marine Corps Color Guard from El Toro Air Station; and James Dean, the artist who created the design.

In addition to the USPS pictorial first-day cancel illustrated here, Disneyland offered a special Christmas envelope designed by Disney artists. When first-day canceled, this cover was offered by mail order for $7.50.

Distribution of both Christmas stamps to post offices on the USPS automatic plan was made in smaller amounts than in 1986. Postmasters were told to place additional requirements carefully, mindful of the impending increases in postal rates coming in 1988.

DEFINITIVES

Of the 12 definitive stamps issued by the United States in 1987, seven were announced and assigned first days early in the year. The latecomers were the 22¢ Flag Over Capitol tagged paper test stamp, the 10¢ Red Cloud, the 17.5¢ Racing Car, the 5¢ Milk Wagon and the 22¢ Flag With Fireworks booklet issues. Five Transportation coils were sent to B Press, four Great Americans stamps came from A Press, Flag With Fireworks stamps in sheet and booklet formats came from the Andreotti gravure press, and the 22¢ Flag Over Capitol prephosphored paper test stamps were printed on C Press.

A half dozen of them accounted for something new in printing, paper or USPS policy.

The 8.5¢ Tow Truck coil had most of its run precanceled in red by the Bureau of Engraving and Printing. Thought to be the first time red was used for a BEP precancel, the bright color was intended to show up better against the dark gray ink of the stamp. Unprecanceled rolls of 500 of the Tow Truck issue were made for collectors.

With the 10¢ Canal Boat coils, rolls of 100 were made especially for the convenience of stamp collectors. Such rolls would be offered for sale by the USPS at post offices with philatelic centers. The collector-size rolls of 100 would not be available at other post offices, and would not be re-run at the Bureau when the special inventory of them was depleted.

The 22¢ Flag With Fireworks stamp was the first denominated definitive made by the gravure process since the 1975 13¢ Eagle and Shield issue of the Americana series. In the long press runs needed for most definitive stamps, gravure printing is cheaper than engraving. Gravure stamps are also available from outside suppliers; engraving is not. The Postal Service said that complex, multicolor gravure designs are even more difficult to counterfeit than the normal three-color engraved definitives.

The 22¢ Flag Over Capitol design was printed on prephosphored paper for a mailing test of more than 100,000 pieces. Each such test stamp was marked with the letter "T" at bottom. The test was to determine if the phosphor-treated paper would adversely affect mail-processing machines in post offices, automatic stamp-affixing devices used by large mailers, or the presses and perforators of the BEP. The test was judged a success, and plans were under way to have all stamps printed on prephosphored paper as soon as possible. The elimination of the tagging varnish, applied after the stamp is printed, would make stamp inks more vibrant in color.

The Flag With Fireworks booklet — the final stamp of the year on November 30 — was the Bureau's attempt to answer a booklet shortage that had plagued the USPS for years. With all of its Goebel booklet machines working 24 hours a day, the BEP supply fell short of booklet demand by some 40 million booklets annually. For the first time since the Goebel devices were installed in 1976-77, the BEP found an automated way to make booklets without them. (See the chapter on this booklet for details.)

The total of 12 definitives in 1987 exactly matched the total issued in 1986 and was only slightly less than the average of 14 definitives per year for the last five years. With a rate increase coming in 1988, the definitive total should jump — possibly as high as the 28 definitive stamps that went to market in the last price-increase year of 1985.

Plate Numbers

The *Yearbook* again includes all known, reported plate numbers for the Transportation series coils and the Great Americans sheet stamps. These are the only current definitives running in series form. The plate numbers listed in the charts take each series back to its beginning — to the 1981 Surrey stamp for the Transportation coils and to the 1980 Sequoyah issue for the Great Americans.

We acknowledge the help of the Bureau Issues Association in compiling the Great Americans plate numbers and the assistance of Stephen Esrati in tracking the plate numbers for precanceled and unprecanceled Transportation coils.

Prior Transportation Coils (not precanceled)

1¢ Omnibus (1983) 1,2,3,4,5,6
1¢ Omnibus (1986) 1
2¢ Locomotive (1982) 2,3,4,6,8,10
3¢ Handcar (1983) 1,2,3,4
3.4¢ School Bus (1985) 1,2
4¢ Stagecoach (1982) 1,2,3,4,5,6
4¢ Stagecoach (1986) 1
4.9¢ Buckboard (1985) 3,4
5¢ Motorcycle (1983) 1,2,3,4
5.2¢ Sleigh (1983) 1,2,3,5
5.5¢ Star Route Truck (1986) 1
5.9¢ Bicycle (1982) 3,4
6¢ Tricycle (1985) 1
7.4¢ Baby Buggy (1984) 2
8.3¢ Ambulance (1985) 1,2
9.3¢ Mail Wagon (1981) 1,2,3,4,5,6
10.1¢ Oil Wagon (1985) 1
10.9¢ Hansom Cab (1982) 1,2
11¢ Caboose (1984) 1

11¢ Stutz Bearcat (1985) 1,2,3,4	
12¢ Stanley Steamer (1985) 1,2	
12.5¢ Pushcart (1985) 1	
14¢ Iceboat (1985) 1,2,3,4	
14¢ Iceboat (1986) 2	
17¢ Electric Auto (1981) 1,2,3,4,5,6,7	
17¢ Dog Sled (1986) 2	
18¢ Surrey (1981) 1 through 18 complete	
20¢ Fire Pumper (1981) 1 through 16 complete	
25¢ Bread Wagon (1986) 1	

Prior Transportation Coils (precanceled)

3.4¢ School Bus (1985) 1,2
4¢ Stagecoach (1982) 3,4,5,6
4.9¢ Buckboard (1985) 1,2,3,4,5,6
5.2¢ Sleigh (1983) 1,2,3,4,5,6
5.5¢ Star Route Truck (1986) 1,2
5.9¢ Bicycle (1982) 3,4,5,6
6¢ Tricycle (1985) 1,2
7.4¢ Baby Buggy (1984) 2
8.3¢ Ambulance (1985) 1,2,3,4
8.3¢ Ambulance (1986) 1
9.3¢ Mail Wagon (1981) 1,2,3,4,5,6,8
10.1¢ Oil Wagon (1985) 1,2
10.9¢ Hansom Cab (1982) 1,2,3,4
11¢ Caboose (1984) 1
12¢ Stanley Steamer (1985) 1,2
12.5¢ Pushcart (1985) 1
17¢ Electric Auto (1981) 1,2,3,4,5,6,7

1987 Transportation Coils (not precanceled)

8.5¢ Tow Truck (1987) 1
7.1¢ Tractor (1987) 1
10¢ Canal Boat (1987) 1
5¢ Milk Wagon (1987) 1
17.5¢ Racing Car (1987) 1
2¢ Locomotive (revised from 1982 design) 1

1987 Transportation Coils (precanceled)

8.5¢ Tow Truck (1987) 1
7.1¢ Tractor (1987) 1
17.5¢ Racing Car (1987) 1
12¢ Stanley Steamer (1987 B Press) 1

Prior Great Americans Sheet Stamps

1¢ Dix (1983) 1,2
1¢ Mitchell (1986) 1
2¢ Stravinsky (1982) 1,2,3,4,5,6
3¢ Clay (1983) 1,2
3¢ White (1986) 1
4¢ Schurz (1983) 1,2,3,4
4¢ Flanagan (1986) 1
5¢ Buck (1983) 1,2,3,4
5¢ Black (1986) 1
6¢ Lippmann (1985) 1
7¢ Baldwin (1985) 1
8¢ Knox (1985) 3,4,5,6
9¢ Thayer (1985) 1
10¢ Russell (1984) 1
11¢ Partridge (1985) 2,3,4,5
13¢ Crazy Horse (1982) 1,2,3,4
14¢ Lewis (1985) 1
17¢ Carson (1981) 1,2,3,4,13,14,15,16
17¢ Lockwood (1986) 1,2
18¢ Mason (1981) 1,2,3,4,5,6
19¢ Sequoyah (1980) 39529, 39530 (BEP numbers)
20¢ Bunch (1982) 1,2,3,4,5,6,7,8,10,11,13
20¢ Gallaudet (1983) 1,2,5,6,8,9
20¢ Truman (1984) 1
22¢ Audubon (1985) 1
25¢ London (1986) 1
30¢ Laubach (1984) 1
35¢ Charles Drew (1981) 1,2,3,4
37¢ Millikan (1982) 1,2,3,4
39¢ Clark (1985) 1, 2
40¢ Gilbreth (1984) 1, 2
50¢ Nimitz (1985) 1,2,3,4
50¢ Nimitz (1986) 1
56¢ Harvard (1986) 1
$1 Revel (1986) 1
$2 Bryan (1986) 2

1987 Great Americans Sheet Stamps

14¢ Julia Ward Howe (1987) 1, 2
2¢ Mary Lyon (1987) 1
10¢ Red Cloud (1987) 1
$5 Bret Harte (1987) 1
22¢ John J. Audubon (1987 perfect-perf variety) 3

141

8.5¢ TOW TRUCK

Date of Issue: January 24, 1987

Catalog Numbers: Scott 2129   Minkus 869

Color: dark gray

First-Day Cancel: Tucson, Arizona (ARIPEX 87)

FDCs Canceled: 224,285

Format: Coils of 500 and 3,000 precanceled; 500 only unprecanceled

Perf: 10 (rotary perforator)

Designer: William Bond

Art Director: Howard Paine (CSAC)

Engravers: Vignette: Edward P. Archer (BEP)
            Inscriptions: Michael Ryan (BEP)

Typographer: Bradbury Thompson (CSAC)

Printing: intaglio B Press

Quantity Ordered: Coils of 500 precancel 46,000,000
                    Coils of 3,000 precancel 303,000,000
                    Coils of 500 unprecancel 16,000,000
Quantity Distributed: Coils of 500 precancel 81,100,000
                         Coils of 3,000 precancel 306,048,000
                         Coils of 500 unprecancel 17,600,000

Plate Number Detail: Single-digit plate number on every 52nd stamp

Tagging: block over vignette on unprecanceled stamps; none on precancels

The Stamp

With an estimated 300 million automobiles throughout the world — more than one-third of them in the United States — tow trucks are as vital as plumbers. With all manner of cars, trucks, buses, ambulances and moon vehicles having already appeared on nearly 20 U.S. stamps, perhaps it was time to call for the tow truck.

Originally intended for an 8.7¢ denomination, the Tow Truck coil in the Transportation series was changed to 8.5¢ when non-profit postage rates were revised April 20, 1986. The 8.5¢ value matched the current rate for basic non-profit mail presorted to three digits of the five-digit ZIP Code. No such stamp had existed for that rate in the ensuing months; mailers had used the 6¢ Tricycle Transportation coil of 1985 and paid for the difference.

Since the stamp's heaviest usage would be for non-profit mail, the bulk of the press run was made in coils of 500 and 3,000 on B press, precanceled "Nonprofit org." in red by a flexographic rubber mat installed on the unit that is usually used for applying phosphor tagging. A lesser quantity of unprecanceled Tow Truck stamps, intended primarily for collectors, was made in coils of 500. These were tagged by the same unit used to make the precancel.

Though Bureau of Engraving and Printing precancels are usually black, red ink was used for this stamp to show up better against the dark gray of the vignette. This is thought to be the first time that the Bureau has applied a precancel in red.

At least for this stamp, the Bureau returned to the basic method of applying precancels that was used in the days of Cottrell-made precancels: by a letterpress unit installed on the press. By eliminating the engraved precancel, of the type applied on 1986's 5.5¢ Star Route Truck coil, the BEP was able to use just one printing plate and produce both uncanceled and precanceled stamps on a single press run.

The first automobile (the word means "self-propelled") was a steam-powered tractor built in 1769 by French Army Captain Nicolas Cugnot. It hauled cannon at three miles per hour, but had to stop every ten minutes or so to build up another head of steam.

Applied by a flexographic rubber mat installed on the unit usually used for phosphor tagging, this "Nonprofit Org." was thought to be the first printed by the Bureau in red ink.

Next on the scene in England came steam carriages — in effect, buses — that could transport up to 22 persons. They were noisy and dirty, and their hot coals occasionally set fire to bridges, trees, bushes and crops. Railroad officials, wary of their competition, helped pass England's Locomotive Act of 1865, which limited the speed of these carriages to 4 miles an hour on country roads and 2 mph in towns. The law also required a signalman, carrying a red flag by day and a red lantern by night, to walk ahead of each carriage to warn of its approach. This law stymied English automobile progress for more than three decades.

Steam autos first appeared in the United States in the late 1800s. Their pioneer makers were J.N. Cathcart, Richard Dudgeon, Sylvester Roper, Ransom Olds and the Stanley brothers.

In the late 1890s and early 1900s, the electric auto challenged steam. The new electrics started at once (without waiting for steam to build), were quiet, easy to operate and didn't smell. But few of them went faster than 20 mph, and their batteries had to be recharged after every 50 miles or so of operation.

In Germany, Gottlieb Daimler and Karl Benz were pioneering internal combustion gasoline engines. By 1885 Daimler offered a gasoline-powered two-wheeled motorcycle and Benz a three-wheeled carriage. A gasoline auto, with the engine mounted in front, appeared in 1891 in France. All these vehicles used bicycle-like chain drives to deliver power to the wheels, until France's Louis Renault replaced the chains with a driveshaft.

Here in America, many were at work on a gasoline horseless carriage. Auto historians generally agree that Charles and Frank Duryea built the first successful one in 1893-94. The Duryeas also established the first American company to make gasoline autos, in 1895.

Henry Ford, Charles King, Olds and Alexander Winton introduced their versions of the gasoline auto in 1896. Olds built 425 cars in 1901, and began the mass production of automobiles as we know it today. Sales of the new cars were aided greatly by the almost simultaneous discovery of vast new oil fields in east Texas. The price of gasoline dropped sharply.

Ford later improved on the Olds assembly line concept. In 1913 he placed workers on each side of the main assembly line, along which the car's chassis moved. These workers affixed parts that had been delivered to them by smaller conveyor belts. By 1914 Ford was building his famed Model T — first introduced in 1908 — in about an hour and a half. Ford sold his first Model T for $850; by 1916 he was able to market it, at a profit, for less than $400.

William C. Durant founded General Motors in 1908, combining firms that had produced Cadillac, Buick, Oakland, Oldsmobile and seven other brands of cars. General Motors grew into the nation's largest automaker in the late 1920s. Durant's 1912 Cadillac introduced the first electric starter, doing away with the difficult and dangerous task of cranking autos by hand. The coming of the pneumatic tire in 1922 and the automatic transmission in 1939 made cars faster, more comfortable and easier to operate.

Auto sales in the United States spurted to 1,905,000 in 1920, to 4.5 million annually by 1929, and to a yearly average of about nine million in the mid-1970s. Ford's Model T, the best-seller from the beginning, was cheaper but unchanging. Other makers concentrated on new models every year, emphasizing style and comfort improvements. In 1927 the GM Chevrolet passed the Model T in sales. Ford quickly came out with his Model A and regained the lead for one year, but Chevrolet has taken the top sales spot in almost all the years since.

In 1923 more than 100 different automakers were in business. The Depression eliminated most of them. By 1939, GM, Ford and Chrysler manufactured 90 percent of all the cars sold in the United States. Today, of the nine million cars and 3.5 million trucks sold in the United States in an average year, foreign makers have seized more than 25 percent of the business. Japan, West Germany, France and Italy provide most of the imports, followed by relative newcomers Yugoslavia and Korea.

Call a tow truck! In the early 1900s, mud was the greatest driving hazard. By 1909 only about 190,000 miles of U.S. roads were surfaced, compared with 2.4 million miles today.

Foreign or domestic, at one time or another most cars will need towing. The 1920s lightweight, spindly tow truck shown on this stamp has grown larger and more powerful — but it is still an integral part of an industry that employs some 15 million Americans in the making, selling, servicing and refueling of more than 100 million automobiles and trucks now registered in the United States.

Collectors had a hard time finding this Tow Truck stamp at smaller post offices. The unprecanceled coils of 500 were sent automatically only to those post offices with philatelic centers. Precanceled stamps had to be ordered in minimums of 100,000 (for coils of 500) or 96,000 (coils of 3,000), so few post offices stocked them. The Philatelic Sales Division, however, offered both styles.

The Design

Artist William H. Bond of Arlington, Virginia, also designer of the Iceboat, Buckboard and Bread Wagon Transportation coils, created this design in pen and ink, using several photographs of tow trucks as models. The stamp thus does not depict any actual tow truck. Typographer Bradbury Thompson — in accordance with a recent 1986 USPS policy — made the figures of value twice as large as "USA."

First-Day Facts

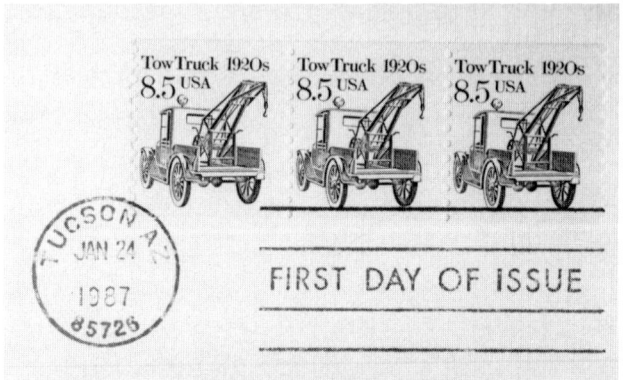

The Tow Truck stamp was released on the second day of the ARIPEX 87 stamp show in Tucson, Arizona.

The Tow Truck stamp was released on Saturday, January 24, 1987, during the second day of the January 23-25 ARIPEX '87 philatelic exhibition in Tucson, Arizona.

Michael McGovern, executive director of the Towing and Recovery Association of America, and Joseph R. Caraveo, postmaster general of the USPS Western Region, spoke at the first-day ceremonies. Guests included designer William Bond, American Philatelic Society President F. Burton Sellers and Robert Myers, president of the Arizona Federation of Stamp Clubs.

7.1¢ TRACTOR (UNPRECANCELED)

Date of Issue: February 6, 1987

Catalog Numbers: Scott 2127   Minkus 870

Colors: dark red

First-Day Cancel: Sarasota, Florida (SARAPEX '87 stamp show)

FDCs Canceled: 167,555

Format: Coils of 500 only. Printing cylinders of 936.

Perf: 10 (rotary perforator)

Designer: Ken Dallison

Art Director: Jack Williams (USPS)

Engravers: Vignette: Gary M. Chaconas (BEP)
             Inscriptions: Robert G. Culin, Sr. (BEP)

Modeler: Clarence Holbert (BEP)

Printing: Intaglio B Press (A separate cylinder was used for this unprecanceled stamp.)

Quantity Ordered: Coils of 500; 16,000,000
Quantity Distributed: Coils of 500; 17,600,000

Plate Block Detail: Single-digit red plate number every 52nd stamp.

Tagging: block over vignette

7.1¢ TRACTOR (PRECANCELED)

Date of Issue: February 6, 1987

Catalog Numbers: Scott 2127a   Minkus none

Color: dark red, black

First-Day Cancel: Sarasota, Florida (SARAPEX 87 stamp show)

FDCs Canceled: unknown

Format: Coils of 500 and 3,000. Printing cylinders of 936.

Perf: 10 (rotary perforator)

Designer: Ken Dallison

Art Director: Jack Williams (USPS)

Engravers: Vignette: Gary M. Chaconas (BEP)
          Inscriptions: Robert G. Culin, Sr. (BEP)

Modeler: Clarence Holbert (BEP)

Printing: intaglio B Press (A separate cylinder was used for this precanceled stamp.)

Quantity Ordered: 500-stamp coils: 10,000,000
                    3,000-stamp coils: 105,000,000
Quantity Distributed: 500-stamp coils: 47,200,000
                         3,000-stamp coils: 150,144,000

Plate Number Detail: single-digit plate number every 52nd stamp

Tagging: none on a precanceled stamp

The Stamps

Two versions of this coil in the Transportation series were produced by the BEP: one with the black non-profit precancel, and one without. The Bureau worked as they had for a similar "with and without" 5.5¢ Star Route Truck stamp in late 1986. Two separate cylinders were made for the intaglio B Press, which can print three colors with one revolution of its printing cylinder. One cylinder printed the dark red unprecanceled 7.1¢ Tractor coil. Another cylinder laid down the red design and the black precancel.

The stamp's 7.1¢ value met the third-class non-profit rate for bulk mail presorted to five-digit ZIP Codes. It replaced the 4.9¢ Buckboard coil of 1985. Originally intended for this new 7.1¢ coil was the Dog Sled design, which was pressed into service on a 17¢ Transportation coil in 1986. This is the fourth and last stamp of a non-profit series delayed by the uncertainty about the size of payment to be voted by the Congress to repay the USPS for losses sustained in handling discounted non-profit mailings.

As with the 5.5¢ unprecanceled stamps of last year, few would be postally used. Most of the unprecanceled Tractor stamps were destined to find their way onto album pages instead of envelopes. The precanceled version, however, would be heavily used by bulk non-profit mailers who need a coil at the correct rate for automatic affixing to mass mail.

Distribution of the new unprecanceled Tractor coils was made only to post offices having a philatelic center. Smaller post offices typically could often not supply the stamp, since there was little demand for it except from U.S. collectors. Both varieties of the stamp were available, however, from the Philatelic Sales Division.

The first successful gasoline-powered tractor was this "Old No. 1," built by the Hart & Parr Company in 1901. Like the John Deere tractor on the stamp, it has a large flywheel on its side to start the engine.

The 1920s Tractor, pictured on the stamp, changed the very concept of what a tractor was. Prior to the 1920s, a tractor was considered a movable source of power to be applied to threshing cylinders, or occasionally to be used in the place of horses or oxen. With the introduction of a power takeoff, power from the engine could be transmitted through a flexible shaft to such in-the-field implements as combines, hay balers and hay mowers.

The word "tractor" was coined by combining parts of the words TRACtion and moTOR. Such a device was first patented in the United States in 1890. The word is used today to describe the motorized cabs that pull huge truck trailers, and even for the mechanized two-wheeled garden apparatus controlled by a walking operator. In the early days of flight, an airplane was said to have a tractor motor if it pulled the plane instead of pushing it forward. "Tractor" first appeared in advertising when the Hart & Parr Company of Charles City, Iowa, used it in 1906.

The 1920s tractor shown on the stamp has steel wheels with large lugs to provide ground traction. The advent of pneumatic tractor tires in 1932 — with widely spaced rubber lugs around the tire — disturbed the soil less and made power transmission more efficient. The large wide tires used on power wheels did not burrow into the ground the way the steel tires did.

Tractors sent American farms into the mechanical age. The tractor was more powerful than the horse, did not have to be watered and fed, and never tired. More land was brought under cultivation more easily, and crop yields increased. With mechanization, one farm worker could now produce enough food for 20 people — with enough left over for export or use in chemical processes.

Not all tractors these days use rubber tires. Crawlers, or tracklaying tractors, run on continuous metal treads, much like military tanks. Such machines have better traction with less ground pressure than regular wheeled tractors. They work better on very light soils (where tires could not get a good grip), and on heavy soils (where they can exert more drawbar pull to break up the soil). Crawler tractors are most often used for changing land contours, building dams, and for clearing brush from virgin land.

Tractors have evolved into many shapes and sizes for specialized jobs. Huge crawler tractors are used in land and construction projects. Regular tractors, tilling soil and pulling hay rakes, now outnumber horses on farms. Special tractors are made small enough to go between rows of grapevines, or big enough to straddle one or more rows.

Once strictly a farm implement, smaller versions of the tractor have moved into the cities to make lawn tending and gardening better and less strenuous.

The Design

Veteran stamp designer Ken Dallison of Indian River, Ontario, Canada, created the tractor stamp. Dallison is himself a fan and collector of tractors and automobiles. He drew his stamp tractor from a

Two different tractors were considered for the stamp: the 1920s John Deere (which made it) and this 1918 Waterloo Boy Model N (which failed because it was too detailed).

photo of a 1920s John Deere machine. The USPS, of course, removed the brand name from the stamp.

Dallison's designs have all been involved with transportation of one kind or another. He began in 1978 with 31¢ stamps for the Wright brothers and a *Wright Flyer*. An Octave Chanute and glider pair came next in 1979, along with two 25¢ stamps for Wiley Post and his plane, the *Winnie Mae*. A 35¢ stamp for Glenn Curtiss followed in 1980, and a 33¢ issue for Alfred Verville in 1985.

All of these were airmail stamps, and all had another element in common: They pictured people as well as machines. With his 11¢ Stutz Bearcat and 12¢ Stanley Steamer Transportation coils of 1985, Dallison drew the machines only. This new Tractor coil is his third "unperson" stamp in the Transportation series.

First-Day Facts

The Tractor stamp was released on February 6, 1987, during SARAPEX 87 at the Sarasota Exhibition Hall in Sarasota, Florida. Regional Postmaster General Harry C. Penttala spoke for the Postal Service. Also in attendance were Arthur G. Smith, Tampa postmaster, and Ken Dallison, designer of the stamp.

14¢ JULIA WARD HOWE

Date of Issue: February 12, 1987

Catalog Numbers: Scott 2177   Minkus 871

Color: red

First-Day Cancel: Boston, Massachusetts (Perkins School for the Blind)

FDCs Canceled: 454,829

Format: Panes of 100, vertical, 10 across, 10 down. Printing cylinders of 800.

Perf: 11 (Eureka off-press perforator)

Selvage Markings: U.S. Postal Service© 1987, Use Correct ZIP Code

Designer: Ward Brackett

Art Director: Bradbury Thompson

Engravers: Vignette: Joseph Creamer, Jr. (BEP)
Lettering: James Goodbody (BEP)
Numerals: Robert G. Culin, Sr. (BEP)

Modeler: V. Jack Ruther (BEP)

Printing: intaglio portion of intaglio/gravure A Press

Quantity Ordered: 1,250,000,000
Quantity Distributed: 429,320,000

Plate Number Detail: single-digit number alongside corner stamp

Tagging: block over vignette

The Stamp

This 14¢ stamp for Julia Ward Howe, author and social reformer, was the 36th stamp in the Great Americans series. It heralded the demise of the 14¢ Sinclair Lewis issue of 1985, though from a technical standpoint, replacing Lewis seemed unnecessary. His stamp had been produced on the webfed A Press, as was Howe's; his stamp, therefore, would have processed through the faster, cheaper Eureka perforators, as did Howe's.

Or so it might seem. Actually, the Lewis stamp had been laid out in printing cylinders of 920. This was the standard definitives layout on A Press before it had been reduced to 800 stamps, to allow for the wide horizontal gutters necessary for perforating stamps on the Eurekas. The 920-stamp cylinder format had forced the Lewis stamps to be perfed on the handfed L perforators. New printing cylinders were needed for Eureka processing, so along came a new design, for Julia Ward Howe.

The stern visage of Sinclair Lewis had not made an attractive stamp. The new Howe stamp tied in with two February 12 anniversaries: Lincoln's birthday and the 125th anniversary of the publication of *Battle Hymn of the Republic*, Lincoln's favorite Civil War song, written by Howe.

Julia Ward Howe in her eighties.

Mrs. Howe was born on May 27, 1819, to a prominent and wealthy New York City banking family. Nothing was too good for her. She was raised with governesses and the finest private schools and tutors. She even had expert training for a possible operatic career.

At 24, she married a Bostonian, Dr. Samuel Gridley Howe, who was nearly 20 years her senior. She moved to Boston, had six children, and somehow found time to help her husband edit an anti-slavery periodical, *The Commonwealth*. After the Civil War began, her husband traveled often to Washington as an official of the Sanitary Commission, which was then involved with battlefield supervision of the treatment of war wounds.

On one of these trips with him, Julia Ward Howe was invited to review some Union troops at Bailey's Crossroads, now a part of Arlington, Virginia. Enemy patrols were reported in the neighborhood, and the viewing party scrambled into its carriages to leave. To pass the time while returning to Washington, the trained, mezzo-soprano voice of Julia Ward Howe led the group in singing *John Brown's Body*, originally written by William Steffe, as a camp meeting hymn.

Steffe had taken its beat and some of its melodies from old plantation chants. At the suggestion of some of her companions, Mrs. Howe wrote a patriotic lyric for the old song. That was the genesis of *Battle Hymn of the Republic*, composed at the Willard Hotel in Washington after Mrs. Howe had fled Confederate troops on November 20, 1861.

Mrs. Howe often said it was the easiest poem she had ever written. After awakening in the middle of the night, the words seemed to flow from her mind, she said. Grabbing a pen, she wrote the first line quickly: "Mine eyes have seen the glory of the coming of the Lord." Previous efforts at poetry had taken hours and days; this one wrote itself. Changing only four words of the scribbled notes, she sent the poem to the *Atlantic Monthly*. When the magazine published it in February 1862, they sent Mrs. Howe $5 for her contribution.

The new song spread through the ranks of Union soldiers. A Captain Charles McCabe of the Ohio Infantry is thought to have used it first as a marching song. The words and music moved from soldiers to civilians — and, ultimately, to the White House. It is said that Lincoln, on hearing it for the first time, wept openly — and asked to hear it repeated. The song was later sung at Lincoln's funeral and is now closely associated with the martyred Civil War president.

When the war ended, Julia Ward Howe became a writer, lecturer and social reformer, working primarily in the women's rights movement. She founded the New England Women's Club, the American Women's Suffrage Association, and was president of the American branch of the Women's International Peace Association. Her writings include *A Trip to Cuba* (1860), *Sex and Education* (1874), *Modern Society* (1881) and *Reminiscences* (1899).

While Anna Jarvis is usually credited with originating the nationwide celebration of Mother's Day in 1908, Julia Ward Howe had started the holiday in 1872. For several years, Mrs. Howe held an annual Mother's Day meeting in Boston on June 2. (History says that Mother's Day did not start in America at all. England had observed a Mothering Sunday for years, and a few European countries had long before established similar days.)

Julia Ward Howe died at the age of 91 on October 17, 1910, in Newport, Rhode Island.

The Design

The Julia Ward Howe design was commissioned several years ago, as the 20¢ value on this essay indicates. Type was rearranged so that the numerals of value were twice as large as USA, and the "¢" symbol was eliminated.

Ward Brackett of Westport, Connecticut, took his design for the stamp from a photograph of Mrs. Howe made at approximately the time she wrote *Battle Hymn of the Republic*. Brackett's design was a pencil sketch based on the photo.

This is Brackett's seventh stamp design. He began in 1962 with the 4¢ Girl Scout commemorative, followed by a 1968 6¢ Law and Order, a 1970 6¢ Women's Suffrage, a 1981 17¢ Rachel Carson, a 1983 3¢ Henry Clay and a 1984 40¢ Lillian Gilbreth. None of his designs has been for more than two colors.

Brackett is the husband of Dolli Tingle, a designer of Christmas stamps for the Postal Service.

First-Day Facts

Though bearing a Boston cancellation, the Howe stamp was released in Watertown, Massachusetts — a 40,000-person suburb west of Boston.

The stamp's first day was held February 12, 1987, at Dwight Hall, in the Howe Building of the Perkins School for the Blind, Watertown, Massachusetts. Featured USPS speaker was John G. Mulligan, Northeastern regional postmaster general.

Samuel Gridley Howe, Julia's husband, had founded the Perkins School, the first such institution in the United States. He served as its director from 1832 to 1876.

2¢ MARY LYON

Date of Issue: February 28, 1987

Catalog Numbers: Scott 2169   Minkus 872

Color: blue

First-Day Cancel: South Hadley, Massachusetts (Mount Holyoke College)

FDCs Canceled: 349,831

Format: Panes of 100, vertical, 10 across, 10 down. Printing cylinders of 800.

Perf: 11 (Eureka off-press perforator)

Selvage Markings: U.S. Postal Service© 1984, Use Correct ZIP Code

Designer: Ron Adair

Art Director: Jack Williams (USPS)

Engravers: Vignette: Joseph S. Creamer, Jr. (BEP)
Inscriptions: Robert G. Culin, Sr. (BEP)

Modeler: Clarence Holbert (BEP)

Printing: intaglio portion of intaglio/gravure A Press

Quantity Ordered: 330,000,000
Quantity Distributed: 101,560,000

Plate Number Detail: single-digit plate number on corner stamps

Tagging: block over vignette

The Stamp

The 2¢ Mary Lyon stamp, the 37th in the Great Americans series, replaced the 2¢ Igor Stravinsky issue of 1982 — also a Great Americans pane stamp. Stamps of 1¢ to 6¢ denomination, called "change makers" by the Postal Service, are needed to meet the almost infinite number of possible rates on parcel post items. They are also kept on hand for use during a possible rate increase.

Of the 37 Great Americans stamps to date, seven have been for women: social reformers Dorothea Dix and Belva Ann Lockwood; authors Pearl Buck, Rachel Carson and Margaret Mitchell; and management engineer Lillian Gilbreth. Mary Lyon is the only pure educator to be so honored.

The stamp's issue date, February 28, 1987, marked the 190th anniversary of her birth, in Buckland, Massachusetts, in 1797. It also coincided with the 150th anniversary of Mount Holyoke College, which Lyon founded. As such, the stamp masked another school anniversary forbidden by stamp selection criteria.

Mary Lyon began to teach at 17. Living at the family homestead with her brother, she also did spinning and weaving to make money. At 20 she had saved enough for a year's training at Sanderson Academy in Ashfield. She supported herself there, and at other academies she attended, by her teaching income.

Detail from an old painting of Mary Lyon by an unknown artist. (Mount Holyoke College collection)

Her success as a teacher and the demand for the young women she trained led her to plan her own permanent school. Aided by Edward Hitchcock, a geologist, she had raised more than $12,000 by 1835 — most of it coming in small donations. It was enough to build a five-story structure that opened in 1837 as Mount Holyoke Female Seminary, located in South Hadley, Massachusetts, with Mary Lyon as principal. A faculty of four welcomed 80 students in the first year. The school's name was shortened to Mount Holyoke College in later years.

Yale, Harvard, and William and Mary had been going for more than 100 years when Mary Lyon's women's college began to offer a program of liberal arts and sciences comparable to those of a men's college. Hers was the first American college-level school for women.

Advocates of advanced education for women comprised a small minority in those times; Mary Lyon had to overcome obstacles of prejudice and derision to open Mount Holyoke.

She served as its principal for 12 years, leaving behind at her death an institution that was out of debt, endowed with $68,000, and staffed with experienced, dedicated teachers. Educational historians admit that the strongest influences on elementary and secondary education in the East, during the mid-1800s, came from teaching graduates of Mary Lyon's school.

This stamp was designed in 1984, and unveiled October 12, 1985. No issue date was set then, although the Postal Service guessed that the stamp would be released sometime during 1987. The unveiling took place at Wheaton College in Norton, Massachusetts, a school that Mary Lyon helped organize before she founded Mount Holyoke.

Automatic distribution of the stamp was made only to those post offices having philatelic centers.

The Design

Left, the stamp design as originally unveiled in 1985. Right, the final design.

The Mary Lyon stamp was designed by Ron Adair of Richardson, Texas. He also designed the 15¢ Everett Dirksen and 20¢ John Hanson commemorative stamps of 1981 and the 1986 1¢ Margaret Mitchell stamp in the Great Americans series.

Ron is the twin brother of Don Adair, designer of the 1986 Republic of Texas stamp. Both brothers had been asked by the Postal Service to submit designs for the Texas issue, and Don's won. The Adair twins, 39, are the only twins designing U.S. stamps.

While Adair based his stamp on several likenesses of Lyon, his principal image came from a daguerrotype taken in 1845 by an unknown photographer. As the illustrations show, the stamp's layout changed from its unveiling until its final issuance. The lettering and portrait decreased in size, and the denomination moved to the right corner of the stamp, becoming much larger than on the first design.

First-Day Facts

These Mary Lyon and Fire Pumper stamps were used on the official first-day program.

The Chapin Auditorium on the campus of Mount Holyoke College in South Hadley, Massachusetts, was the venue for the February 28, 1987, first-day ceremony. Featured speaker for the USPS was John G. Mulligan, postmaster general for the Northeast Region.

When collectors did not affix their own stamps, the Postal Service applied one 2¢ Mary Lyon stamp and a 20¢ Fire Pumper coil to make the first-class rate.

10¢ CANAL BOAT

Date of Issue: April 11, 1987

Catalog Numbers: Scott 2259   Minkus 874

Color: blue

First-Day Cancel: Buffalo, New York (Marine Midland Bank Auditorium)

FDCs Canceled: 171,952

Format: Coils of 3,000 and 100. Printing cylinders of 936.

Perf: 9.9 (coils of 100 on guillotine perforator; others on rotary perforator)

Designer: William Bond

Art Director: Howard Paine (CSAC)

Engravers: Vignette: Edward Archer (BEP)
              Inscriptions: Robert G. Culin, Sr. (BEP)

Typographer: Bradbury Thompson (CSAC)

Printing: intaglio B Press

Quantity Ordered: Coils of 3,000: 130,000,000
                       Coils of 100: 12,000,000
Quantity Distributed: Coils of 3,000: 21,888,000
                           Coils of 100: 10,920,000

Plate Number Detail: single-digit number every 52nd stamp

Tagging: block over vignette

The Stamp

Although it bears no legend saying so, this stamp seemed to be issued as much for the Erie Canal as for canal boats. The Postal Service releases and bulletins honed in on the Erie Canal, and the first-day ceremonies went to Buffalo, New York, where the Erie Canal originated. For the U.S. collector, who has seen five canals on U.S. stamps, it brought the number of stamps for man-made waterways and locks to nine.

The Erie is canal number 5 in that litany. First came postage stamps for the canals and locks at Sault Ste. Marie, Michigan (1901 and 1955), the Panama Canal (1913 and 1939), the Ohio River canals (1929), the St. Lawrence Seaway (1959 and 1984), and the Erie Canal (1967 and 1987).

This 1967 stamp for the Erie Canal marked 150 years since the groundbreaking. It was far more stylized and colorful than the new Canal Boat issue.

This 10¢ Canal Boat stamp, picturing the first watercraft in the Transportation series, replaced no other issue. At the time of its release, no other 10¢ coil was on active sale. The stamp was intended to pay the 10¢ surcharge for oversized items on first-class mail and single piece rate third-class mail which weighed one ounce or less. The *Domestic Mail Manual* states that first-class and third-class mail is non-standard if its length exceeds 11½ inches, or if its height exceeds 6⅛ inches, or if its thickness is greater than ¼ inch.

The USPS announced that, beginning with this stamp, all future coil stamps would be produced in coils of 100 for the convenience of stamp collectors. This was to be a limited production at the BEP, and such 100-stamp coil rolls would be offered for sale at philatelic centers only. They would not be available to other post offices, and would not be re-run after first production inventory had been depleted.

The Erie Canal was far from the first to be built in the United States. It was, however, the largest, longest and most important to the commercial growth of its environs. Smaller canals had been constructed in Massachusetts and South Carolina in the 1790s and 1800s, but the Erie Canal's connecting of the Hudson River, at Troy and Albany, New York, with Lake Erie, at Buffalo, New York, brought the economies and importance of canal transportation to national attention.

The Erie Canal, begun in 1817 in Rome, New York, was finished in 1825. It ran for 363 miles, was 42 feet wide and 4 feet deep. It could float boats that were 80 feet long, 15 feet wide, and had a draft of no more than 3½ feet. Its cost, $7,143,780, was paid for entirely by the state of New York. By the time toll charges were abolished in 1882, the state had collected 17 times that cost in fees.

The canal was improved and enlarged several times. It provided cheap transportation for manufactured goods flowing towards the Midwest, and for the raw materials that came back to the East. The Erie Canal helped develop New York City into the financial center of the United States. Long before the coming of the St. Lawrence Seaway, the Erie Canal unlocked the Great Lakes to the Atlantic Ocean.

Canal boats were low and wide. Necessarily, they had flat, shallow bottoms. The bows were rounded, but the sterns were blunt. Cabins in the rear of the boats were seldom more than 30 inches above deck level. As this stamp shows, passenger space was greatest on the cabin roof, which often had tables, chairs and an awning for comfort. The boats were steered by a rudder, and pulled by horses, donkeys or mules that walked on towpaths alongside each bank of the canal.

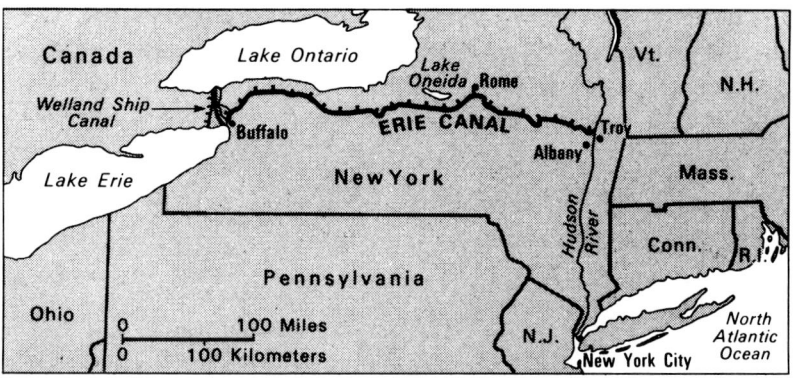

The original Erie Canal ran between the Hudson River and Lake Erie.

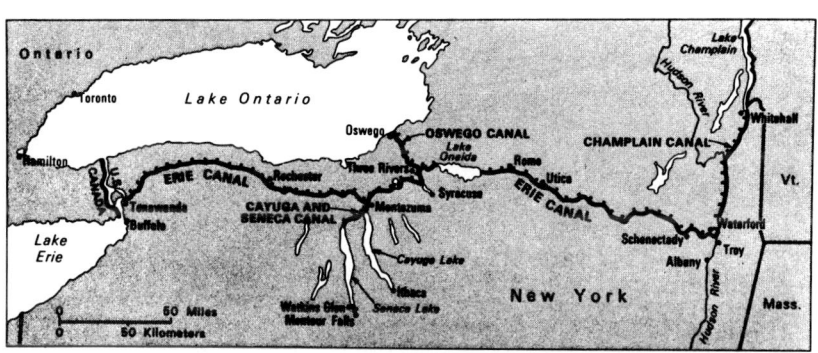

Today's New York State Barge Canal System consists of the Erie Canal and three other canals. The system connects major waterways of New York.

The standard charge on the Erie Canal for freight was 3¢ per ton per mile. Many other canals charged less. In 1826, $4 a day would pay for the boat captain, a mule and mule driver, the mule's feed, and the rental of a 25-ton canal boat. Stagecoaches were faster, but the canal boats carried passengers who preferred the safety, comfort and serenity of a smooth, four-mile-per-hour ride.

The canal era came to an end when railroads crossed the Appalachian Mountains in the 1850s. By 1918 the Erie Canal was combined with three shorter canals in New York to form the New York State Barge Canal System. The system connects the state's principal natural waterways on a toll-free operation. The old Erie Canal depth has been increased to 12 and 14 feet in different portions of the system. About two million short tons of freight and thousands of pleasure boats still move through remnants of the Erie Canal each year.

The Design

In this nearly completed design stage, artist Bill Bond was asked to lighten the contrast lines in the water and separate them from the hull. The lettering was changed to read "1880s" instead of "1880." The proper 10¢ denomination was added.

With this stamp, William H. Bond of Arlington, Virginia, completed his fifth design for the Transportation series. David Stone has also designed five, while Jim Schleyer remains the ranking Transportation coil designer with nine stamps. Bond's only design, other than for the Transportation series, was the 20¢ Alaska Statehood stamp of 1984.

The Canal Boat stamp's inscription, "Canal Boat 1880s," makes for a larger craft than appeared on the 1967 issue. As years went by, the canal was deepened, widened and improved. There is more above the waterline on the 1880s boat than on the 1967 commemorative for the anniversary for the beginnings of the Erie Canal.

First-Day Facts

The 10¢ Canal Boat stamp was released during the ALPEX stamp show of the Plewacki American Legion Post Stamp Society on April 11, 1987, at the Marine Midland Bank auditorium in Buffalo, New York. Although construction of the canal began in Rome, New York, Buffalo was its western terminus.

Gordon Morison, assistant postmaster general for philatelic affairs and a former resident of upstate New York, spoke for the USPS. He noted the popularity of Transportation series stamps with collectors, saying, "We sell these stamps to collectors by the yard."

For collectors who did not affix their own postage to first-day covers, the Postal Service attached two Canal Boat stamps and one 2¢ Locomotive issue.

22¢ FLAG WITH FIREWORKS

Date of Issue: May 9, 1987

Catalog Numbers: Scott 2276   Minkus 875

Colors: yellow, red, royal blue, background blue

First-Day Cancel: Denver, Colorado (ROMPEX 87)

FDCs Canceled: 398,855

Format: Panes of 100, vertical, 10 across, 10 down. Printing cylinders of 800.

Perf: 11.2 (Eureka off-press perforator)

Selvage Markings: U.S. Postal Service© 1987, Use Correct ZIP Code

Designer: Peter Cocci (BEP)

Program Manager: Don McDowell (USPS)

Typographer: Peter Cocci (BEP)

Modeler: Peter Cocci (BEP)

Printing: Andreotti 7-color gravure press

Quantity Ordered: 2,300,000,000
Quantity Distributed: 729,500,000

Plate Block Detail: 4-digit plate number on corner stamps

Tagging: block over vignette

The Stamp

The production of this 22¢ Flag With Fireworks definitive on the Andreotti gravure press poses a question. Has the United States ever printed a definitive stamp heretofore that was not engraved? We have been told for years that the heavily used regular issues were engraved because that was the hardest printing medium for counterfeiters to duplicate. Which spawns a second question: Isn't that true any more?

From 1847 until 1918, all U.S. definitives had been engraved. As a result of World War I, the quality of printing inks available to the Bureau of Engraving and Printing deteriorated. Gritty substances in the inks were chewing up engraved printing plates. From a normal life expectancy of six to eight weeks, the abrasive inks were now wearing out plates in just ten days. The Bureau received permission from the Post Office Department to print the 1¢, 2¢, and 3¢ Washington regular issues via offset — the first and last time that U.S. definitives were made wholly by the offset process.

As gravure entered U.S. stamp production in the early 1970s with the installation of the Andreotti press, the newly organized United States Postal Service had no hesitancy in placing its new emblem on the first gravure-made definitive, the 8¢ U.S. Postal Service stamp of 1971. Several gravure Christmas issues followed, but gravure was not again seen on a definitive until the 10¢ ZIP Code stamp of 1974. Since then, gravure definitives have included the 13¢ Eagle and Shield stamps in the Americana series, plus sheet varieties of the non-denominated A, B, C and D issues. Since 1979, all U.S. airmail stamps have also been printed via gravure. So much for the first question — many U.S. definitives have been produced without engraving.

The second question is a bit more difficult to answer: Aren't engraved definitives still the toughest to counterfeit? Here's the official USPS answer to that query: "When used for complex, multicolor designs, gravure is much harder to counterfeit than three-color intagalio (engraved) printing."

Other factors might have influenced the Postal Service's decision. Gravure creates more colorful stamps; customers have told the USPS they prefer colorful stamps. On the longer press runs of definitives, gravure is more economical than intaglio printing. The Postal Service expects to save $1 million annually by using a gravure-printed Flag stamp as its bellwether issue for first-class mail. Should production get tight during a postal rate increase, outside producers could step in to help with creating definitives with new values, possibly eliminating the need for non-denominated issues.

This stamp is the first American issue to portray the U.S. flag against a nighttime, darkened background. It is also the first to combine fireworks and the flag. Definitive issues with a flag design have been continuously available since 1968. The American flag — first seen on a U.S. stamp in 1869 — has been featured on 34 U.S. stamps and has appeared as a recognizable element on 20 others.

This Flag With Fireworks sheet stamp replaces the 22¢ Flag Over Capitol sheet stamp. Production of the Flag Over Capitol coils and booklet stamps was to continue for the foreseeable future.

The Design

The workhorse 22¢ definitives that go on billions of letters — compared to mere millions for a commemorative — need to be designed and refined for the best possible press operation. Perhaps that is why the BEP's in-house designers take over when new designs are needed. The Bureau's Frank Waslick crafted the 22¢ Flag Over Capitol stamp; the Bureau's Peter Cocci designed the 22¢ Seashells booklet. Cocci returns to design this new Flag With Fireworks issue, a design that may be used on coils and booklets later.

Cocci has also created the 18¢ Flag and Anthem issues of 1981 and the 15¢ Organized Labor stamp of 1980, among others.

First-Day Facts

The stamp was issued May 9, 1987, in Denver, Colorado, at the ROMPEX 87 stamp exhibition. The first-day ceremony took place in the Sheraton Denver Tech Center Hotel. Against a background of 50 U.S. flags, Gordon C. Morison, assistant postmaster general for philatelic affairs, presented the first pane of the new stamps to Denver Postmaster Jose Perez, who promised to Express Mail them to the White House that afternoon. The second pane went to designer Cocci.

22¢ PREPHOSPHORED PAPER TEST STAMP

Date of Issue: May 23, 1987

Catalog Numbers: Scott 2115b   Minkus 876

Colors: red, blue, black

First-Day Cancel: Secaucus, New Jersey (NOJEX 87 stamp show)

FDCs Canceled: 151,686

Format: Coils of 100 and 3,000. Printing cylinders of 960

Perf: 10 (100's on guillotine, 3,000's on rotary perforator)

Designer: Frank Waslick (BEP)

Art Director: Leonard Buckley (BEP)

Engravers: Vignette: Thomas Hipschen (BEP)
   Inscriptions: Robert G. Culin, Sr. (BEP)

Modeler: Frank Waslick (BEP)

Printing: 3-color intaglio C Press

Quantity Ordered: 20,000,000
Quantity Distributed: 20,000,000

Plate Number Detail: Letter "T" appears at bottom of each stamp. Plate number every 48th stamp appears as "T1."

Tagging: Phosphor-treated paper used. No varnish or tagging applied on press.

The Stamp

The first use of a phosphor-tagged U.S. stamp took place in Dayton, Ohio, in August 1963. A test quantity of 8¢ carmine airmail stamps, treated with phosphor, was used to determine if airmail handling could be improved. Could these airmail letters be plucked out of the normal mailstream by new National Cash Register automatic devices and sped on their way faster if airmail stamps were tagged? The test proved that they could.

From that simple task of separating one class of mail from another, the use of phosphor-tagged stamps now extends to commemoratives, special stamps, definitives, airmails, officials, envelopes, postal cards and aerogrammes that are not precanceled. The tagging that was first intended only to pick out airmail letters now triggers automatic facer-canceler machines that can locate a stamp, correctly position or "face" the envelope, and apply a cancellation. Post offices could not function today without tagged stamps, postal cards and envelopes.

Those first airmail stamps were tagged with calcium silicate phosphor. In recent years all U.S. unprecanceled stamps have been coated after printing with a varnish that serves as a carrier for zinc orthosilicate, an inorganic phosphor that emits a signal when exposed to shortwave ultraviolet light. The brief instant of that signal operates high-speed, high-tech mail-processing equipment.

But laying on the phosphor-varnish after the stamp is printed has major drawbacks. The tagging roller slows down press speeds, takes up a printing station on the press that might otherwise print another color, dulls the brightness and "snap" of stamp inks, corrodes cutting knives and perfing pins, and coats the surface of the stamp so that cancel inks do not penetrate the paper as they should. This makes it easier to remove cancellations. The USPS estimates a loss of revenue in "washed" stamps at somewhere around $200 million annually. For both the Postal Service and the Bureau of Engraving and Printing, tagging is indeed a necessary evil.

This close-up view of the "Ts" on the test coils also shows the "T1" plate number that occurred every 48th stamp.

The Netherlands was the first country to use a prephosphored paper in 1962. The paper used by the United States for the Flag test stamps will contain the same zinc orthosilicate phosphor that had been used heretofore. Others were tested — and more may be tested — but this zinc orthosilicate treated paper will have a weaker formula of tagging material than the liquid phosphor/varnish used on press. The paper was supplied to the BEP by Harrison and Sons Limited of Buckinghamshire, England. This company makes prephosphored paper for several customers, and was more conveniently able to supply test quantities quickly than an American supplier.

The test stamps were printed by the BEP on its intaglio C Press, often termed the "most productive intaglio press in the world." Each stamp bears a "T" at the bottom where the plate number usually appears. As with other coils from C Press, a single plate number appears every 48th stamp — but this time grouped with the "T," i.e., "T1." The Flag Over Capitol test stamps were made in coils of 100 and 3,000. They were available in larger philatelic centers and from the Philatelic Sales Division only.

In the last year or so, the tagging varnish had been applied on U.S. stamps in between the perforations — the "block over vignette" format. Prior to that, the abrasive phosphor material was found all over a sheet of stamps — the so-called "random tagging." The prephosphored paper will again have the corrosive phosphor everywhere. It cannot be placed in stamp paper in the block-over-vignette printed form. This is one of the reasons for the extensive testing.

Test coils made with prephosphored paper (top) show no definite luminescent pattern, though the phosphor material is scattered on an overall basis throughout the web of paper. Press-tagged coils (bottom) show a block tagging pattern under ultraviolet light.

The test seeks to determine — by field experience, not scientific guesswork — whether the phosphor-treated paper will adversely affect mail processing machines in post offices, automatic stamp-affixing devices in private concerns, and the presses and perforators of the BEP. Some 100,000 pieces of mail with test stamps are due to be processed, although that number could go higher. Locations of the test mailings were not revealed at press time.

From 20 to 25 million of the test stamps were manufactured by the Bureau, which felt it needed that quantity to get a real fix on how the new paper might affect its printing, perforating and cutting devices. Other phosphors, both organic and inorganic, will probably be tested. Should the present test — or later tests — prove successful, the use of prephosphored stamp paper would expand to include all postage stamps sold by the Postal Service.

The Design
Frank Waslick of the BEP rendered the original Flag Over Capitol design for sheet, coil and booklet stamps in 1985. All that was needed was to engrave the "T" at the bottom of the stamp, and a "T" plus a plate number every 48th stamp.

Coil stamps were probably chosen for the prephosphored paper test since coils now account for half the total stamp production of the United States.

First-Day Facts
The special test stamp was issued May 23, 1987, in conjunction with the NOJEX philatelic exhibition at the Meadowlands Hilton Hotel in Secaucus, New Jersey. William R. Cummings, regional postmaster general for the Northeast region, spoke for the USPS. He said, "Should the test prove successful, we would be able to convert much of our coil stamp production to prephosphored paper within a year, and take the first step toward reducing the Postal Service's losses to cancellation removal. Our ultimate goal is prephosphored paper for all stamp issues."

10¢ RED CLOUD

Date of Issue: August 15, 1987

Catalog Numbers: Scott 2176   Minkus 877

Color: red brown

First-Day Cancel: Red Cloud, Nebraska

FDCs Canceled: 300,472

Format: Panes of 100, vertical, 10 across, 10 down. Printing cylinders of 800.

Perf: 11 (Eureka off-press perforator)

Selvage Markings: U.S. Postal Service© 1987, Use Correct ZIP Code.

Designer: Robert Anderson

Art Director: Richard Sheaff (CSAC)

Engravers: Vignette: Joseph S. Creamer, Jr. (BEP)
 Inscriptions: Robert G. Culin, Sr. (BEP)

Typographer: Bradbury Thompson (CSAC)

Modeler: Clarence Holbert (BEP)

Printing: intaglio portion of intaglio/gravure A Press

Quantity Ordered: 200,000,000
Quantity Distributed: 59,700,000

Plate Block Detail: single-digit plate number alongside corner stamp

Tagging: block over vignette

The Stamp

Red Cloud is the third American Indian to be recognized in the long-running Great Americans series. An Indian began the series when Sequoyah debuted as the first Great American in 1980. Crazy Horse, a contemporary of Red Cloud, appeared on a 1982 stamp. The Great Americans series of definitive sheet stamps is the successor to the Prominent Americans group, which ran from 1965 to 1978 and totaled 25 different varieties.

This stamp for Red Cloud brings the Great Americans series to 38 stamps. By year's end, it was running neck and neck with the popular Transportation coil series. The Great Americans stamps were ahead — unless you counted the precanceled and re-engraved Transportation coils as separate issues. The only other current USPS series coming close was the American Folk Art series. The 1987 Lacemaking stamps brought that category to 32 issues, although they have only been issued on eight occasions, in se-tenant blocks of four.

No other current USPS series is even close. With this year's Du Sable stamp, the Black Heritage series now boasts ten — a figure equalled by the Performing Arts series, thanks to the 1987 Caruso stamp. The Literary Arts series has limped along since its first John Steinbeck issue in 1979. The 1987 Faulkner stamp is only its sixth.

The Great Americans series has encompassed values running from the 1¢ Dorothea Dix and Margaret Mitchell stamps to the $2 William Jennings Bryan and $5 Bret Harte issues. Its stamps have pictured writers, politicians, educators, social reformers, soldiers, Indians, physicians, clergymen, a historian, a biologist, a diplomat, a physicist, a composer, an editor, an engineer, a sailor, a painter, a jurist and one U.S. president, Harry Truman. No stamp series has been so catholic in its choice of Americans.

No other 1987 U.S. stamp came upon collectors as quickly as did this 10¢ Red Cloud. It was first listed in the July/August edition of the USPS *Philatelic Catalog* and was not announced until July 13 — just 33 days before it was issued. Obviously, the stamp for the Sioux chief was one of those Great Americans finished designs that are now and then summoned to duty in a hurry.

Red Cloud replaced the 10¢ Richard Russell sheet stamp of 1984. The Russell stamp had been produced on the intaglio portion of the BEP's intaglio/gravure A Press. So was the Red Cloud stamp. Could not the USPS have rerun the Russell stamp rather than creating a new design? The answer to that is: "Yes, but . . ."

Russell cylinders would have produced floating plate numbers, since they had not yet changed to the format of the 25¢ Jack London issue of 1986, which reduced A Press intaglio printing cylinders from 920 to 800 stamps per revolution. The old Russell 10-centers had been perforated on the L perforators, thus creating mismatched perfs in corners. If the Russell cylinders had run again, they could not have been sent to the off-press Eureka perforators, which need space between panes to operate.

Making reruns of older definitives on different presses and different perforating equipment created both engraving and perforation varieties. The USPS said it started producing these varieties (i.e., the 4¢ Stagecoach, the 50¢ Nimitz, the 8.3¢ Ambulance, the 14¢ Iceboat and the 1¢ Omnibus of 1986) in the belief that collectors preferred the varieties to a new issue. The Postal Service maintained that collectors then switched gears and decided they would rather have new issues, so the USPS acquiesced. The Postal Service does not elaborate on how it tracked such collector "preferences" so quickly and so definitely.

Supplies of the Russell stamp were running low. Even though a 10¢ Canal Boat coil was available, a 10¢ perforated sheet stamp was also needed. Red Cloud came out of the great Americans backlog.

One of the tribes of the great Sioux nation was the Oglala. Their home was the Black Hills and, later, the country around Nebraska's Platte River. Red Cloud, the most famous chief of the Oglala Sioux, was born in 1822 near what is now North Platte, Nebraska. He was not a chief by birth; he rose to that position by his bravery in battle and his wisdom in council.

The Oglala Sioux and other tribes were directly in the path of the white man's rush to the West. By 1849 the white tide increased, as the Mormons and those bound for Oregon were added to the thousands seeking gold in California. Brigham Young had passed by in 1848 with 397 wagons and 1,200 people. Other trains were as large or larger.

Asiatic cholera came with these settlers. The Oglala and other Indians thought the white man was poisoning them by some mysterious magic. The growing hostility of the Indians prompted the U.S. government to purchase an old trading post on Laramie Fork — later to become Fort Laramie, Wyoming, on the Upper Platte River. The white man came on. By 1857, some 20 steamboats were plying the Missouri River as far as Sioux City, Iowa. Attempts were being made to void Indian titles to lands in Kansas, Nebraska and the Dakotas.

When the United States started to build a road in 1865 from Fort Laramie, by way of the Powder River, to the gold regions of Montana, Red Cloud led the opposition for his tribe. This new Bozeman Trail, he said, would destroy the best remaining buffalo grounds of the Indians. When the government sent out a small detachment of troops to begin construction work, Red Cloud intercepted them with a large party of Oglala and Cheyenne. Red Cloud held the soldiers for two weeks as prisoners, letting them go when he feared that his own young braves might massacre them.

In the fall of 1865, commissioners were sent to pow-wow with the Oglala for permission to build the road. Red Cloud forbade any negotiations and refused to council. On June 30, 1866, the United States called another council for the same purpose at Fort Laramie. Red Cloud agreed to attend, but repeated his refusal to endanger the hunting grounds of his people. While Red Cloud was speaking, a strong force of U.S. soldiers arrived, saying they had come to build forts and open the road to Montana. Red Cloud seized his rifle. With a defiant outburst, he led the Oglala from the council.

As the building of forts proceeded at Fort Reno, Fort Kearney and

Fort C.F. Smith, Red Cloud harassed the white men. With 2,000 warriors, he encircled the workers at Fort Kearney, so that not even a load of hay could be brought to the building site without a strong guard. On December 21, 1866, an 81-man detachment under Captain Fetterman was cut off from support. Every man was killed. Other skirmishes took place; meanwhile, not a wagon had been able to pass over the new Bozeman Trail.

An etching of Red Cloud, chief of the Oglala Sioux.

By 1868 another commission was named to come to terms with Red Cloud, who demanded the abandonment of the three posts and of all attempts to open the Montana road. A treaty was finally agreed to on this basis, defining the limits of Indian country as claimed by the Sioux. Red Cloud refused to sign or even attend until all U.S. garrisons had been withdrawn. He finally signed the treaty at Fort Laramie November 6, 1868. Red Cloud had kept and won the position he had taken from the beginning.

Red Cloud stayed at peace with the whites. Although he was accused of doing so, he took no active part in subsequent Sioux wars with the white man. He served as an Indian delegate to Washington, where he professed to be a patriot from the Indian standpoint. He has been described as a courtly chief and natural-born gentleman, but he stood first with his people as a warrior, having counted 80 coups (an Indian act of bravery) in battle.

Red Cloud died, blind and decrepit, in 1909. He and his people had been moved to the Pine Ridge Reservation in South Dakota in 1878. Next to Sitting Bull, he is regarded as the premier chief of the Sioux.

The Design

Robert Anderson of Lexington, Massachusetts, designed the Red Cloud stamp. He created a portrait of Red Cloud based on several photographs provided by the Smithsonian Institution. This is Anderson's fourth U.S. stamp design, and all have been for the Great Americans series. He was responsible for 1985's Alden Partridge and Sylvanus Thayer stamps, and for the 1986 John Harvard issue.

First-Day Facts

Red Cloud, named for the Indian chief, is a small village of 1,500 near the Kansas-Nebraska border.

Nebraska has a town named for Red Cloud, and it was there that first-day ceremonies were held. The little city of 1,500 is barely north of the Kansas border, and directly south of Grand Island and Hastings, Nebraska. It was author Willa Cather's childhood home and appears in several of her writings. The Cather home and museum are tourist attractions, and the small town had served as the first day site for the 8¢ Willa Cather stamp of 1973.

Stanley W. Smith, assistant postmaster general for the facilities department, spoke for the Postal Service. Smith, a native Nebraskan born 100 miles from Red Cloud, said the USPS began the Great Americans series with the hope of recognizing many great Americans who may not be as well-known as founding fathers and presidents. "Our hope," he said, "is that many people will look for additional information about individuals, such as Red Cloud, who are honored in this series."

$5 BRET HARTE

Date of Issue: August 25, 1987

Catalog Numbers: Scott 2196   Minkus 878

Color: brown

First-Day Cancel: Twain Harte, California (Twain Harte Elementary School)

FDCs Canceled: 111,431

Format: Miniature sheetlets of 20, vertical, 5 across, 4 down. Printing cylinders of 320.

Perf: 11 (Eureka off-press perforator)

Selvage Markings: United States Postal Service© 1986 (appears at either top or bottom of sheetlet).

Designer: Arthur Lidov

Engravers: Vignette: Thomas Hipschen (BEP)
             Inscriptions: Thomas Bakos

Modeler: Esther Porter (BEP)

Printing: intaglio portion of intaglio/gravure A Press

Quantity Ordered: 40,000,000
Quantity Distributed: 9,908,000

Plate Block Detail: Four single-digit plate numbers at corners of each sheetlet.

Tagging: block over vignette.

The Stamp

By now, U.S. collectors are used to seeing their stamps in a multitude of printing formats. In fact, since the United States first issued a se-tenant block of four holiday stamps for duty on Christmas mailings of 1964, the ensuing 23 years have witnessed 568 more U.S. stamps printed in multiple formats. To look at it another way, more than 52 percent of all U.S. regular and commemorative postage stamps since 1964 have been issued with another different stamp alongside, above or below them. In the last ten years, 1978 through 1987, the percentage has increased to 57 percent.

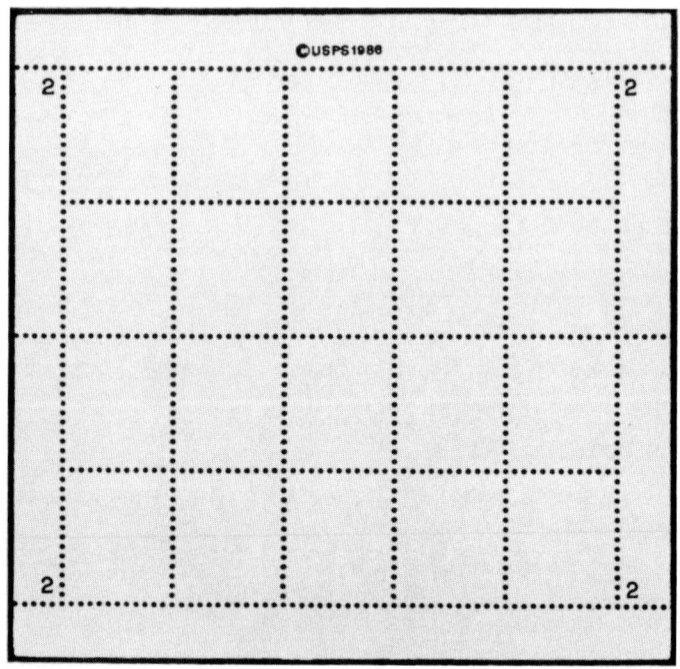

This is the way the U.S. Postal Service said the new $5 Bret Harte stamps would appear: in 20-stamp miniature sheets with a plate number at each corner.

Multiples are now a way of life for the USPS. In that 23-year span, collectors have been offered 53 blocks of four, as well as blocks of eight, sheetlets of nine, and souvenir sheets of five and eight stamps. Pairs of two have appeared seven times, while booklets have variously carried four, five, eight and ten different stamps. Stamps have come to market in strips of three, four, six and ten; entire panes of 50 different issues have come from the presses three times.

(This does not count the souvenir sheets of 1926 through 1956. These items were seldom used for postage and were not sold over regular post office counters. Even so, these began as sheets of 25 stamps with the 2¢ White Plains, and 1¢ and 3¢ Chicago issues. They dropped to sheets of six in the 3¢ Byrd, 3¢ Mount Rainier and 1¢ Yosemite souvenirs. Only four stamps were on the 3¢ TIPEX sheet, and just two stamps on the 1947 CIPEX and 1956 FIPEX sheets.)

Granted, most of these printing formats comprised different, se-tenant stamps. Granted, the $5 Bret Harte miniature sheet of 20 contains nothing but Bret Harte stamps. The fact remains that throughout nearly a quarter century of multiple postal issues, never before has the United States used a format of 20 stamps.

There are no panes of 100 Harte stamps, heretofore the usual definitive pane quantity. The new, smaller format was expected to reduce waste and destruction costs at Philatelic Centers and the Philatelic Sales Division, where the policy has been to require the purchase of only four stamps to get a plate block of issues costing $1 or more each. This has meant that when a request for a plate block of four has come in for the $1 Revel, the $2 Bryan or the $5 Railroad Lantern stamps (which the Harte stamps replace), 96 stamps out of each pane were left over to be sold or destroyed — most likely the latter.

The 20-stamp Harte format provided four plate number blocks, one from each corner, leaving only four singles in the middle vertical row to be sold or destroyed. Some paper was wasted with this new format, since the intaglio cylinder of A Press printed just 16 of the miniature sheets (320 stamps) per revolution. With a normal definitive layout, A Press can produce 800 stamps on the same one revolution. Ink and paper are not major costs in stamp printing, however, and the USPS expected to more than recoup the initial printing deficit by savings in processing and destruction throughout the distribution system.

The BEP actually produced the sheets with no perforations through the selvage between the second and third horizontal rows. The USPS changed to this format, hoping that clerks would be forced to scissor cut all plate block selvage.

The Harte panes of 20 had five vertical rows and four horizontal rows. The USPS 1986 copyright slogan appeared in the top selvage on half the panes, in the bottom selvage on the other 50 percent. Unlike definitive panes of the past, no "Use Correct ZIP Code" lettering was printed. The USPS avowed that it would use this 20-stamp format for high-denomination definitives of the future.

The use of any $5 stamp in the U.S. mailing world is very limited. This Bret Harte stamp was originally scheduled for release in 1986, but was delayed early that year as postal officials sought ways to reduce manufacturing costs. The supply of the former $5 Railroad Lantern stamps was depleted to near exhaustion, though they were not officially taken off sale until October 31, 1987.

Photo of a younger Bret Harte than seen on the stamp.

How will collectors save the new $5 Harte stamps? If they have been saving plate number blocks, they can still do that at no penalty. But underneath all the USPS publicity about efficiency and cost savings, one could suspect that some new marketing motives might have been operating.

Collecting stamps in small sheet formats is enticing. They fit nicely and look imposing on an album page, appealing to those collectors who can afford the higher cost. Liechtenstein has been doing it for years, even with commemorative stamps that offer such popular subjects as the prince and princess, Rubens paintings, Vaduz Castle and royal carriages. Sometimes the sheet of four or eight, or whatever, will use just one stamp from a series (as with Bret Harte from the Great Americans series). Other Liechtenstein sheets will feature a stamp from a set that is not available as a single — only as a sheet. In Liechtenstein and other European nations, such sheets have met with good sales and collector approval. Many collectors told the philatelic press that the Bret Harte 20-stamp sheet was intended primarily to bilk the collector out of a $100 bill. Some felt that if the $5 stamp was a production and handling problem, the Postal Service was trying to recoup its losses from collectors by tempting them to purchase this $100 item.

Harte was born Francis Brett Harte in Albany, New York, in 1836. When only 18 years old he went to California; by the time he was 21, he had already been a schoolteacher and gold miner. In 1857 he became a typesetter on the *Golden Era*, a San Francisco newspaper, and soon began to contribute poems and fictional stories to that paper.

Harte later served as editor of the *Overland Monthly*, a California magazine, to which he also contributed stories such as "The Luck of Roaring Camp," "The Outcasts of Poker Flat," "Brown of Calaveras," and "Plain Language from Truthful James." His tales were peopled with gold miners, gamblers and prostitutes, whose personal characteristics and lively speech Harte captured as no one else had. His descriptions helped shape a form of American fiction that came to be called "local color writing." His stories were lusty, often funny, often tragic, but they became classics of American folk literature.

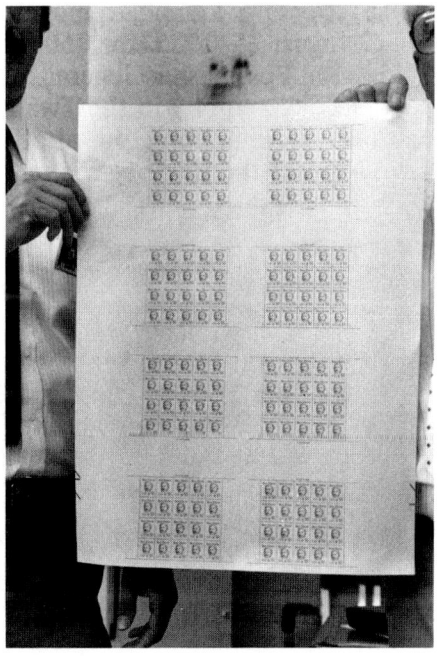

Two Bureau employees hold a sheet of Harte stamps from A Press. Normally, 400 stamps could have been printed on this piece of web which contains just 160 images in the 20-stamp formats.

Harte became nationally famous. He moved to Boston in 1871. He had a $10,000 contract to write for the *Atlantic Monthly*, but his assignments were often late and their quality was below his former standards. His popularity soon declined, and his only novel, *Gabriel*

Conroy, was panned by the critics. Harte's extravagant manner of living and his writing failures left him penniless.

Friends obtained a political appointment for him as U.S. consul in Crefeld, Germany. After two years, he was transferred to Glasgow, Scotland, where he remained until 1885. He lived in London, working as an unsuccessful hack writer, until his death at age 65 in 1902.

The Design

The Bret Harte stamp was the second design to come from the pen of Arthur Lidov of Poughquag, New York. Lidov's first stamp design was for the 8¢ Henry Knox stamp of 1985. As he had with the Knox Great Americans issue, Lidov based this Great American stamp design on portraits of Harte. The stamp shows a middle-aged Harte with long sideburns. For a look at a younger, more clean-cut Harte, see the accompanying photo.

First-Day Facts

In California, some 150 miles straight east of San Francisco in the foothills of the Sierra Nevada range, sits a town of 1,500 people called Twain Harte. Twice the Postal Service journeyed to this hamlet named for Harte and his friend and fellow author, Mark Twain.

On August 25, 1986, the 150th anniversary of Harte's birth, Western Region Postmaster General Joseph R. Caraveo unveiled the Harte design at a ceremony in the Twain Harte Elementary School. Exactly one year later, the same postal official in the same school in the same town released the Harte stamp on August 25, 1987.

Varieties

The second stamp from the left in the top row (arrow) has a darker appearance than the rest of the stamps. Called a double entry, the anomaly occurs when a line-engraved stamp is printed from a plate upon which the transfer roll has impressed the stamp twice in slightly different positions.

5¢ MILK WAGON

Date of Issue: September 25, 1987

Catalog Numbers: Scott 2255   Minkus 879

Color: gray

First-Day Cancel: Indianapolis, Indiana (INDYPEX stamp show)

FDCs Canceled: 162,571 (includes Racing Car first days)

Format: Coils of 100 and 3,000. Printing cylinders of 936.

Perf: 10 (rolls of 100 on guillotine perforator; rolls of 3,000 on rotary perforator.)

Designer: Lou Nolan

Art Director: Derry Noyes (CSAC)

Engravers: Vignette: Gary Chaconas (BEP)
             Inscriptions: Dennis Brown (BEP)

Modeler: Clarence Holbert (BEP)

Printing: intaglio B Press

Quantity Ordered: Coils of 100: 15,640,000
                    Coils of 3,000: 92,000,000
Quantity Distributed: Coils of 100: 15,640,000
                         Coils of 3,000: 8,160,000

Plate Number Detail: single-digit plate number every 52nd stamp

Tagging: block over vignette

The Stamp

The 5¢ Milk Wagon coil in the Transportation series replaced the 5¢ Motorcycle issue of 1983, which had been produced on the Cottrell presses that were scrapped in November 1985. To have continued printing the Motorcycle stamps would have required re-engraving the die to adapt the design for production of B Press. Once again, the Postal Service maintained that its decision to create a new stamp was based on collector input that collectors would rather have new stamps than re-engraved stamps.

Over the last 140 years of U.S. stamp history, wagons have not been a favorite stamp subject. It took 51 years of stamps before one even appeared — the 10¢ Trans-Mississippi stamp of 1898. That one pictured a covered wagon. For another 76 years, only the covered wagon was seen on U.S. stamps — and only on five occasions. (There was a little riding buggy or two on the 1968 Cherokee Strip stamp, but those are too puny to be called wagons.)

What really got the wagon going as a U.S. stamp subject was the advent of the Transportation coils series in 1981. In the ensuing seven years, 32 new Transportation coils have been issued. Within the range of those 32 stamps, collectors have seen an omnibus, a stagecoach, a mail wagon, a buckboard, an ambulance, an oil wagon, a bread wagon and, now, a milk wagon.

Home delivery was the best way for dairies to sell their milk from about 1850 through the 1930s. Milk wagons were a familiar sight on city and village streets in those years. By 1900 New York City could boast more than 1,100 horses pulling wagons that delivered more than a million gallons of milk per day to its residents. Small trucks started to replace the horses in the 1920s, and by the 1940s, store sales of milk were exceeding the amount sold on home delivery routes.

A dairy route truck could deliver from 50 to 100 cases or more of milk to a single store outlet. The same truck would have to travel many blocks of residential streets and make hundreds of stops to sell a like amount. The result was that deliveries could be made cheaper to stores; the housewife could pick up her milk there at a lower cost than by using home delivery service. The resultant price advantage swung the delivery of milk from home to store, and the packaging of milk from glass bottles to paper cartons.

The Design

The 5¢ Milk Wagon stamp was designed by Lou Nolan of McLean, Virginia. Nolan had previously designed two other Transportation stamps, the 1985 3.4¢ School Bus and the 1986 17¢ Dog Sled stamps. Nolan's pen-and-ink drawing of an old milk wagon of the 1900s was based on photographs supplied by the Smithsonian Institution. Nolan also acted as his own typographer.

First-Day Facts

This stamp was released in a double ceremony with the 17.5¢ Racing Car stamp on September 25, 1987, at the INDYPEX stamp show in Indianapolis, Indiana. (For more details, see the First-Day Facts section of the chapter on the Racing Car stamp.)

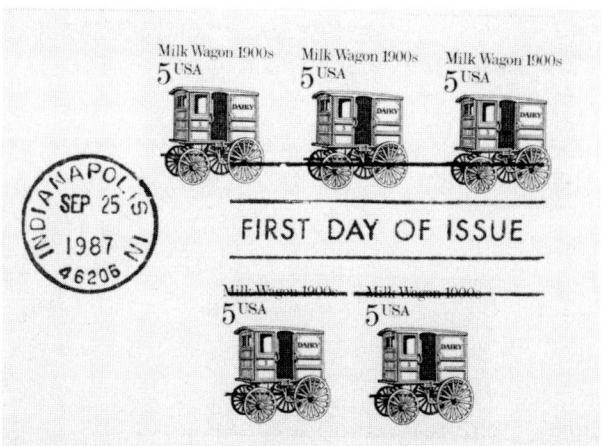

Five Milk Wagon coil stamps were needed to make the first-class rate on first-day covers.

Double releases of two stamps at the same site on the same day are becoming more common. In April 1985, the 10.1¢ Oil Wagon and 12.5¢ Pushcart stamps were released together at Oil Center, New Mexico. No first-day ceremonies were held, however. In June 1985, the 4.9¢ Buckboard and 8.3¢ Ambulance coils were both released at Reno, Nevada. This time full-blown first-day ceremonies were held during the NEVPEX-TOPEX all-topical exhibition in Reno.

First-day cover requests for the 5¢ Milk Wagon stamp had to include at least 17¢ additional postage. The Postal Service, on request, would affix a 17.5¢ Racing Car stamp and a 5¢ Milk Wagon issue with a remittance for 23¢ for each such cover.

17.5¢ RACING CAR (UNPRECANCELED)

Date of Issue: September 25, 1987

Catalog Numbers: Scott 2264   Minkus 880

Color: purple

First-Day Cancel: Indianapolis, Indiana (INDYPEX stamp show)

FDCs Canceled: 162,571 (includes Milk Wagon first days)

Format: Coils of 100 and 500. Printing cylinders of 936

Perf: 10 (guillotine perforator on coils of 100; rotary perforator on coils of 500)

Designer: Tom Broad

Art Director: Jack Williams (USPS)

Engravers: Vignette: Gary Chaconas (BEP)
Inscriptions: Gary Slaght (BEP)

Modeler: Peter Cocci (BEP)

Printing: intaglio B Press (A separate cylinder was used for this unprecanceled stamp.)

Quantity Ordered: Coils of 100: 17,300,000
Coils of 500: 34,000,000
Quantity Distributed: Coils of 100: 17,300,000.
Coils of 500: 13,000,000

Plate Number Detail: single-digit purple plate number every 52nd stamp

Tagging: block over vignette

17.5¢ RACING CAR (PRECANCELED)

Date of Issue: September 25, 1987

Catalog Numbers: Scott 2264a   Minkus none

Colors: purple, red

First-Day Cancel: Indianapolis, Indiana (INDYPEX stamp show)

FDCs Canceled: unknown

Format: Coils of 3,000 only. Printing cylinders of 936

Perf: 10 (rotary perforator)

Designer: Tom Broad

Art Director: Jack Williams (USPS)

Engravers: Vignette: Gary Chaconas (BEP)
              Inscriptions: Gary Slaght (BEP)

Modeler: Peter Cocci (BEP)

Printing: intaglio B Press (A separate cylinder was used for this precanceled stamp.)

Quantity Ordered: 48,000,000
Quantity Distributed: 13,000,000

Plate Number Detail: single-digit purple plate number every 52nd stamp

Tagging: none on a precanceled stamp

The Stamps

Both versions of this Racing Car stamp — the monocolor purple unprecanceled and the bicolor purple and red precanceled varieties — were issued to fit the 17.5¢ rate for mail presorted to the ZIP+4 classification. Since this special rate is used only by major mailers, the overwhelming majority of these stamps would be of the bicolor, precanceled variety. There would be little demand for the unprecanceled, monocolor stamp beyond those sold to collectors.

In 1985 the Postal Service issued a 21.1¢ Letters stamp both with and without a ZIP+4 precancellation. That stamp matched the rate for first-class letters in mailing quantities of 250 that bore nine-digit ZIP Codes but were not presorted. At the time that 21.1¢ stamp was issued, the USPS announced a 17.5¢ denomination for mail presorted by ZIP+4 codes in quantities of 500 or more letters. Nearly two years later, this Racing Car stamp fulfills that promise.

When the Postal Service released this advance design for the Racing Car stamp, collectors thought the engraved Transportation coils had changed to gravure printing. The USPS explained that a photograph of the design before it had been engraved was mistakenly sent out.

This stamp in the Transportation coil series pictures a Marmon Wasp, winner of the first Indianapolis 500 Mile Race in 1911. Now one of the richest auto races in the world, it is held each year on Memorial Day or the preceding Saturday or Sunday. Indianapolis was the site because that Indiana city — not Detroit — was then the automaking capital of the United States.

Howard Marmon had been making motor cars in Indianapolis since 1901. His cars had their motors up front, under a hood, in a day when most makers hung their engines on the rear axle. His cars used a double-frame system, a frame within a frame, which constituted one of the most ingenious suspension systems ever devised. In a time when most cars used tillers for steering, Marmon installed a wheel with spark and throttle controls mounted thereon.

Marmon had an engineer, Ray Harroun, working for him. Harroun, because he was an engineer, climbed into the driver's seat when Marmon started entering his cars in races. Harroun wanted to get the feel of how his machines were performing; along the way he became one of America's renowned racing drivers. But no racer had ever gone 500 miles, and Harroun took the driver's job very reluctantly, only after Marmon promised him a relief driver during the race.

Harroun had a few tricks up his sleeve. He would run without the usual riding mechanic sitting alongside. This would save some 150 pounds of weight, allow a lighter, narrower body with the driver and steering wheel centered. It was almost an unwritten law, and some tracks required that you carry a mechanic. Indianapolis did not, and Harroun took advantage of it. He designed the first rear-view mirror for his Marmon Wasp so that he could keep track of the competitors behind him.

Harroun's choicest piece of strategy involved tires. Racing drivers stepped on the gas and went as fast as their machines would go. If the tires blew, they stopped to change them. Harroun knew that Indy's brick surface was going to be tough on tires, so he began to test them. By driving a lot of practice laps at Indy, he tried to determine the exact speed at which tires began to shred. Tires in those days were primitive compared to today's. Ray Harroun found that they let go somewhere between 75 to 80 miles per hour. He would win by pacing himself at 75 mph to save stopping for tire changes.

Forty cars were entered in the 1911 Indianapolis 500, and 80,000 people — a record racing crowd then — showed up at race time. The winner was to get a $16,000 prize. Forty cars strung out behind the pace car, getting up to speed as they circled the big oval track. As the pace car scurried into the pits, the checkered flag came down, and the race was on.

This Marmon Wasp, the first car to win the Indianapolis 500, rarely leaves its home at the Motor Speedway Museum. Ray Harroun drove it at an average speed of 74.59 mph for his 1911 victory.

Bigger, faster cars, such as a Fiat, a Mercedes, a Simplex and a Lozier, took the early lead. But as the race wore on, Harroun's strategy was vindicated. The big machines had to change tires frequently; their frequent trips to the pits ultimately defeated them. At the 100-mile mark, Harroun and his Marmon Wasp were running a respectable number three. At 150 miles, the Wasp was second, with only Bruce Brown's monster Fiat ahead. At 175 miles, Harroun let his relief driver, Patschke, take over. At the 250-mile mark, Harroun took the wheel again. The canny "Bedouin," as some called Harroun because of his Arabian ancestry, took the lead at the 300-mile mark.

Harroun lost his lead at the 350-mile pole, and regained it again at the 400-mile mark. At 450 miles, just to play it safe, Harroun went to the pits for a last tire change. The right rear power wheel was the only one upon which he changed tires; tires on the other three wheels ran the full race. Harroun was running on Firestones; most of the foreign cars used Michelins.

When Harroun's Marmon Wasp took the winner's flag, only 18 of the 40 starters were still on the track. Harroun's strategy had been to drive a steady 75 mph to save tires and stops. When the race was over, the timer said he had averaged 74.59 mph.

Howard Marmon then made a stunning announcement. The Marmon Company was withdrawing from racing — no Marmon auto would ever run again under sponsorship of the Marmon organization. Racing fans were aghast until the company explained. It was terribly expensive for a small car company to build and support an auto that could win the big races. Once you got to the top, it was even more expensive staying there. Thus, said Marmon, what better time to quit than at the top?

Today, the Marmon six-cylinder Wasp that won the first Indy 500 has a place of honor in the Indianapolis Motor Speedway Museum. With its rear-view mirror and sharply tapering tail that gave the car its name, it is the first among all Indy winners.

The Design

Two designs were developed for the Racing Car stamp and presented to the CSAC. The Marmon Wasp won and appears on the stamp. This 1903 Winton Bullet car lost.

Tom Broad of Chevy Chase, Maryland, designed the Racing Car stamp by making pencil sketches from photos of the Marmon Wasp provided by the Indianapolis Motor Speedway Corporation. Peter Cocci did the modeling (or editing) of the design in the Bureau of

Engraving and Printing's new $2.6 million Design Center (see General Introduction). Using Broad's sketch and the photographs, Cocci and other Design Center technicians moved and sized the design to create a final model from which the master intaglio die was hand-engraved.

Designer Broad has also designed the 1986 $1 Dr. Bernard Revel and $2 William Jennings Bryan stamps in the Great Americans series.

First-Day Facts

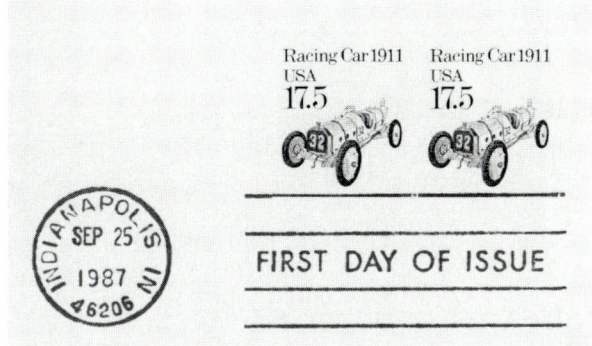

First-day ceremonies for the Racing Car stamp took place alongside the original No. 32 Marmon Wasp that won the first Indy 500.

First-day ceremonies for the 17.5¢ Racing Car and the 5¢ Milk Wagon coils, both in the Transportation series, took place September 25, 1987, the opening day of the INDYPEX stamp show at the Convention-Exposition Center in Indianapolis. Ray Harroun's Marmon Wasp was brought to the 500 Ballroom at the Center where it remained on display throughout the stamp exhibition.

Harold J. Hughes, deputy general counsel for the Postal Service, spoke at the single ceremony for both stamps. He took the occasion to note that a racing car was ideal for a stamp since the "Postal Service" and "speed" are synonymous. "We thought it only fair," said Hughes, "to honor our parcel competitors for their speed . . . so we chose the milk wagon."

Varieties

This imperforate pair of Racing Car coils was discovered in October 1987 in Kansas City. A roll of 100 stamps contained 26 imperf copies. Since coils are printed, perforated, sliced and wrapped in one automatic process, they cannot be seen until the purchaser unrolls the stamps.

22¢ FLAG WITH FIREWORKS BOOKLET

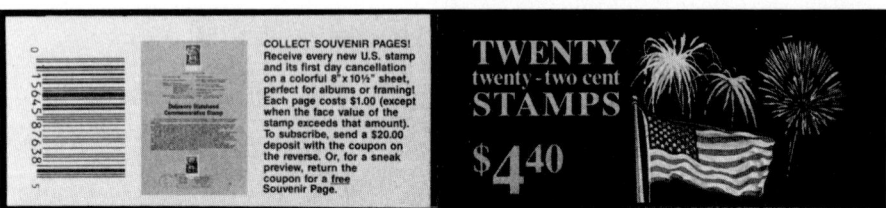

Date of Issue: November 30, 1987

Catalog Numbers: Scott 2276a   Minkus 875

Colors: yellow, red, royal blue, background blue

First-Day Cancel: Washington, D.C. (no first-day ceremony)

FDCs Canceled: unavailable

Format: One booklet pane of 20 stamps. Printing cylinders of 800.

Perf: 11.2 (Eureka off-press perforators whose perfing pins were removed from alternating horizontal rows)

Selvage Markings: U.S. Postal Service© 1987, Use Correct ZIP Code (Each appears on one-tenth of booklet panes produced.)

Designer, Typographer and Model: Peter Cocci (BEP)

Printing: Andreotti 7-color gravure press

Quantity Ordered: 1,000,000,000
Quantity Distributed: not available

Plate Number Detail: 4-digit plate number (appears on one-tenth of panes produced)

Tagging: block over vignette

The Booklet

The use of stamp booklets by the American mailing public has soared in just the last four years from 19 percent to 25 percent of all stamps issued. A shortfall of 40 million booklets a year inspired the Bureau of Engraving and Printing to find a way to increase its booklet production from 560 million annually on the Goebel booklet-making equipment to at least 600 million or more.

With the Goebel machinery running at maximum capacity, the BEP evolved a method to print, perf, slice and form booklets that bypassed the Goebel equipment until more booklet-forming machines could be secured. Much of the philatelic press heralded this new single-pane, 20-stamp booklet as a "conversion of sheet stamps into booklets." That was not literally true. No existing sheets of the Flag With Fireworks stamps were made into booklets. They couldn't have been; they were already perforated incorrectly for booklet panes.

The booklet stamps went back to the same Andreotti press that had made the sheet stamps. The same cylinders printed the stamps via gravure on paper that rolls through the press as a continuous web. The stamps were arranged on that web in full sheets of 400 stamps each, each sheet containing four panes of 100 stamps each.

After these stamps, intended for booklet production, came off the press, the rolls of printed stamps were transferred to a Eureka off-press perforator whose perfing pins had been removed from alternating horizontal rows. Each pair of horizontal stamp rows of ten was perforated between stamps, but not at the top or bottom.

Two panes on the left side of the web and two on the right formed a sheet of 400. The selvage on the left side of the two left panes, and on the right side of the two right panes, held a plate number, a "Use Correct ZIP Code" slogan, and the USPS copyright. But because the booklet panes of 20 stamps had to be attached to booklet covers by selvage from the left side only of each pane, all right-hand selvage was trimmed from all four panes. For those reasons, each of the three kinds of marginal markings appears only twice in the 20 booklet panes sliced from each full sheet of 400 stamps. Even when it does appear, trimming occasionally can cut away portions of the markings.

With a minimum of ten varieties to look for (possibly more after the booklets have been seen by collectors), the BEP would appear to have solved its booklet shortage while handing the booklet collector an as-yet unknown number of varieties. The USPS ordered its clerks not to honor customer requests for booklets with plate numbers, ZIP slogans or copyrights. The distribution of booklets was random, and the Postal Service did not want its employees taking the time to search for production varieties. The same random sale of booklets applied to the shipment of booklet orders from the Philatelic Sales Division in Washington. No special requests were to be honored by postal employees anywhere.

A *Postal Bulletin* notice told window clerks to reduce the sale of existing booklets produced for small booklet vending machines. Those were in short supply and not to be used for over-the-counter sales. The clerks were urged to substitute the new Flag With Fireworks booklet whenever possible.

The Postal Service said that this was the first in a series of new kinds of booklets, which will not all be of one standard size. Some will contain panes of five, ten or 20 stamps. The stamps also will vary in size, said the USPS.

The Booklet Cover

Standard commercial bookmaking equipment was used to affix unseparated covers and panes of stamps. Once both had been glued together, the equipment sliced through the covers and panes at the same time to form the individual booklets.

The covers, normally printed on the Goebel booklet machine, were produced on a six-color Goebel webfed offset Optiforma press. It produced color considerably superior to those covers made on the Goebel booklet device.

Peter Cocci, the stamp's designer, modeled the booklet front cover on the BEP's electronic design equipment. He used the stamp artwork as the design basis, adding one additional blue fireworks burst, the lettering and the denomination. The cover is printed in yellow, magenta, cyan and self-blue. Esther Porter of the Bureau modeled the complete booklet cover layout, inside and out.

The booklet cover also carries a promotion for the collecting of souvenir pages and the Universal Product Code (UPC) for recording the price and inventory data at checkout counters. At the lower right corner inside the booklet cover, collectors will see the initials "SBF." This is a source code indicating "Stamp Booklet Flag With Fireworks." A similar source code, "SBL," was added to the Locomotive booklet. Both these and future such markings will indicate to the USPS Marketing Division which product the return inquiry cards were taken from.

First-Day Facts

Although the regular first-day-of-issue cancel was available from Washington, D.C., no first-day ceremonies took place. Since the entire pane is almost nine inches wide, collectors who prepared their own FDCs had to use a Number 10 business or a large mailing envelope. Any single stamp with a straight edge at top, bottom or side was identifiable as coming from the Flag With Fireworks booklet.

REVISED DEFINITIVES

Two factors have caused the Bureau of Engraving and Printing to reprint former definitive stamps in a different manner throughout 1986 and 1987. The first factor was the removal of the Cottrell presses in late 1985. Without the Cottrells, some heavily used Transportation coils had to be rerun on B Press.

The second factor was the decision of the BEP to run all sheet stamps through its new Eureka off-line perforators, huge machines that operate independent of any press. They perforate perfectly, inspect, slice and stack press rolls of printed stamps into sheets. This year they were even used to produce a Flag with Fireworks booklet.

Prior to the arrival of the Eurekas in 1984, sheet stamps could be perforated on on-press rotary perforating drums (which produced perfect perfs) or on L perforators (which did not). The rotary on-press drums with hundreds of perfing pins affixed required too much maintenance, slowed down potential printing speeds and, as a result, were too costly. The L perforators were hand-fed, sheet by sheet. They perfed in one direction and then the paper was turned 90 degrees to be perfed in another direction. Where intersecting holes met, the L perforators would most often make two holes. The BEP — for cost, speed and efficiency reasons — wanted all perfing done by the Eurekas.

When Cottrell-made Transportation coils had to be shifted to B Press, some designs wider than .73 inches had to be re-engraved into a reduced design. This was true for the 2¢ Locomotive stamp, which had been on sale since 1982. Since re-engraving was necessary, the USPS made updated changes in the value lettering as well. Other changes are noted in the 2¢ Locomotive chapter.

Factor two came into play for the revised 22¢ Audubon stamp. The original 1985 version had been produced on the intaglio portion of A Press, which prints roll-to-roll. The original Audubon stamps had to be sent to the L perforators because the printing cylinder layout was so tight and close that the Eureka perforators could not accept A Press-printed stamps.

No change in the stamp design was necessary, but new Audubon cylinders made 800 stamps per revolution as opposed to the 920 subjects from the 1985 production. The result was perfect Eureka perfs and the elimination of floating plate numbers caused by the tight layout on the first Audubon issues.

In the case of the Stanley Steamer coil, no re-engraving was necessary — but the design changed nonetheless. Because the original die was impressed directly into printing cylinders, the image looked narrower than the Cottrell-made coils. The same die had made flat-plate impressions for the Cottrells, and when the flat plate was curved to fit press mandrels, the image was stretched and widened.

No announcements are usually made of the press and/or perforation changes on every stamp. Collectors are left to discover the changes that still occur when re-engraving is not necessary. Among former stamps whose perforations have been made perfect by processing on the Eurekas for the first time are the 39¢ 1985 Grenville Clark and the 1984 40¢ Lillian Gilbreath. The Clark stamp was remade in December 1986. No one is quite sure when Gilbreth got reperfed by the Eurekas.

Tagging sometimes changes as well when stamps are rerun. In the 2¢ Locomotive stamp it went from random overall tagging (1982) to block-over-vignette tagging (1987).

At left is a 1984 Gilbreth stamp made on A Press; at right is the same stamp, rerun on A Press at an unknown date. Though made on the same press, the 1984 issue has a floating plate number and imperfect perfs. (At that time, the layout on the web was too tight to be perfed by the Eureka off-press perfect perforators, and so tight that plate numbers floated.) When the Bureau decided to perf all stamps on the Eurekas, the stamp at right was the result. The layout was altered so that gutters were provided for the Eureka perfect-perf operation. That also opened up the layout so that A Press made fewer stamps per revolution, enabling it to place plate numbers in pane corners.

2¢ LOCOMOTIVE

Revised 1987 stamp

Original 1982 stamp

Date of Issue: March 6, 1987 (original: May 20, 1982)

Catalog Numbers: Scott 2226 (original: 1897A)
Minkus 873 (original: 790)

Color: black

First-Day Cancel: Milwaukee, Wisconsin (original: Chicago, Illinois)

FDCs Canceled: 169,484 (original: 290,020)

Format: Coils of 3,000 and 100 initially; 500 when needed.

Perf: 10 (3,000-stamp coils on rotary perforator; coils of 100 on guillotine perforator)

Designer: David Stone

Typographer: Bradbury Thompson (CSAC) (original: none listed)

Engravers: Vignette: Gary Chaconas (BEP) (original: John Wallace)
Inscriptions: Michael Ryan (BEP) (original: Robert G. Culin, Sr.)

Printing: intaglio B Press (original: Cottrell presses)

Quantity Ordered: 33,072,000
Quantity Distributed: not available

Plate Number Detail: Plate number on every 52nd stamp. (original: plate number on every 24th stamp, adjacent to line marking.)

Tagging: block over vignette (original: random overall)

The Stamp

A 2¢ black Locomotive coil stamp in the Transportation series first appeared on May 20, 1982. Coil rolls of 500 and 3,000 stamps were produced at the Bureau on a Cottrell press. When this new re-engraved 2¢ Locomotive coil reappeared in 1987, it did so only in coils of 100 and 3,000. Ample supplies of the Cottrell-made, 500-stamp coils still existed, but these too would one day have to be made on B Press. The last Cottrell had been turned off November 20, 1985.

The demise of the Cottrells had resulted in five revised definitives in 1986. Four coil stamps were switched to B Press; one Nimitz pane stamp was sent to A Press. The reason for using these presses was simple: They were both webfed. Huge rolls of printed stamps could be shifted easily to the webfed Eureka perforator, a 300-foot-per-minute machine that perfed, sliced and inspected the stamps far faster, better and cheaper than the handfed L perforators.

B press was a natural for coils; it had been a major supplier of all regular coil stamps. But it had limitations different from the old Cottrells. Coils with an image area wider than .73 inches had to be reduced in size. That meant re-engraving the vignette in the die. Even when a former Cottrell product did not have to be reduced, new cylinders were necessary with shallower ink recesses for intaglio printing.

Because of the size of B Press cylinders, a plate number appears every 52 stamps, instead of every 24 stamps, as on the old Cottrells. Because the cylinders on B Press are solid, no joint line occurs. Old Cottrell plates were cast in two 180-degree sections, then fitted on a press mandrel. Where the seams came together, an ink recess was created that printed a line between two stamps. It was really a plate joint, hence the term "joint line pair."

Since re-engraving was necessary anyway to turn the 1982 2¢ Cottrell Locomotive stamp into 1987's B press variety, other aesthetic changes were made as well. "USA 2¢" on the old stamp became "2 USA" on the new. The figure "2" was enlarged to twice its former size, in keeping with a 1986 USPS mandate to make stamp numerals as large as possible. The "¢" marking was eliminated, and the locomotive on the 1987 stamp is obviously narrower in design, as is the legend "Locomotive 1870s" across the top of the stamp.

The locomotive pictured on the 1982 and 1987 stamps is the same, a coal-burning, high-wheeled American type used for hauling passenger trains in the 1860s and 1870s. (Locomotives are typed by their wheel arrangement, in this case, 4-4-0 — meaning four pilot wheels, four drivers and no trailer truck wheels under the cab. That is termed an "American" type.)

According to the Smithsonian Institution, the locomotive closely matches a photograph of No. 71, built for the Atlantic & Great Western Railway and leased to the Erie Railroad, which used the engine on runs out of New York City.

The Design

The original stamp was designed by David Stone of Chapel Hill, North Carolina. Stone's concept was based on several of about 50 lithographed railroad prints produced by Currier and Ives publishers. Two of them, *The Express Train* and *The American Express Train*, gave Stone the basics and ornamentation detail of the design.

Both of those Currier and Ives sketches were done by F.F. Palmer — actually Fanny Palmer, an Englishwoman credited with more than 200 prints for Currier and Ives, and ranked as one of their most versatile artists. Without her work, Stone's somewhat simplified design would not have been as accurate as it was.

First-Day Facts

This Locomotive stamp was a substitute issue for the first-day ceremony planned for the March 6-8 MILCOPEX 87 stamp show in Milwaukee, Wisconsin. MILCOPEX had been scheduled as the first-day site for a 14¢ Flag postal card, but heavy scheduling of a new four-color offset press at the Government Printing Office forced the card's delay. The 2¢ re-engraved Locomotive thus became the first re-engraved stamp to have a first-day ceremony. The release took place in Kilbourn Hall of Milwaukee's MECCA Auditorium.

Jerry K. Lee, regional postmaster general for the Central Region, spoke for the Postal Service. The ceremony also included the unveiling of five 22¢ stamps for the Locomotives booklet, issued October 1, 1987, as the kickoff for National Stamp Collecting Month.

First-day cover collectors who did not attach their own stamps for canceling received one 2¢ Locomotive and one 20¢ Fire Pumper coil on their covers.

22¢ JOHN J. AUDUBON (PERF VARIETY)

The revised Audubon stamp at left features the perfect perfs typical of the off-press Eureka perforators. The Audubon block at right shows the mismatched center perfs of the L perforators.

Date of Issue: June 1, 1987 (original: April 23, 1985)

Catalog Numbers: Scott none (original: 1863)
Minkus none (original: 839)

Color: blue

First-Day Cancel: none (original: New York, New York)

FDCs Canceled: unknown (original: 516,249)

Format: Panes of 100, 10 across, 10 down. Printing cylinders of 800. (original: printing cylinders of 920)

Perf: 11 Eureka off-press perforator (original: 11 L perforator)

Selvage Markings: U.S. Postal Service© 1985, Use Correct ZIP Code

Designer: Christopher Calle

Art Director: Jack Williams (USPS)

Engravers: Vignette: Thomas Hipschen (BEP)
Inscriptions: Gary Slaght (BEP)

Modeler: V. Jack Ruther (BEP)

Printing: intaglio portion of intaglio/gravure A Press

Plate Block Detail: single-digit plate number alongside corner stamps (original: single-digit floating plate numbers)

Tagging: block over vignette

The New Stamp

Collectors had spotted a new variety of the 1985 Audubon stamp — without floating plate numbers and with perfect perforations — long before the November-December issue of the *Philatelic Catalog* brought it to their attention. The catalog listed an A Press variety that had four plate number positions, and noted the upcoming withdrawal on December 31, 1987, of the old 1985 Audubon stamp. According to United States Postal Service records, the new stamp went to press on June 1, 1987. No first-day release was held; the stamp merely went to the Bureau vaults for shipment as needed along with the older 1985 Audubon issues.

No changes in the master die were made, or necessary. The original 1985 Audubon stamps also had been printed on the intaglio portion of A Press in printing cylinders of 920 subjects. That layout format was so tight that three sides of a pane had straight edges, there being no room between stamps for selvage and normal perfing. Since the cylinder revolved every 920 stamps, no way could be found to print a plate number consistent in location on sheets of 100.

With the Jack London stamp of 1986, all of that changed on A Press. The stamps were repositioned on the cylinders so that wide horizontal gutters occurred every 100 stamps. (These gutters were needed so that perforation could be done on the Eureka perforators.) The new layout produced 800 stamps per cylinder revolution — four panes of 100, two wide across the printing web of paper.

Now, with cylinder subject stamps evenly divisible by 100, plate numbers could be placed in corners and would stay there. With the new Audubon stamps processing through the Eureka perforators instead of the old L perforators, the perforations would be cleaner and would meet perfectly at all intersections.

It was worth making new cylinders for the Audubon stamp so that full, printed rolls from A Press could be perfed, sliced and automatically inspected on the BEP's Eureka perforators.

No announcements on these changes were forthcoming from the Postal Service ahead of the press date. There is no "first day," since no one knows at this time when the first new Audubon printing was affixed to an envelope and mailed. Since tagging on both the 1985 and 1987 varieties was the same block-over-vignette style, stamps standing alone will be difficult to categorize. Only in blocks of four can the perforation differences be identified readily and easily.

12¢ STANLEY STEAMER

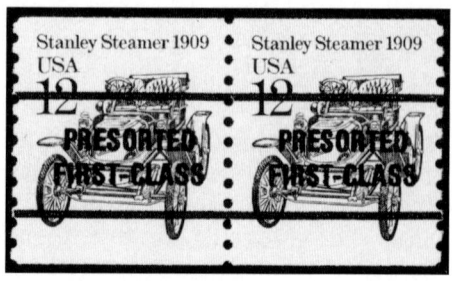

Date of Issue: September 3, 1987 (original: April 2, 1985)

Catalog Numbers: Scott not available (original: 2131); Minkus none (original: 831)

Color: blue

First-Day Cancel: no first-day ceremony (original: Kingfield, Maine)

FDCs Canceled: not known (original: 173,988)

Format: Coils of 3,000 only (original: coils of 500 and 3,000)

Perf: 10 rotary perforator; (original: perf 10 on rotary perforator)

Designer: Ken Dallison

Art Director: Howard Paine (CSAC)

Engravers: **Vignette:** Gary Chaconas (BEP)
  Inscriptions: Gary Slaght (BEP)

Modeler: Esther Porter (BEP)

Printing: intaglio B Press (original: Cottrell intaglio press)

Quantity Ordered: 54,000,000
Quantity Distributed: not available

Plate Number Detail: single-digit plate number on every 52nd stamp (original: plate number and line marking every 24th stamp)

Tagging: no tagging on precancels (original: random overall, none on precancels)

The Stamp

When it was first produced in 1985, the 12¢ Stanley Steamer stamp was sent to the Cottrell presses for 17.5 million plain and 32 million precanceled varieties. Before fiscal 1985 was finished, both types were run again on the Cottrell presses. Sales of the stamps for 1985 were approximately 30 million plain and 86 million precanceled. Final runs on the Cottrells apparently loaded inventories before the Cottrells were taken out of production in November 1985.

Precanceled stocks could not handle a large order from a major mailer who needed the stamps for the first-class, postcard presort rate in May 1987. The order was sufficient to warrant rescheduling the stamps on B Press. A sleeve was made from the original master die and quietly sent to press. The first the collecting community knew about the B Press 12¢ precanceled Stanley Steamer issue was when it appeared in a list of B Press precancels in the September-October *Philatelic Catalog*.

This is not a re-engraved stamp. Only those coils having an image area wider than .73 inches had to have the master die re-engraved. The Stanley Steamer image fell well short of that guideline. The same master die produced a narrower image on these 1987 issues, however, because the die was impressed directly into cylinders. The same die made flat plates for the Cottrells, which had to be curved to fit the press mandrel. In that curving, the Cottrell plates were stretched, thus widening the image on the older stamps.

Just a few weeks after the USPS said it would issue no more varieties, this B-Press version of the 12¢ Stanley Steamer appeared. The stamps went to press at the BEP May 12, 1987. All were precanceled; no plain stamps were printed. Printing sleeve number 1 was used. The stamps were delivered to the vaults on June 18 and mixed in with the earlier Cottrell versions of the 12¢ precanceled Stanley Steamer issues.

The quickest way to tell old Cottrell-made stamps from the 1987 B Press variety is to compare the words "Stanley Steamer 1909." The wording on 1987 stamps is about a half millimeter shorter than the wider Cottrell-made issues. Cottrell stamps have joint lines and plate numbers every 24 stamps. Stamps from B Press have no joint lines and have plate numbers at 52-stamp intervals.

The Design

Since the same master die made the 1985 and 1987 stamps, the design information does not change. Designer Ken Dallison looked through hundreds of photos of Stanley Steamers and examined several 1909 models of the car still in existence. All personnel listed for the first stamp hold the same positions on this re-issued stamp.

First-Day Facts

Since this stamp had neither a formal release nor a ceremony, the term "first day" is not entirely accurate. What the September 3, 1987, date means is first known day of use — and that might change in years

This cover bears a B Press precanceled 12¢ Stanley Steamer stamp between two older Cottrell varieties. The September 3, 1987, date is thought to be the earliest usage discovered to date.

to come. The stamps went on sale in Washington at the USPS philatelic center the afternoon of September 3. Robert Brown, manager of the Philatelic Sales Division, said there were no sales from Kansas City, Missouri, or Merrifield, Virginia, prior to the new stamps being shipped to Washington postal headquarters. The cover illustrated bears what is thought to be the first day of use. It was canceled in Washington at 1 p.m., September 3, 1987. If the stamp escaped from another post office in Washington ahead of that time, it likely would be found on an advertising postcard that was overcanceled in error.

Charles Yeager, *Linn's* Washington correspondent who secured the cancel illustrated, estimates that fewer than 200 first-day-of-use covers were serviced at the USPS philatelic center on September 3.

$10 MIGRATORY BIRD HUNTING (DUCK) STAMP

Date of Issue: July 1, 1987

Catalog Numbers: Scott RW54   Minkus RH54

Colors: Front: orange, yellow, brown, light blue, dark blue (offset); black (intaglio)
Back: black (offset)

First-Day Cancel: no official first day

FDCs Canceled: not known

Format: Panes of 30, arranged 5 across, 6 down.

Perf: 11 (Eureka off-press perforators)

Selvage Markings: none

Designer: Arthur G. Anderson

Engravers: Vignette: John S. Wallace (BEP)
   Inscriptions: Gary J. Slaght (BEP)

Modeler: Esther Porter (BEP)

Printing: 6-color offset, 3-color intaglio D Press

Quantity Ordered: 4,000,000

Plate Block Detail: One 6-digit intaglio plate number at pane corners.

Tagging: none

Plate Numbers:
   Intagalio: 178171-1 (black)
   Offset: 178206-1 (orange), 178207-1 (yellow),
       178208-1 (light blue), 178209-1 (brown)
       178210-1 (dark blue)
   Lettering on back: 178286-3 (offset black)

The Stamp

Both Duck stamp artists and Duck stamp collectors may be falling victim to an inexorable law of supply and demand that says, "As prices rise, demand falls."

To enter the contest for the 1985 Duck stamp, artists had to pay a fee of $20. More than 1,600 entries were received. For the 1986 contest, the entry fee rose to $50. The submitted art declined by almost 400 pieces. In this contest for the 1987 Duck stamp, Wisconsin artist Arthur G. Anderson prevailed over just 798 other contenders.

To help stem the continuing loss of wetlands for America's wildlife, Congress passed the Emergency Wetland Resources Act of 1986, which raised the cost of this year's Duck stamp from $7.50 to $10. The act also calls for increasing the stamp's price to $12.50 for 1989 and to $15 for 1991. The $10 price proposal has been on Capitol Hill since 1984. In 1985 the Fish and Wildlife Service suggested that the USPS issue semipostal stamps to help the wildlife fund. They got a resounding "No."

Printing on the back of Duck stamps appeared in 1946. Note the 1987 "Take Pride in America" slogan, which ties in with a 1987 postal card.

Top sales years for the Duck stamps were 1955 through 1957, three consecutive years when sales exceeded 2½ million stamps per year. Sales have been averaging about 1.8 million stamps per year recently, and based on past results when prices increased, officials are expecting a temporary drop in sales this year to 1.65 million. More than 90 million Duck stamps have been sold in total, providing more than $300 million for the purchase of more than 3½ million acres of wetland habitats for wildfowl.

Prices for Duck stamps began at $1 in 1934, doubled to $2 in 1949, rose to $3 in 1959, jumped to $5 in 1972, and soared to $7.50 in 1979. That's an increase of 750 percent. Meantime, the average price for an acre of wetland in that period has increased more than 1,000 percent. More than 90 percent of Duck stamps are thought to be purchased by wildlife hunters, the balance by collectors and wildlife fans.

Many more aspects of the stamps than their numerals of value have changed over 54 years of Duck stamps. The first five stamps were issued by the Department of Agriculture and are so inscribed. When that department's Bureau of Biological Survey was transferred to the

Department of the Interior by presidential order in 1939, the inscription changed to Interior. Lettering on the backs of Duck stamps started with the 1946 issue. While it has changed in form and content several times, it has always carried an instruction for the hunter to sign the stamp. It also now urges him to buy Duck stamps, save wetlands, send in all bird bands and take pride in America.

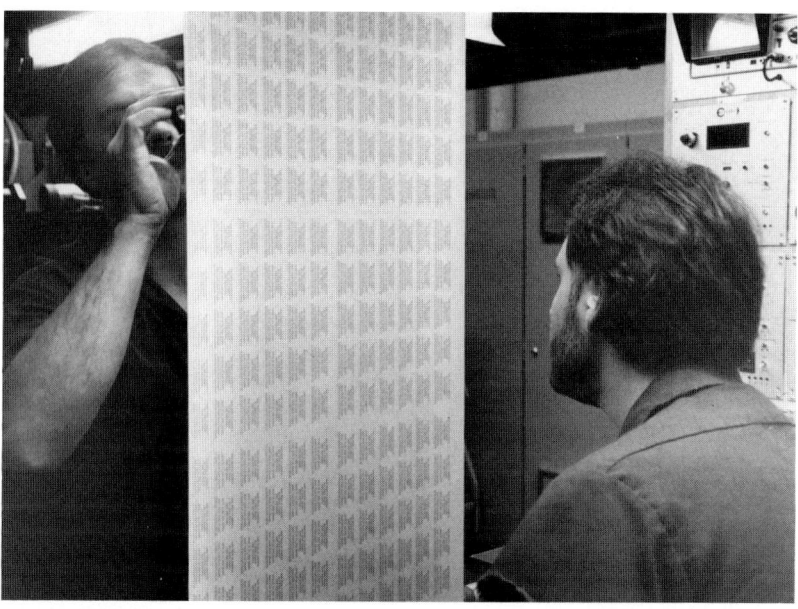

Because it is printed on both sides, two inspectors examine the web as the Duck stamp goes through D Press.

Over the years, the stamps have chalked up these firsts:
1935: First stamp to require a signature across its face.
1940: First year that Duck stamps were sold by the Philatelic Sales Division.
1946: First Duck stamp to sell two million copies.
1949: The only year Duck stamps were delayed until September, while Congress dawdled over an increase from $1 to $2.
1950: First stamp to show a species forbidden to hunters, the trumpeter swans.
1952: First stamp to bear the name of the species shown.
1954: First Duck stamp to have the back inscription printed on top of the gum instead of underneath it.
1958: First to show wildlife that had already been depicted on a Duck stamp. (The Canada Goose had appeared on a 1936 issue.)
1959: First multicolored Duck stamp, and the first to feature a major subject other than waterfowl.

1977: First name change of the stamp. "And Conservation Stamp" was added to "Migratory Bird Hunting."

1978: First Duck stamp to show only one bird.

For the last 25 years or so, the Bureau of Engraving and Printing has produced Duck stamps on sheetfed rotary presses — one applying offset printing and another intaglio. With those two types of printings, the Duck stamp was a natural for the offset/intaglio D Press. Offset colors are orange, yellow, brown, light blue and dark blue. Intaglio is black. The lettering on the back is printed in black via offset.

Judges for the contest this year were Colonel Robert Brantly, executive director of the Florida Game and Freshwater Fish Commission; Peter Coors, chairman, Ducks Unlimited, Inc.; Martha Hill, picture editor, *Audubon* magazine; James Norine, director of the hunter services division of the National Rifle Association; and Beatrice Pickens of the National Fish and Wildlife Foundation's board of directors.

The Design

Artwork for the 1987 Migratory Bird Hunting stamp before lettering, titles and numerals were added.

Arthur G. Anderson of Onalaska, Wisconsin, had tried four times previously to win the Federal Duck Stamp Contest. When told of his victory in this 1986 competition by telephone from Fish and Wildlife Service Director Frank Dunkle in Washington, Anderson whooped, "This is great, just great! I was painting a bald eagle when the phone rang, and I was so engrossed in my work I'd almost forgotten about the contest."

Anderson, 50, who "hunts mostly with a camera," moved his family to Onalaska to be close to the marsh habitat frequented by redheads, canvasbacks and other waterfowl during their annual migrations. His winning art featured three redhead ducks, two males and one female. Redheads had not appeared on the Duck stamps since 1960, and had been pictured before that in 1946.

In a pressroom at the BEP, Arthur Anderson, designer of the 1987 Duck stamp, examines a sheet of the stamps from D Press. (Courtesy U.S. Fish & Wildlife Service)

Born in Eau Claire, Wisconsin, Anderson started painting at age 12 with a set of oils borrowed from an uncle. He studied art at the University of Wisconsin and an art school in St. Paul. Supporting himself as a commercial artist, he did wildlife painting at home in evenings and on weekends until 1983, when he became economically able to devote all of his time to wildlife art. He likes to paint eagles and white-tailed deer, and was runner-up in Wisconsin's 1982 lake trout stamp contest.

Anderson says his winning design was inspired by his wife, Virginia. "She's a redhead," he says, "and I told her I'd enter redheads until I won." His three redhead ducks are depicted flying low over water in late afternoon. The place is a typical river marsh habitat, a scene that Anderson selected because "just about anyone would be able to identify with it."

The redhead is a common duck found in all four North American waterfowl flyways. Hunters call them "fool ducks," because they can be lured so easily. The female redhead lays her eggs in another duck's nest. She depends on other ducks to hatch her eggs and care for her young. Since ducklings look much alike, usually the foster mother will accept them. Redheads dive for their food. Their bodies are round and heavy, so they have to run along the surface of the water for some distance to get airborne.

First-Day Facts

No first-day ceremonies are held for Duck stamps. Post offices selling the Duck stamps would apply regular July 1, 1987, circular date-stamp cancels, so long as 22¢ in postage was also affixed to the cover. The PSD offered only the mint stamps for sale.

22¢ SAVINGS BOND ENVELOPE

Date of Issue: March 2, 1987

Catalog Numbers: Scott UO75   Minkus PDEN 76

Colors: blue, black

First-Day Cancel: Washington, D.C. (no first-day ceremony)

FDCs Canceled: 34,799

Size: 7⅞ by 3⅝ inches, with window

Watermarks: none

Designer: Bradbury Thompson (CSAC)

Printing: Westvaco-USEnvelope Division on a VH machine

Quantity Ordered: 4,000,000
Quantity Distributed: 3,789,000

Tagging: vertical bar to left of indicium

The Envelope

This Savings Bond envelope's appearance was so swift and surprising that the envelope itself was available several days before the USPS got around to issuing a March 13 release about its coming. Even so, the envelope missed its announced release date of March 2, 1987. First-day cancels read March 2, but the envelope was not really available until a few days later.

The size and the placement of its window restrict its use to the mailing of U.S. savings bonds. That's all it was intended for — that and to improve the accuracy of postal costs. Heretofore, savings bonds had been mailed in penalty envelopes, those that bear "Penalty for Private Use $300" in the upper right corner instead of an imprinted stamp. Each post office, however large or small, either counted and recorded all of this mail or took random statistical samplings thereof.

Each calendar quarter, all post offices reported totals to the USPS in Washington. The breakdown of each government agency costs was a lengthy recap. The chances for error were horrendous. Accurate accountability was impossible.

Top, a specimen design of the Savings Bond Official envelope. Bottom, by the time it got to press, the lettering was changed and repositioned.

This stamped Official envelope was to be sold to agencies sending out smaller quantities of U.S. savings bonds. Offices mailing large quantities of bonds were to use an imprinted permit envelope, which requires an accurate statement and record of mailing when mailed. The permit envelope was made of brown paper, with the legend "First-Class Mail, Postage & Fees Paid, Bureau of Public Debt, Permit No. x-xxxx" in the upper right corner.

"Bureau of the Public Debt" also appears on the Official stamped envelope, but as a return address rather than in place of the stamp. The bureau prepares Department of the Treasury circulars offering public debt securities, formulates regulations pertaining to security issues, maintains accounting control over public debt receipts and expenditures, and authorizes payment of principal and interest.

A large space on the envelope under the bureau return address allows for handstamping a more specific address.

This stamped Savings Bond envelope was produced on Westvaco-USEnvelope's VH machine. The Williamsburg, Pennsylvania, plant has four of the machines, which can emboss, print, knife, cut out windows, apply the transparent overlay, and finally lay down gum and dry it before folding the flaps. This Savings Bond envelope was not embossed, however. Neither was it printed on watermarked paper, since that would have meant securing a special web width of "custom watermarked" paper.

The Postal Service vacillated on instructing collectors how to obtain this envelope. First instructions said that collectors could purchase the envelopes from the Philatelic Sales Division and mail them in for canceling. Those who did not want to purchase the envelopes first were told to send peelable return address labels and 27¢ for each envelope wanted.

That was quickly amended. The new envelope would not be for sale in post offices or philatelic centers. None was to be mailed in under cover. Instead, collectors were told to send a No. 10 size, self-addressed, stamped envelope — along with 27¢ for each mint or canceled cover wanted — to a special Washington ZIP Code.

The changes were necessary because of the Bureau of Public Debt return address. That limited the envelope's use to that agency. None could be returned to collectors in the mailstream. Collectors had to supply the return envelope to place the Saving Bond envelopes under cover while in the mailstream.

The Design

Designs for all Official stamps, envelopes and postal cards are similar, though not precisely alike. Bradbury Thompson, design coordinator of the Citizens' Stamp Advisory Committee, set design standards for all Official items in 1983, when he selected the Great Seal of the United States as the basis for their design.

The eagle on the Great Seal is far different, however, from the one seen on postal items. Its wings and tail are thinner. Its head is smaller, and the device above the eagle's head on the Great Seal is nothing like the one seen on postal paper.

First-Day Facts

First-day of issue cancels read March 2, 1987, but like the 11 Official stamps, two postal cards and two envelopes that preceded it, this one too had no first-day ceremony. And like all the others, the cancels read Washington, D.C.

POSTAL CARDS

There was a time — when postal cards sold for 1¢ — that the Government Printing Office printed two billion cards per year. Lately, the annual volume has been more like 500 million, but in 1987 the GPO and USPS took some giant strides to make postal cards more colorful for users, more attractive for collectors and possibly less costly to produce.

What makes all of this attainable is a new, $2 million, five-color, sheetfed, offset Roland Man 800 press installed for printing postal cards in the Washington plant of the GPO. Three 16,000-pound printing units print two colors each, or five colors plus a tagging material. Top and bottom, each unit has a two-ton inking system. From this new multicolor, single-pass press came the striking postal cards of 1987 — the Steel Plow, Constitutional Convention, Flag, Take Pride in America and Timberline Lodge cards.

For the first time, a definitive postal card was printed in multi-splendid color. The Flag postal card replaced a 14¢ George Wyeth card printed on the former nearly 80-year-old Potter rotary press. The insipid printing on the Wyeth card, when compared to the Flag card, shows why the GPO installed a new press.

With all postal cards now capable of being printed in three, four or five colors, the differences between commemorative and regular postal cards may be blurred. Because of the two passes needed for multicolor cards heretofore, regular cards had to be printed in one color for cost reasons.

The cost of producing multicolor commemorative cards should drop by 50 percent, while the cost of a multicolor regular card (like the Flag) goes up slightly versus the old single-color cards (like the Wyeth). The commemorative cards produced on the old two-color presses could not be made in quantities large enough to sell them to commercial users in sheets of 40 cards for privately printed messages. Postal cards in more colors may become a mailing instrument for mass mailers that did not exist before. And as volume rises, unit costs come down.

Almost as important as the new press is a processing system costing $1 million. It was custom-designed for the GPO by a Japanese firm, Unomatic Seisakusho Company. This Cut-Pack System can process 6,500 to 7,000 80-card press sheets hourly, stacking them into bricks of 250 finished postal cards. In a series of operations that involve collating, cutting, banding, stacking and shrink-wrapping, the machine finally stuffs the bricks of 250 cards into shipping cartons that hold 2,000, 5,000 or 10,000 postal cards. The Cut-Pack unit keeps up with the press in processing 520,000 to 560,000 cards per hour.

Speeds are such that human inspection is next to impossible, so the machine itself searches for freaks and printing mistakes. It automatically sorts the rejected cards into a separate stack for destruction.

Tagging changed on the 1987 postal cards. Previous commemorative cards have been block tagged over the stamp area; definitive cards have had the tagging material mixed with the design inks. Beginning with the first card of 1987, all postal cards had a vertical phosphor bar, about ¼-inch wide and ½-inch high, placed to the right of the stamp design. And until 1987, U.S. postal cards had pictured and usually identified specific persons, events and locales. Two postal cards of this year do neither: the Take Pride in America and Steel Plow cards.

The total of five face-different postal cards issued by the USPS in 1987 is less than the average of six cards per year for the past decade.

14¢ STEEL PLOW POSTAL CARD

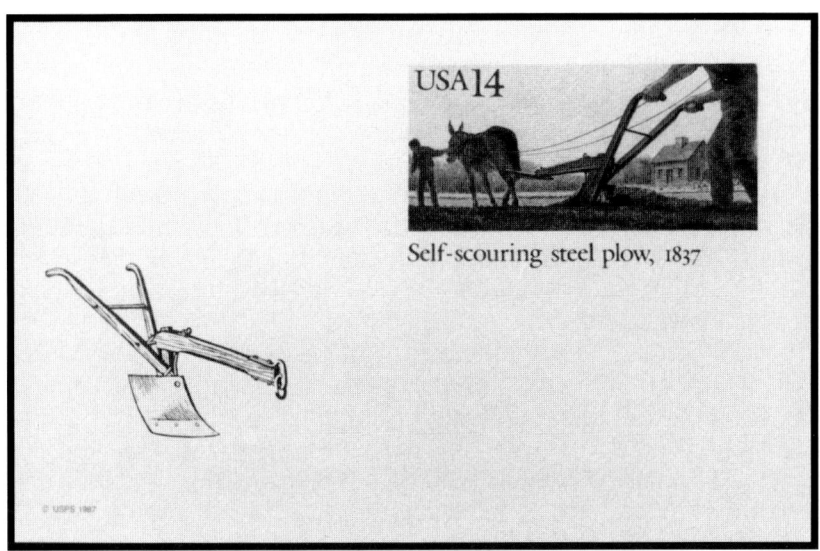

Date of Issue: May 22, 1987

Catalog Numbers: Scott UX115   Minkus PC111   UPSS S132

Colors: cyan, magenta, yellow, dark brown

First-Day Cancel: Moline, Illinois (Deere & Company Administrative Center)

FDCs Canceled: 160,099

Size: 3½ by 5½ inches

Format: Printed in 80-card sheets, 8 by 10, but available to collectors only in single cards.

Designer: William H. Bond

Art Director: Howard E. Paine (CSAC)

Inscriptions: Howard E. Paine (CSAC)

Printing: U.S. Government Printing Office in one pass through new 4-color, Roland Man 800 press.

Quantity Ordered: 8,000,000
Quantity Distributed: 7,660,000

Tagging: vertical bar to right of indicium

The Postal Card

The first postal card to be issued from the Government Printing Office's new $2 million, four-color offset press (see Introduction) was this 14¢ Self-Scouring Steel Plow postal card. It marked the 150th anniversary of John Deere's refinement of a centuries-old device that was undoubtedly the most important agricultural tool ever invented. Never mind the motorized cotton pickers, hay mowers, reapers and combines. Without the plow, they wouldn't need to exist.

The ancient precursor of the bladed plow was a simple digging stick, which was later equipped with handles for pushing or pulling it along the ground. By the time of the Roman Empire, light, wheelless plows with iron plowshares (the blade that digs into the ground to turn the soil) were drawn by oxen. But they could not break up the heavier soils of northwest Europe.

That was left to the wheeled plow, first pulled by oxen and later by horses, which made the worldwide spread of agriculture possible. The 18th-century development of the moldboard — that part of the plow against which the soil is lifted, turned and pulverized — occupied the talents of Thomas Jefferson. With his love of gardening and his bent for mathematics, Jefferson revised the shape of moldboards and plows of his day so that they would pull more easily through the soil and spread it more effectively. Moldboards were still being made of wood, as witness Jefferson's comment that his new moldboard "could be made most easily by the most bungling carpenter."

John Deere — twice a failure as a blacksmith — developed the plow that was to become the start of John Deere & Company.

John Deere, a blacksmith by trade, moved from Vermont to Illinois in 1834. New England was a depressed area in those times, and tales of the rich prairie land in Illinois had spawned a substantial movement westward. Deere, who had gone broke twice as a blacksmith, faced a court order for seizure of his property. He had nothing to lose, so he joined the emigrants, coming by canal boat and stagecoach to Grand Detour, Illinois, a hamlet about 100 miles west of Chicago.

When he opened his blacksmith shop in 1836, he learned that nearby farmers were dissatisfied with their plows. The heavy, gummy soil stuck to rough surfaces of the moldboard, which was used to turn the prairie dirt. When crops were cultivated in the wet Illinois springtimes, the muddy earth clung even more.

John Deere's first plow was cut from an old sawmill blade. Deere shaped it by bending and pounding it over a log. Its plowshare was steel, not iron. As the moving soil polished the steel in use, the dirt fell away more readily; it became a "self-scouring" plow. Later, Deere made a curved moldboard from steel, making the plow more efficient in shedding mud and dirt. From that plow grew the multimillion-dollar John Deere & Company.

This is the first U.S. postal card to feature a cachet-like, "second" design on the front of the card. While the stamp shows a plowman, a plow, and a mule being led by another person, a line drawing of one of the first self-scouring steel plows appears at lower left.

Placement of the phosphor tagging is also different on this postal card. Previous commemorative cards have been block tagged over the stamp area. Definitive postal cards have had the tagging material mixed in the design inks. On this Steel Plow card, a phosphor bar, approximately ¼ inch wide by ½ inch high, was placed along the right edge of the stamp design. It abuts the design at the top right corner.

Bar tagging on the left side of the stamp has been used only on envelopes. But since the stamp design area on postal cards varies in width and size, placing the tagging bar to the left of the design might require different bar positions, which could confuse the facer/canceler machines in post offices.

The Design

William H. Bond of Arlington, Virginia, rendered his third postal design for the year with this postal card. His other 1987 designs are the 8.5¢ Tow Truck and 10¢ Canal Boat, both stamps in the Transportation series. Though this was Bond's first postal card design, he has also crafted the 4.9¢ Buckboard, 14¢ Iceboat, and 25¢ Bread Wagon stamps in the Transportation series and the 1984 20¢ Alaska Statehood commemorative.

Bond created both the stamp design and the line drawing of a plow that appears at lower left. Program manager for the USPS on this card was Joe Brockert.

First-Day Facts

This postal card was issued at the John Deere & Company's Administrative Center in Moline, Illinois, on May 22, 1987. Deere's self-scouring plow had been so successful that he moved his company to

Designer Bill Bond made these preliminary sketches for the Self-scouring Steel Plow postal card.

Moline in 1848. At the time, Deere was selling 13,000 of the plows annually. Today, Deere & Company does not manufacture plows of any type.

Deputy Postmaster General Michael S. Coughlin spoke for the USPS at the ceremony.

The Postal Service said that these postal cards would be first-day canceled in Moline, Illinois, rather than the usual practice of machine canceling most first days in the Philatelic Sales Division's Merrifield, Virginia, facility. Two other postal cards and three stamps were bumped from Merrifield back to first-day sites for canceling.

Robert Brown, PSD manager, said the steps were taken in anticipation of a probable overload situation at Merrifield when the Wildlife 50-stamp panes were issued. First-day issues of postal cards are not plastic wrapped as are stamp covers, so postal stationery collectors perhaps did not know of the switch.

14¢ CONSTITUTIONAL CONVENTION POSTAL CARD

Date of Issue: May 25, 1987

Catalog Numbers: Scott UX116   Minkus PC112   UPSS S133

Colors: yellow, black, magenta, cyan

First-Day Cancel: Philadelphia, Pennsylvania (Independence Hall)

FDCs Canceled: 138,207

Size: 3½ by 5½ inches

Format: Printed in 80-card sheets, 8 by 10, but available to collectors only in single cards.

Designer: David K. Stone

Art Director: Joe Brockert (USPS)

Inscriptions: Bradbury Thompson (CSAC)

Printing: U.S. Government Printing Office in one pass through new 4-color, Roland Man 800 press.

Quantity Ordered: 25,000,000
Quantity Distributed: 16,793,000

Tagging: vertical bar to right of indicium

The Postal Card

There are those who contend that the United States of America was not born with the Declaration of Independence in 1776, but with the Constitutional Convention in 1787. In May 1787, 11 of the 13 original colonies gathered in Philadelphia. (New Hampshire didn't show up until July, and Rhode Island never came at all.) The 55 delegates were there to fashion a new framework for a nation that had just been drifting along since 1781 under the Articles of Confederation.

The Articles provided for no president, no power to tax, no method for raising an army and no national courts. The only government outside the 13 state governments was the Continental Congress, which, by the 1780s, was vainly trying to resolve trade barriers and even talk of war between the individual states. There was no national currency, and foreign trade was regulated by the separate states. Economic depression had resulted. In 1785, when George Washington looked over the land he had led to victory over the British, he could only remark, "The wheels of government are clogged." Rhode Island stayed away from the convention solely because of fear that its own lucrative trade practices might be regulated under a newly formed national government.

Among the 55 who came to Philadelphia were many historic names: Washington, James Madison, Alexander Hamilton and Benjamin Franklin. Others just as famous had business elsewhere. John Adams was in London, on diplomatic duties for the Continental Congress. Thomas Jefferson was U.S. minister in Paris. Looking at the delegate list, he called the convention "an assembly of demigods."

James Madison of Virginia. His pre-convention Virginia Plan became the convention's agenda.

Most delegates did not look forward to spending a sticky summer in Philadelphia. George Mason of Virginia said that he "would not, upon pecuniary motives, serve in this convention for a thousand pounds per day." A few who were not very well-known for anything else stood out at the convention: Gouverneur Morris, James Wilson,

Oliver Elsworth, John Dickinson. Alexander Hamilton left the proceedings June 29 because of the "pigheadedness" of his fellow delegates from New York. He made one unexplained appearance on August 13 and hastened back in early September in time for the closing ceremonies. He was a convention nonentity.

Independence Hall as it looks today. The card pictures it as it looked in 1787, with a spire rather than a tower.

Virginia was the most influential colony, with delegates like George Washington, George Mason, James Madison, George Wyeth, Edmund Randolph and John Blair. Madison, in fact, worked harder and smarter than anyone else to bring about the convention, and then melded diverse feelings into agreement on a Constitution. Then 36 years old, Madison outlined his proposed system for governing, called the Virginia Plan, while early delegates waited for a quorum to arrive at Philadelphia's State House, since renamed Independence Hall. As the convention finally began on May 25, Washington was named its president, Madison its unofficial daily secretary.

The delegates agreed quickly on three branches of government: the executive, the judicial and a legislature. Over time, however, they began to form into groups with selfish desires. The smaller states, such as Maryland, New Jersey, Connecticut and Delaware, leaned toward the status quo — a loose federation of states. The larger colonies — Massachusetts, Pennsylvania, North Carolina and Virginia — wanted a strong central government. Bouncing one way and then another were medium-sized New York, South Carolina and Georgia. The convention split into Federalists and Nationalists.

The makeup of Congress became the divisive issue. Federalists wanted equal representation for all states; Nationalists felt voting power should reflect population. For his part, Madison was determined to do away forever with the one-state, one-vote principle. The delegates were meeting for five hours a day, six days per week, in an assembly room made almost unbearable by the long, hot summer.

Tempers were short. Debates were both heated and inspired, but often bitter and personal. Delaware's John Dickinson charged that Madison, whose plans for a strong central government had so far enjoyed much support, was "pushing things too far." He seriously threatened to lead the smaller states into an alliance with a foreign power rather than go along with the Virginia Plan. But the large states pushed for representation by population in both legislative houses.

The matter was settled when Ben Franklin observed that the larger states felt their money would be in danger with equality in both houses, while the smaller states felt their liberties would be at risk with proportional representation. These were fair differences, said Franklin, and ought to be compromised. They were resolved when it was decided that the Senate would consist of two members per state, and representation in the House of Representatives would be according to each state's population.

The large states were mollified with a proviso that only the lower house could originate bills concerning money, and the Senate had no power to change them.

Alexander Hamilton of New York. Says one historian, "He had so much to give, and gave so little." The most disappointing delegate.

The hassle over Constitutional details seemed endless. On one day, the delegates voted on several matters — then decided at day's end to invalidate all of the votes taken. Finally, two more crucial and controversial issues were put to rest. The acts of the U.S. legislature and all treaties, it was agreed, were to be the supreme law of the several states. The jurisdiction of the Supreme Court would extend to all cases arising under laws passed by the legislature of the United States. By August 6, 1787, the 55 men had the draft of a Constitution with a preamble and 23 articles. Article by article, the debate went on for another five weeks.

At the last minute, it was proposed that a Bill of Rights be added. Worthwhile as that may have sounded to the delegates, they were simply too exhausted to cope with it. They proposed that such a bill could be added later, while the Constitution was going through the prescribed amendment process. On Monday, September 17, 1787, the Constitution was signed "in the unanimous consent of the states present" — that last clause being the final motion of Ben Franklin.

By June 21, 1788, the required nine states had ratified the Constitution as the law of the land. Within three years the Bill of Rights became part of it. A few years ago, former Chief Justice Earl Warren remarked that if the Bill of Rights came up for legislative approval today, the Congress would probably never pass it. Noted attorney Edward Bennett Williams went the chief justice one better. "Pass it?," he said. "It would never even get out of committee!"

The Design

Artist David Stone prepared these pencil sketches for the Constitutional Convention postal card for consideration by the CSAC.

For David K. Stone of Chapel Hill, North Carolina, this was his ninth postal design but his first for a postal card. Stone prepared a number of proposed pencil sketches for the card, some of which are illustrated here. The one finally approved by the CSAC and postmaster general shows five delegates — George Mason, Gouverneur Morris, James Madison, the seldom-present Alexander Hamilton and Charles C. Pinckney — discussing convention matters outside the State House, now Independence Hall.

At the left side of the stamp design is Independence Hall, site of the convention deliberations. Atop the hall is the base of a spire, which is as the hall appeared in 1787. The full tower was added later. The names of the men in the group are printed in black in the lower left corner of the card — the second consecutive postal card with an added design on its face.

Though this postal card was issued after the Steel Plow card, it was actually the first postal card to be produced on the GPO's new four-color offset press.

First-Day Facts

The courtyard behind Independence Hall in Philadelphia was the site for the May 25, 1987, first-day ceremony that marked exactly 200 years since George Washington had called the Constitutional Convention to order. Johnny F. Thomas, regional postmaster general for the USPS Eastern Region, was the Postal Service speaker.

Also appearing on the first-day program were Benjamin Franklin and George Washington, portrayed by two actors. Each made a few pithy remarks about the convention hall. A Marine Corps Color Guard and David K. Stone, designer of the card, were honored guests.

All first-day cancels for this postal card were actually applied in Philadelphia, rather than in the Philatelic Sales Division's Merrifield operation. (For reason, see chapter on Steel Plow postal card.)

14¢ FLAG POSTAL CARD

Date of Issue: June 14, 1987

Catalog Numbers: Scott UX117   Minkus PC113   UPSS S134

Colors: special red, special blue, black

First-Day Cancel: Baltimore, Maryland (Fort McHenry)

FDCs Canceled: not available

Size: 3½ by 5½ inches

Format: Printed in 80-card sheets, 8 by 10, but available to collectors only in single cards.

Designer: Stevan Dohanos

Art Director: Joe Brockert (USPS)

Printing: U.S. Government Printing Office in one pass through new 4-color, Roland Man 800 press.

Quantity Ordered: 155,000,000
Quantity Distributed: 65,232,000

Tagging: vertical bar to right of indicium

The Postal Card

Compared to the one it replaces, this Flag postal card is indeed a many-splendored thing. The flag comes alive in color, thanks to the new multicolor offset press on which it was printed. The colors are intense and striking. Ironically, it replaces the 14¢ George Wyeth issue of 1985 — as olive drab and poorly printed a postal card as had been seen since earlier that year when the Government Printing Office issued a pale green disaster for Charles Carroll. Both came from Potter presses, installed in 1909, and whose latest modifications dated back more than 60 years.

The new GPO postal card press may cause some problems of definition among collectors, however. This Flag item is a definitive postal card that will stay on sale for a long period and be rerun as needed. Heretofore, U.S. definitive postal cards were a dull, monocolor lot easily recognized from the multicolor commemorative cards. That definition no longer works. It is now possible to print all postal cards in more than one color. The Flag card is the first definitive U.S. postal card to be so printed.

The only difference between the September 1 double-reply Flag postal card (top) and the June 14 single Flag card (bottom) was in the size of the copyright inscription (lower left). It was reduced slightly to conform to new standards for a smaller copyright notice on postal cards.

For the last quarter century, the U.S. Flag has been the subject of commemorative stamps, definitive stamps, sheet stamps, coil stamps, booklets and postal cards. It is a safe subject in a country whose varied makeup renders many possible stamp subjects objectionable to somebody, somewhere. Perhaps that non-controversial aspect is why nearly half of all U.S. stamps now printed feature the flag.

At first, the Flag postal cards were obtainable only as single cards. Message-reply (double) cards were not available until September 1 because of the close proximity of issue for the Flag, Plow and Constitutional Convention cards. (All appeared within 24 days.) Fine-tuning the new GPO press was really not a factor. The quantities of new postal cards scheduled was.

The U.S. Flag first appeared as part of a stamp design on the 30¢ issue of 1869. The first stamp to picture the flag alone and in full color was the 4¢ Flag issue of 1957. The flag has never been featured on an envelope, and has been the principal design on only one postal card, the 11¢ airmail card of 1966. Even then, it was seen as part of the emblem of the Commerce Department's travel service.

The Design

Left, Art Director Joe Brockert's quick sketch for the Flag postal card gave artist Stevan Dohanos size requirements. It also told him to let the flag "float free — no edges or borders." Dohanos' first design, at right, went to press without being changed.

The red, white and blue national ensign on the postal card was designed by Stevan Dohanos of Westport, Connecticut. Dohanos, a former chairman of the Citizens' Stamp Advisory Committee, is a prolific artist whose work includes more than 30 stamps and postal stationery items. His flag designs include the 4¢ 49-star Flag stamp of 1959, the 4¢ 50-star Flag issue of 1960, the 5¢ Savings Bonds/Servicemen stamp of 1966, and the 6¢ definitive Flag Over White House issue of 1968.

This Dohanos design, however, duplicates no other flag design exactly, including those of his own creation. The postal card flag waves almost straight out, with only small wind crinkles at upper right and lower center. A copyright notice appears at lower left on the card.

Other flag designs by Stevan Dohanos are (left to right) the 4¢ 49-star Flag stamp of 1959, the 4¢ 50-star Flag issue of 1960, the 5¢ Savings Bonds/Servicemen stamp of 1966, and the 6¢ Flag Over White House definitive of 1968.

First-Day Facts

When the 1987 postal program was first announced by the USPS in 1986, this 14¢ Flag postal card was scheduled for release on March 6, 1987, at the opening day of MILCOPEX 87 in Milwaukee, Wisconsin. By early February 1987, the Postal Service said the card would be delayed until later in the year. No other information was forthcoming until early May, when a USPS release revealed that the card would be issued June 14 — Flag Day — at Fort McHenry in Baltimore harbor.

This design, along with a circular datestamp, was used on some 14¢ Flag first-day cancels in an effort to gauge collector interest in pictorial FDCs.

The first-day ceremony for the card formed a small part of an evening-long program that began at 6 p.m. Music by an Air Force band, a procession of 50 state flags, a parachute drop, a 42- by 30-foot Star Spangled Banner and a Flag Day message by John O. Marsh, Jr., Secretary of the Army, bracketed the card's release by Assistant Postmaster General Stanley W. Smith. A concert and fireworks display took the ceremonies over the three-hour mark.

All first-day covers were canceled at Baltimore, not at the Philatelic Sales Division in Merrifield, Virginia. This was part of an effort that also involved two other postal cards and three stamp releases. All were canceled at actual issue sites to keep PSD canceling equipment free for the expected deluge of 50-stamp Wildlife stamps.

14¢ TAKE PRIDE IN AMERICA POSTAL CARD

Date of Issue: September 22, 1987

Catalog Numbers: Scott UX118   Minkus PC114   UPSS S135

Colors: yellow, magenta, cyan, black

First-Day Cancel: Jackson, Wyoming (National Elk Refuge)

FDCs Canceled: 47,281

Size: 3½ by 5½ inches

Format: Printed in 80-card sheets, 8 by 10, but available to collectors in single cards only.

Designer: Lou Nolan

Art Director: Derry Noyes (CSAC)

Inscriptions: not credited

Printing: U.S. Government Printing Office in one pass through new 4-color, Roland Man 800 press.

Quantity Ordered: 11,000,000
Quantity Distributed: 7,139,000

Tagging: vertical bar to right of indicium

The Postal Card

This card urging U.S. citizens to "Take Pride in America" was announced in late 1986, but never received a date of issue until a July 13, 1987, postal release scheduled it for September 22. July 13 was a popular date for late-coming stamps and postal cards. The 10¢ Red Cloud definitive and coils of a 5¢ Milk Wagon and 17.5¢ Racing Car also went unannounced for their August and September release dates until July 13.

Launched by President Reagan in his 1986 State of the Union speech, Take Pride in America is a major campaign to fight and correct abuses against the hundreds of millions of acres of public land. A tremendous toll of damage has taken place against these national treasures and resources. According to the Department of the Interior, more than 80 percent of the prehistoric ruins in the Southwest have been vandalized.

The Design

At bottom is a proof of the Take Pride in America postal card produced on standard, off-white postal card stock. At top is the same design as it was printed on a new bright-white stock.

Lou Nolan of McLean, Virginia, who has also designed the School Bus and Dog Sled coils in the Transportation series, plus 1987's Milk Wagon coil and the CPA commemorative, rendered his third design of the year for this Take Pride in America postal card.

Nolan had no specific place in mind when he rendered his vista of mountains, lake, trees and rolling hills for this card's imprinted stamp, says Joe Brockert, USPS project manager for the postal card. Until 1987, U.S. postal cards had pictured and usually identified specific persons, events and locales. Two postal cards of this year — this one and the Self-scouring Steel Plow card — do not.

First-Day Facts

The first-day postmark of Jackson, Wyoming, doesn't just represent a scenic beauty spot. It is also the national refuge for the American elk.

The Take Pride in America card was released September 22, 1987, at the National Elk Refuge in Jackson, Wyoming, the southern gateway to Yellowstone National Park. In winter, herds of American elk move from their normal habitats of high mountain valleys to lower valleys. Here, where snow is not too deep, bulls and cows of all ages spend the winter. Located just north of Jackson, Wyoming, the National Elk Refuge is the largest of six Wyoming wildlife refuges.

Assistant Postmaster General John J. Davin, USPS speaker, compared the scenery to the marble monuments of his workplace, Washington, D.C. He said, "They cannot compare to the massive majesty of mountains. The statues around us today are live, made of pine and cedar. This memorial was built by nature, standing as a tribute to wildlife and freedom."

Davin also noted that the National Elk Refuge was celebrating its 75th anniversary. Its nearly 25,000 acres "offer winter sanctuary for about 7,500 elk, 45 species of mammals and 75 species of birds."

14¢ TIMBERLINE LODGE POSTAL CARD

Date of Issue: September 28, 1987

Catalog Numbers: Scott UX119   Minkus PC115   UPSS S136

Colors: yellow, magenta, cyan, black

First-Day Cancel: Timberline, Oregon (Timberline Lodge)

FDCs Canceled: 63,595

Size: 3½ by 5½ inches

Format: Printed in 80-card sheets, 8 by 10, but available to collectors in single cards only.

Designer: Walter D. Richards

Art Director and Typographer: Bradbury Thompson (CSAC)

Printing: U.S. Government Printing Office in one pass through new 4-color, Roland Man 800 press.

Quantity Ordered: 10,000,000
Quantity Distributed: 7,585,000

Tagging: vertical bar to right of indicium

The Postal Card

This four-color postal card for the 50th anniversary of Franklin D. Roosevelt's dedication of Timberline Lodge is the sixth to be issued in the Historic Preservation series. Others have been for the Cincinnati Music Hall (1978), Iolani Palace in Honolulu (1979), the Mormon Salt Lake Temple (1980), Old Post Office in St. Louis (1982) and Rancho San Pedro (1984). The first three appeared in as many years; the last three have stretched over six years.

Announcement of the card and its design were made at Mount Hood, Oregon, on October 11, 1986. From the first, the postal card was scheduled for release on September 28, 1987, at Mount Hood. The date never varied, but the site changed from Mount Hood to Timberline, Oregon, in early March 1987.

Timberline Lodge was built as part of the Works Progress Administration (WPA) and Civilian Conservation Corps (CCC) programs during the Great Depression years of the 1930s. Constructed entirely of native Northwest wood and stone, the lodge sits at the timberline (6,000-foot level) of Mount Hood in the Mount Hood National Forest about 50 miles east of Portland, Oregon. With its picturesque setting and architecture, it has been used as background for several television programs and motion pictures including "Lost Horizon," "Bend in the River" and "All the Young Men." It became a national historic landmark in 1977.

Construction began June 13, 1936, and the lodge was finished in September 1937. Workers on the project were changed every two weeks so that the maximum number could gain at least temporary employment. Pay was 90¢ per hour plus three meals a day and a heated tent to sleep in. Artisans in Portland handcrafted many of the lodge's decorations and furnishings. Women sewed applique curtains, and wove hundreds of yards of drapes and furniture fabrics.

The lodge's steep, sloping roofs and heavy walls — intended to hold back deep snows and 80-knot winds — were also an attempt by its architects to establish a new and distinctive American style. Called Cascadian, it was a take-off on the long tradition of European Alpine design. Construction of the 53-room lodge took 760,000 hours of labor. Built and owned by the federal government, its management was assigned to the U.S. Forestry Service.

But the lodge was not profitable. When it was closed for three years during World War II, vandals did extensive damage. Refurbished and reopened, not enough trade came to keep it in operation. It closed again in 1955 for non-payment of utility bills. The Internal Revenue Service padlocked the doors.

Enter now the man who has run Timberline Lodge for 31 of its 50 years: Richard Kohnstamm, prosperous businessman, Oregonian and lover of the lodge. A weekend skier himself, Kohnstamm took over operations and was immediately appalled at the deterioration of Timberline. Handmade drapes had been used to stuff broken windows, handmade furniture was used for firewood and the only ski lift was a shambles. Between 1955 and 1966, Kohnstamm and family spent a half million dollars on Timberline, installing a new pool and chairlifts, and buying new Sno-Cats to transport tourists and skiers.

But Kohnstamm is quick to spread the credit for Timberline's rebirth around. "This place runs on the devotion of many, many people who work here — and they are not doing it just for the money," he says. "Imagine, week after week, digging your car out of the snow to go to work, working eight hours, and then digging your car out of the snow to go home. Think about spending all day plowing out the parking lot, and then having it snow four feet that night. That's what it's like to work here. Nothing comes easy at Timberline."

Kohnstamm calls Timberline "a ski resort that is primarily an architectural monument and, believe it or not, a museum." The ski boom and back-to-nature fetishes of the 1960s brought new life to Timberline. By 1969 it was drawing 750,000 visitors annually. A much-needed day lodge came later, after Kohnstamm told congressional committees that "running Timberline without a day lodge is like trying to run an exclusive restaurant in the Lincoln Memorial."

At 6,000 feet, the winds howl and temperatures plummet. The snow can drift to 30 feet. But Timberline Lodge can cater to skiers all year around, and it attracts more than 30,000 each summer. In the 50 years it has been open, Timberline Lodge — hotel, ski resort, architectural monument and museum — has been host to 30 million visitors. It is a rustic, handmade, lovely old WPA project that works, but not without a lot of planning and dedication.

The Design

Stamp designers often tend to specialize: Chuck Ripper for wildlife, Howard Koslow for "poster art" designs, Ken Dallison for airplanes and racing cars. Walter DuBois Richards of New Canaan, Connecticut, designer of the Timberline Lodge postal card, has specialized in buildings and architecture for the USPS.

Of his 23 stamp designs since 1967, 16 have been for the American Architecture series from 1979 through 1982. When the 18¢ and 20¢ James Hoban commemoratives of 1981 honored the Irish-born architect of the White House, Richards teamed up with Irish designer Ron Mercer on the stamp. Mercer did the Hoban likeness, Richards, of course, did the White House.

Richards' view of Timberline Lodge is from the front, and shows it as it looks in winter. Mount Hood looms magnificently in the background, as it does in actuality. It is only a few miles from the lodge.

First-Day Facts

On October 11, 1986, Postmaster Dallas Keck of the Portland Division unveiled the design for the Timberline Lodge postal card at the lodge itself. On September 28, 1987, Regional Postmaster General Joseph R. Caraveo came to Timberline Lodge to release the postal card. Caraveo said, "Timberline Lodge marks a moment in time when life was simpler and more difficult. Television and computers had not come into the lives of every American, but the Great Depression certainly had."

SOUVENIR CARDS

In the late 1960s, the U.S. Post Office Department and the Bureau of Engraving and Printing reached a gentlemen's agreement whereby the Postal Service would supply souvenir cards for international philatelic events, and the Bureau would print cards for national stamp and coin exhibitions. While there have been a few exceptions to that understanding, it has held true generally that USPS cards are for overseas stamp events while BEP cards are used within the United States for both numismatic and philatelic shows.

The *Yearbook* lists all souvenir cards issued by the Postal Service since these are strictly philatelic and almost always picture one or more stamps. The *Yearbook* does not list all souvenir cards issued by the BEP, however. In 1987 the majority of BEP cards were printed for coin and currency collectors — six for the numismatists and only one (SESCAL) for stamp collectors.

You will, however, find three BEP cards recorded here. One is a card marking the 125th anniversary of the Bureau; it was available all year long. Another, of course, is the philatelic SESCAL card. The third BEP souvenir, for the Hawaii State Numismatic Association's Honolulu show, had a numismatic theme but pictured a die proof of the 1937 3¢ Hawaii Territory commemorative stamp. Whenever a BEP numismatic card features anything relating to stamps and stamp collecting, the *Yearbook* will show it to you and tell you about it.

The USPS issued only three souvenir cards in 1987, and with the advent of exhibition cards (various U.S. postal cards overprinted to honor overseas stamp shows), it seems likely that the USPS will use the postal card in place of the souvenir card for other philatelic happenings. The exhibition cards (see that section) have been well-received. There is another advantage to overprinting postal cards. Postal cards seldom sell out anyway, so the overprinting of them for stamp shows offers an alternative to their destruction.

125th ANNIVERSARY CARD (BEP)

Date of Issue: January 7, 1987

First-Day Cancel: Orlando, Florida (Florida United Numismatists exhibition; BEP Center, Washington)

Colors: blue, green, red (offset); black (intaglio)

Size: 8 by 10 inches

Printing: 6-color Miller offset press; 3-color intaglio press (not die-stamped)

Quantity Produced: 20,000

This multicolor offset and intaglio card was used all year long by the Bureau of Engraving and Printing to mark its 125th anniversary. Congress authorized the BEP's establishment on July 11, 1862. The special anniversary logo had first been used on the LOBEX 86 souvenir card of October 2, 1986, but that was an advance appearance. The BEP's 125th anniversary year began in 1987 with this handsome card.

The view shows the BEP, as seen from the 15th Street side across the Tidal Basin. Cherry blossom trees bloom overhead in close-up and across the basin in front of the Bureau. Black intaglio printing outlines the BEP, tree trunks and blossoms, shadows on the water, some gray clouds and the BEP anniversary inscription. All the rest is offset printed.

All 20,000 cards were printed in this manner at one time. Throughout the year, the cards received the show logos of the following events: Florida United Numismatists FUN 87, Lake Buena Vista, Florida; American Numismatic Association, Charlotte, North Carolina; WMPG 87, New Carrollton, Maryland; International Paper Money Show, Memphis, Tennessee; American Numismatic Association convention, Atlanta, Georgia; and Great Eastern Numismatic Association's GENA 87, Cherry Hill, New Jersey. These show names were applied at the top left of the card just prior to each show by the BEP's Heidelberg Letter Press. The six cards with show lettering were obtainable only at the show sites, not by mail.

Anniversary cards without any show lettering were priced at $10 at shows or the BEP Visitor's Center, or $11.50 by mail. The specially embossed show cards were $15 at show sites only.

The BEP kicked off its 125th anniversary celebration with a formal program featuring Secretary of the Treasury James A. Baker, U.S. Treasurer Katherine Ortega, Federal Reserve System Chairman Paul A. Volcker, and Postmaster General Preston Tisch. The January 29, 1987, affair in the Bureau's recently refurbished auditorium was attended by some 400 guests. The anniversary year continued with a monthly series of events for Bureau personnel, culminating with a family day in August for family members and retirees.

CAPEX 87 SOUVENIR CARD (USPS)

CAPEX '87

Toronto, Ontario, Canada
June 13-21, 1987

The United States issued this Buffalo stamp in 1923. It was the first U.S. regular issue to feature American Wildlife.

Ce timbre représentant un bison a été émis par les États-Unis en 1923. Il s'agit du premier timbre courant américain ayant pour sujet un animal sauvage.

The U.S. Postal Service is pleased to issue this souvenir card, featuring American Wildlife, in honor of CAPEX '87.

L'Administration postale des États-Unis est heureuse d'émettre cette carte-souvenir sur la faune américaine, en l'honneur de CAPEX '87.

This stamp was issued by Canada in 1981 as part of its Endangered Wildlife series. It depicts the Vancouver Island Marmot.

Ce timbre a été émis par le Canada en 1981 dans le cadre d'une série consacrée aux espèces menacées d'extinction. Il reproduit une marmotte de l'île de Vancouver.

Date of Issue: June 13, 1987

First-Day Release: Toronto, Canada (CAPEX 87); Philatelic Sales Division; all USPS Philatelic Centers

Colors: yellow, cyan, magenta, black, red (offset); brown (intaglio)

Designer: Joe Brockert (USPS)

Engravers: Vignette: Gary Chaconas (BEP)
    Lettering: Michael J. Ryan (BEP)

Modeler: Clarence Holbert (BEP)

Size: 6 by 8 inches

Printing: Miller offset press and 2-color, high speed intaglio press (die-stamped)

Quantity Delivered: 90,000

This first USPS souvenir card of 1987 was created for and issued at CAPEX 87, the international philatelic exhibition that took place in Toronto, Canada, from June 13 to 21. This show was the venue for issuing 50 new U.S. Wildlife stamps. To buttress the USPS's wildlife show theme, the souvenir card also pictures wildlife. When canceled, the card carried a randomly selected U.S. Wildlife stamp; even the cancellation incorporated an eagle and a beaver in its design.

At left, the card almost reproduces the sepia 30¢ Buffalo stamp of 1923. By law, the design of a U.S. stamp cannot be shown in its entirety if it is produced in actual color in a size more than three-fourths and less than one and one-half times the size of the real stamp. The "30" numerals were eliminated from the two circles at the bottom corners of the reproduction on the card.

The card states that this was the first U.S. regular issue to portray wildlife. According to most stamp collectors, catalogs and stamp albums, that statement is not so. The 1869 pictorial definitives pictured horses and eagles, with the latter, at least, qualifying for wildlife status. The USPS evidently classifies the 1869 issues as "commemoratives." The great majority of collectors, catalog makers and philatelists consider the Columbians as the first U.S. commemoratives.

The Canadian stamp at right shows the Vancouver Island Marmot on a 1981 issue that was part of Canada Post's Endangered Wildlife series. Both stamps are printed on the card as they were in actuality — the U.S. Buffalo stamp in brown intaglio engraving, and the Canadian stamp in multicolor offset printing.

The CAPEX card was printed by the BEP on off-white parchment stock composed of the same acid-free material currently used for BEP souvenir cards. The USPS said that any future souvenir cards it issues will be printed on a whiter version of the same stock.

Mint cards were available from the Philatelic Sales Division for $2 each, canceled cards for $2.22.

This cancel was applied to CAPEX souvenir cards. The eagle represents the United States; the beaver symbolizes Canada.

SESCAL '87 SOUVENIR CARD (BEP)

Date of Issue: October 16, 1987

First-Day Release: Los Angeles, California (SESCAL 87 stamp exhibition); Washington, D.C. (BEP Center)

Colors: gray, blue, magenta, black (offset); black (intaglio); silver (letterpress)

Size: 8 by 10 inches

Printing: Offset by 6-color Miller press; metallic silver by Kluge letterpress; intaglio by high-speed intaglio press (die-stamped)

Quantity Produced: 6,500

    This is the first souvenir card issued by the Bureau of Engraving or the U.S. Postal Service to carry an actual die proof of a U.S. stamp. All other U.S. stamps heretofore pictured on BEP or USPS souvenir cards have been either enlarged, reduced, modified in some manner, or have had denominations and other legends eliminated. On this card, the BEP said it used the Number 951 original die for the 1937 3¢ Constitution Sesquicentennial stamp to produce the stamp.

No matter that it was done 50 years after the stamp was issued; no matter that an acid-free "modern" paper was used; no matter that an offset press later placed a black cancel over the numerals. The stamp shown on the SESCAL card is a legitimate die proof for one simple reason: It was printed from the original die.

With only a small white border around it, it would be cataloged as a small die proof. Value of such a small die proof of this stamp is listed at $650 (without the overprinted cancel slashes). The overprinting still does not change the fact that this is a die proof of the 1937 issue.

Perhaps with this additional collector attraction in mind, the Bureau said that it would be using original die proofs on some of its future cards.

The centerpiece art is a blowup of the stamp, showing the signing of the Constitution at Philadelphia, September 17, 1787. In the background is a copy of the handwritten Constitution. Haloed in white at upper right is an adaptation of the state seal of California.

The color scheme on this SESCAL card makes it the most unusual looking souvenir card ever. A dull gray background supports two bright violet highlights: the oval seal and the large, fuzzy portrait of Washington, Franklin, et al. SESCAL lettering and the BEP seal are in silver; all other lettering in dropout white. The combined result is more sickening than striking.

The mint card sold for $4 at the exhibition or at the BEP Visitors' Center in Washington. The canceled version was $4.25. When purchased by mail, the mint card was $5.50 and the canceled card $5.75.

HAFNIA 87 SOUVENIR CARD (USPS)

Copenhagen, Denmark
16-25 October, 1987

USA udgav dette dampskibsfrimærke over emnet "Hurtig søgående skibsfart" i 1901. Det havde den højeste værdi i serien, der blev udgivet det år i anledning af den Pan-Amerikanske Udstilling.

The United States issued this Steamship stamp, depicting "Fast Ocean Navigation," in 1901. It was the highest value of the series issued that year in honor of the Pan American Exposition.

USA's Postvæsen har den glæde at udgive dette souvenir kort med søgående skibe i anledning af HAFNIA '87.

The U.S. Postal Service is pleased to issue this souvenir card, featuring seagoing vessels, in honor of HAFNIA '87.

Dette frimærke blev udgivet af Danmark i 1976 som del af en serie til minde om 200-året for den Amerikanske Frihedskrig. Det havde den højeste værdi i serien, der var udgivet over emnet "Danske søgående skibe."

This stamp was issued by Denmark in 1976 as part of its series honoring the bicentennial of the American Revolution. This was the highest value of the series, which depicted Danish ocean-going vessels.

Date of Issue: October 16, 1987

First-Day Release: Copenhagen, Denmark (HAFNIA 87 international stamp show)

Colors: blue, red, black (offset); brown, black (intaglio)

Designer: Joe Brockert (USPS)

Engravers: Vignette: Gary Chaconas (BEP)
Inscriptions: Dennis Brown (BEP)

Modeler: Clarence Holbert (BEP)

Size: 6 by 8 inches

Printing: Miller offset press and 2-color, high speed intaglio press (die-stamped)

Quantity Delivered: 6,000

This card for the HAFNIA 87 international stamp exhibition in Copenhagen, Denmark, features a maritime theme with stamps from the United States and Denmark that were issued 75 years apart.

The 10¢ stamp from the U.S. 1901 Pan American series shows the steamship *St. Paul* of the International Navigation Company. The ship was the first merchant marine vessel taken over in 1898 by the U.S. government for use during the Spanish-American War. Launched in 1895, the *St. Paul* sailed the seas until 1923 when it was sold to a German firm for scrapping.

The Denmark stamp pictures the Danish naval training ship *Danmark* as it appears on a 1976 Danish semipostal stamp issued in honor of the American bicentennial celebration. The *Danmark* came into American hands in World War II when Denmark fell to the Germans. The United States used it as a training ship for the Coast Guard at New London, Connecticut. At war's end, the ship was returned to Denmark.

The *Danmark* has since been a frequent visitor to the United States. It appeared here in 1964 during the second New York World's Fair, came back in 1976 for the bicentennials' Operation Sail, and most recently returned in 1986 for the Statue of Liberty centennial.

Not since its St. Lawrence Seaway souvenir card of mid-1984 has a USPS card borne an English translation of a foreign language text. USPS cards have journeyed to many foreign shows, and collectors have found texts in French, Hebrew, Spanish, German and Italian — but no English translations of same. This card handles its Danish and English in an unusual manner: One Danish paragraph is followed by its English translation. The paragraphs alternate in that fashion until the entire text is translated.

The HAFNIA card was printed on white parchment stock, the same acid-free stock used for Bureau of Engraving and Printing cards. This card was sold at the Philatelic Sales Division and philatelic centers in post offices around the country for $2 mint, or $2.25 when struck with the HAFNIA 87 cancellation over a 22¢ Flag With Fireworks stamp.

HSNA 87 SOUVENIR CARD (BEP)

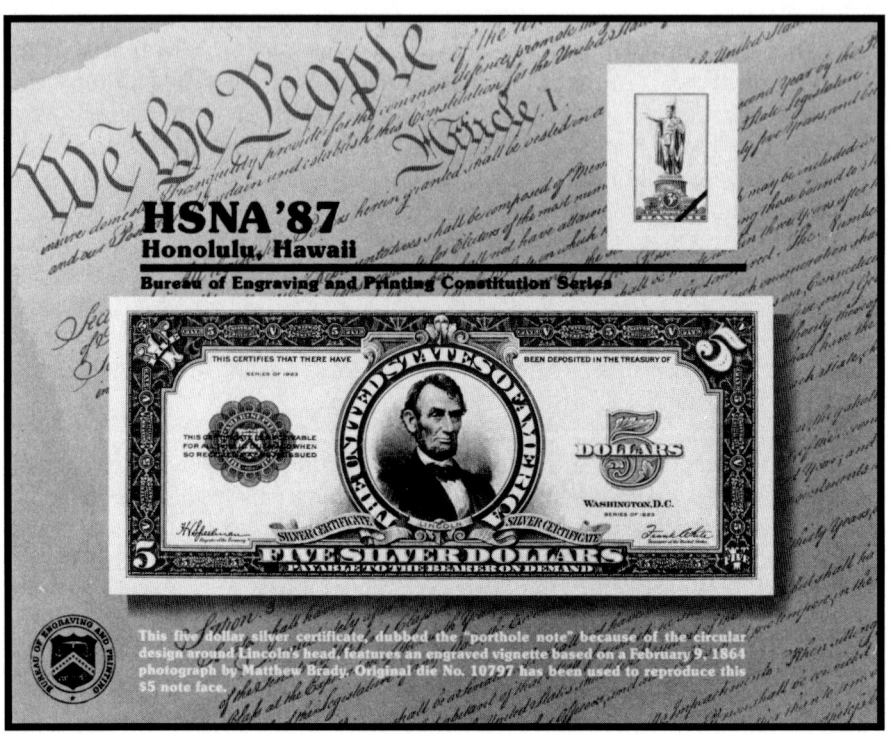

Date of Issue: November 12, 1987

First-Day Release: Honolulu, Hawaii (Hawaiian State Numismatic Association coin show); Washington, D.C. (BEP Center)

Colors: brown, dark brown, black (offset); brown foil (letterpress); black, purple (intaglio)

Size: 8 by 10 inches

Printing: Offset by 6-color Miller press; brown foil by Kluge letterpress; intaglio by high-speed intaglio press (die-stamped)

Quantity Produced: 7,500

Although this card was created for the Hawaiian State Numismatic Association's 24th annual coin show November 12-15, 1987, in Honolulu, Hawaii, the *Yearbook* includes it because of the stamp pictured thereon.

The card focuses on the image of Abraham Lincoln, as it appeared on the $5 silver certificate of 1923. Because of the heavy circular design around the Lincoln vignette, the note came to be known as the porthole note.

In the upper right corner is a die proof of the 1937 3¢ Hawaii Territory commemorative stamp, printed with the original die. As with the original die proof on the SESCAL card, this one has been canceled with an overprinted slash marking across the stamp. Designer of the 1937 issue picturing King Kamehameha I was A.R. Meissner. Charles Chalmers engraved the vignette; James T. Vail cut the lettering.

After the chief of Hawaii died in 1782, Kamehameha conquered the island. He won other islands in the Hawaiian chain, climaxed by his victory in 1795 over the island of Oahu. Kamehameha used cannon-fire to drive Oahu's defenders off a cliff near Honolulu. He brought the island of Kauai into the Hawaiian kingdom peacefully in 1810.

Kamehameha tried to keep the old customs and religion of his people alive, but after his death, missionaries started to spread Christianity throughout the islands. A statue of the king represents Hawaii in Statuary Hall in the U.S. Capitol in Washington, D.C.

Both the stamp and the banknote are placed over a background consisting of an angled copy of the Constitution.

Mint copies of the card were available for $4 at the coin show and the BEP Visitors' Center in Washington. Canceled copies of the card were not sold at the Hawaiian show, but were available for $4.25 at the Visitors' Center. Both versions were sold by mail for $5.50 for the mint card and $5.75 for the canceled variety.

MONTE CARLO SOUVENIR CARD (USPS)

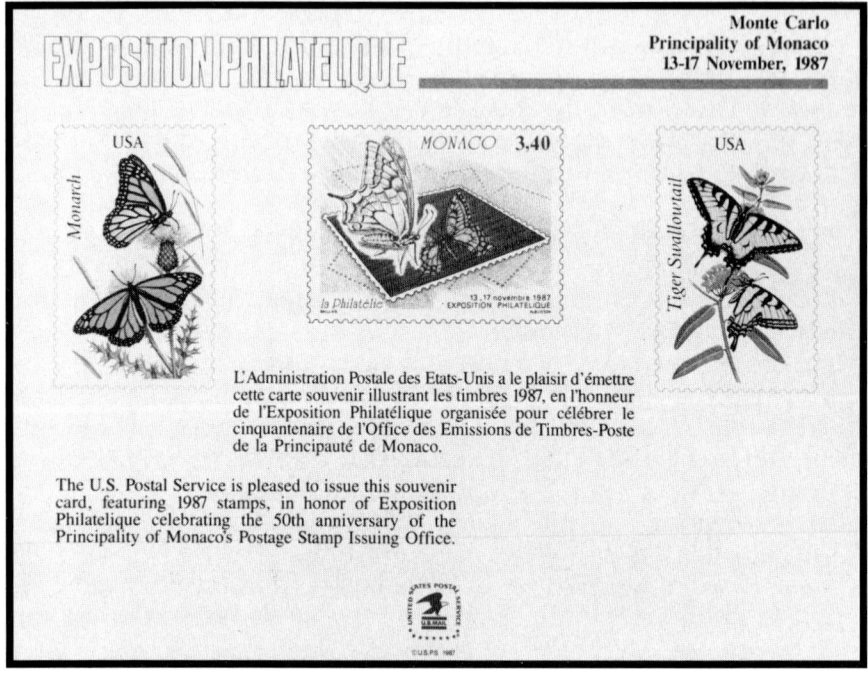

Date of Issue: November 13, 1987

First-Day Release: Monte Carlo, Monaco (Exposition Philatelique)

Colors: process yellow, magenta, cyan, black, special blue

Designer: Joe Brockert (USPS)

Modeler: Ronald C. Sharpe (BEP)

Size: 6 by 8 inches

Printing: 6-color Miller offset press

Quantity Delivered: 86,000

Only a few hours before issuing it, the USPS announced this souvenir card honoring the international exhibition, *Exposition Philatelique*, in Monte Carlo, Monaco, November 13-17, 1987. The card, which first surfaced in the November-December listings of the *Philatelic Catalog*, also celebrates the 50th anniversary of the Principality of Monaco's Postage Stamp Issuing Office.

The card design, by Joe Brockert of the USPS, features large, undenominated copies of the Monarch and Tiger Swallowtail butterfly stamps from the Wildlife pane of 50 issued June 13, 1987. In between the two U.S. stamps is a 3.40-franc stamp that also features a butterfly. This stamp was issued by Monaco especially for the stamp show.

Monaco, surrounded by the French Riviera on the Mediterranean Sea, is one of the smallest countries in the world. It stretches along the shore for about 2½ miles, but at some spots is no wider than 200 yards. For decades it has been a popular and expensive tourist resort, as well as host to two of the world's best-known auto races, the Monte Carlo Rally and the Monaco Grand Prix.

Monaco, termed a principality since it is ruled by a prince, is both a country and a town within that country. The city of Monaco, an old town and former fortress, sits on a rocky point 200 feet high. It is dominated by the royal palace.

The city of Monte Carlo has the famous gambling casino, plus most of the hotels, shops, beaches and an opera house. It is ironic that each year thousands of visitors come to play roulette, baccarat or other games of chance. Since Monte Carlo became famous for gambling in the mid 1800s, no citizen of Monaco has been allowed to gamble at the famous club.

In addition to these two cities, Monaco has a port area, La Condamine, and an industrial zone called Fontvieille. All of that lies in an area of slightly more than one-half square mile. Perhaps more so than for any other country, postage stamps are important to Monaco. The colorful stamps of the principality are collected around the world and are a vital source of income to the tiny state.

The $2 mint version of the card was available at the show, at philatelic centers or by mail order from the Philatelic Sales Division. Customers could also purchase the card by mail with a randomly selected Wildlife stamp affixed and canceled with the exposition imprint. The BEP charges more for its cards, but the USPS's PSD insisted on a $10 minimum order, plus a 50¢ postage and handling fee.

MAXIMUM CARDS

With the eight maximum cards issued by the USPS in 1987 (three for the Pan American Games and five for the Locomotive booklet), the total of these special postcards now jumps to 38, including 16 in 1983, nine in 1984, and five in 1986.

Maximum cards have been popular in Europe for many years and are now a recognized part of FIP (Federation Internationale de Philatelie) international exhibits. The collecting and showing of these cards is termed *maximaphily* in Europe and other foreign locales. What the USPS creates, however, are not true maximum cards.

International rules state that legitimate maximum cards may not have been produced intentionally to duplicate a stamp. European collectors seek out cards, however old, that match stamps as closely as possible in design and layout. Under that exhibiting definition, the USPS cards are not maximum cards; they are special postcards, designed and produced about the same time as the stamps they picture.

The Locomotive Cards

Five maximum cards — each showing one of the locomotives pictured on the five stamps of the Locomotive booklet — went on sale at the PSD October 1, 1987. They were not sold at local post offices or philatelic centers.

Each card shows an enlarged version of the same designs used on the stamps. The cards could be obtained as a mint set for $2.50, or canceled with appropriate stamps for $3.60. All cards were based on artwork by Richard Leech, designer of the Locomotive stamps.

The Pan American Games Cards

The maximum card shown at top duplicates the runners seen on the Pan American Games stamp that was issued January 29, 1987, in Indianapolis, Indiana. The card was issued with the same special red color that predominates on the stamp. Designer Lon Busch designed the stamp and all maximum cards, which went on sale first on August 7, 1987, at the games.

The second card pictures cyclists and is printed primarily in oranges and yellows. The third card shows a swimmer and is produced largely in blue tones. Both of these cards were designed originally by Lon Busch as possible stamps — not maximum cards.

The set of three cards was available by mail from the Philatelic Sales Division for $1.50.

ITEMS WITHDRAWN FROM SALE IN 1987
Commemoratives:
1986 22¢ Sojourner Truth 2/28
1986 22¢ Arkansas Statehood 2/28
1986 22¢ Republic of Texas 2/28
1985 22¢ Veterans World War I 2/28
1986 22¢ Public Hospitals 4/30
1986 22¢ Duke Ellington 4/30
1986 22¢ Polar Explorers (4) 4/30
1986 22¢ Statue of Liberty 4/30
1986 22¢ T.S. Eliot 10/31
1986 22¢ Love 6/30
1985 22¢ AMERIPEX 6/30
1986 22¢ Christmas (contemporary) 10/31
1986 22¢ Christmas (traditional) 10/31
1986 22¢ Stamp Collecting booklet 10/31
1986 22¢ Navajo Art (4) 12/31
1986 22¢ Woodcarved Figurines (4) 12/31

Definitives:
1983 3¢ Henry Clay 2/28
1979 $1 Rush Candleholder 2/28 (plain and precanceled)
1982 2¢ Stravinsky 4/30
1985 3.4¢ School Bus 4/30 (plain and precanceled)
1981 17¢ Electric Auto 4/30 (coils of 100)
1965 25¢ Paul Revere 4/30 (coils of 3,000)
1979 30¢ Schoolhouse 4/30 (precanceled)
1979 50¢ Whale Oil Lamp 4/30
1985 14¢ Sinclair Lewis 6/30
1981 17¢ Electric Auto precancel 6/30
1986 50¢ Chester Nimitz (A Press version) 8/31
1985 39¢ Grenville Clark 8/31
1981 35¢ Charles Drew 10/31
1981 17¢ Electric Auto (coils of 500) 10/31
1981 20¢ Fire Pumper (coils of 3,000) 10/31
1979 $5 Railroad Lantern 10/31 (last of the Americana series)
1985 22¢ John J. Audubon 12/31
1984 10¢ Richard Russell 12/31

Envelopes:
1986 6¢ Old Ironsides 4/30 (all varieties and watermarks)

Postage Dues:
All 1¢ through $5 single denominations 2/28

Duck Stamp:
1984-85 $7.50 Wigeon 8/31

Souvenir Cards:
1984 $2 Philakorea 10/31

EXHIBITION CARDS

In 1983 the U.S. Postal Service issued a souvenir card entitled "International Philatelic Memento Card 1983-1984." It featured an American Bald Eagle and quotations from Franklin D. Roosevelt and Postmaster General William Bolger. Generic in nature and text, it was intended for use primarily by USPS foreign sales representatives at foreign international exhibitions. A 1985 International Philatelic Memento Card replaced it, bearing a reproduction of the U.S. 1847 10¢ George Washington stamp, and a salute to collecting and AMERIPEX 86 from Postmaster General Paul Carlin.

Such international, generic souvenir cards were abandoned by the Postal Service in 1986. Instead, in September 1986, the USPS issued its first exhibition card. It took the form of a regularly issued postal card (in this case the 1986 14¢ Stamp Collecting card), which was then officially overprinted for a specific stamp show (in this case the NAJUBRIA 86 show in Villingen-Schwenningen, West Germany).

In its *United States Postal Card Catalog,* the U.S. Postal Stationery Society has given its official recognition to this NAJUBRIA and subsequent overprinted exhibition cards as listable varieties eminently collectible for postal card collectors.

The NAJUBRIA card has long since sold out. According to the Postal Service, it will not be reprinted. The second, third and fourth cards in this new series of postal card exhibition salutes to international stamp shows are shown here.

The CUP-PEX 87 Card

The U.S. Postal Service ordered 50,000 of the 25¢ Clipper *Flying Cloud* postal cards to be overprinted in honor of the CUP-PEX 87 National Stamp Exhibition in Perth, Australia, January 31 through February 7, 1987. The cards were overprinted by a contract printer secured by the Philatelic Sales Division in Merrifield, Virginia.

Ordered in December 1986, the cards became available in January 1987 and quickly sold out. The Postal Service ordered another 50,000 in February 1987. Until the CUP-PEX cards go off sale, there will be no way of knowing a printing and sales total.

The overprinted cards were available from the PSD for the face value of the postal card.

The SUDPOSTA 87 Card

The 1986 33¢ AMERIPEX postal card was authorized for an overprint honoring SUDPOSTA 87, which took place October 22-25 in Sindelfingen, West Germany. The card was available at the show from Hermann Sieger, sales representative for the U.S. Postal Service in Austria and West Germany. The card was available in the United States from the Philatelic Sales Division for the 33¢ face value of the postal card. The $10 minimum order and 50¢ service charge for mail orders applied, however.

The PHILATELIA 87 Card

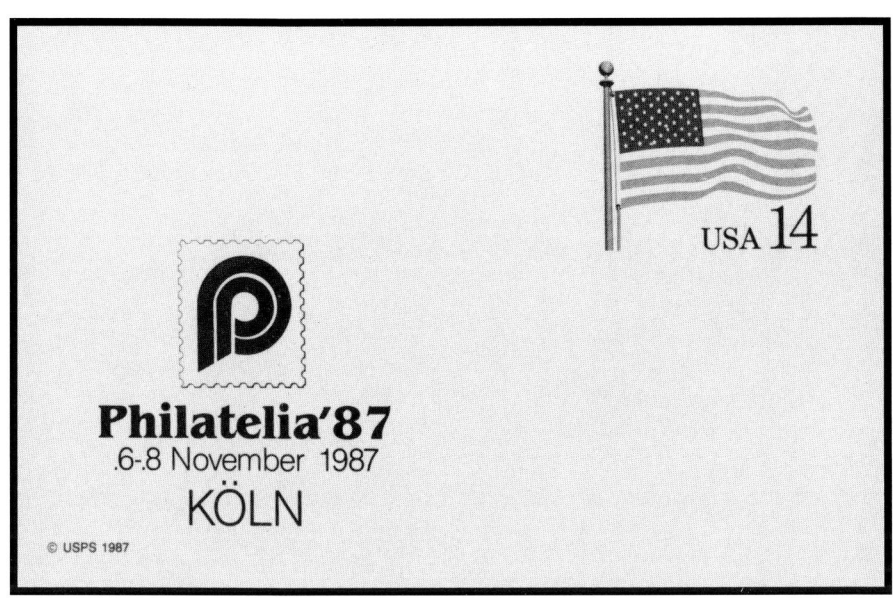

At the same time the USPS announced the overprinted exhibition card for SUDPOSTA 87, they also revealed that the 14¢ Flag postal card of 1987 would be overprinted to note PHILATELIA 87, a stamp show scheduled for November 6-8 in Cologne, West Germany.

This exhibition card was available from Hermann Sieger, USPS sales representative in West Germany, and from the PSD in Merrifield, Virginia, for the 14¢ face value of the Flag postal card.

With this PHILATELIA 87 overprint, the number of such USPS exhibition cards rose to four during 1986-87.